Modernism and
the Anthropocene

Ecocritical Theory and Practice

Series Editor: Douglas A. Vakoch, METI

Ecocritical Theory and Practice highlights innovative scholarship at the interface of literary/cultural studies and the environment, seeking to foster an ongoing dialogue between academics and environmental activists.

Recent Titles

Modernism and the Anthropocene edited by Jon Hegglund and John McIntyre

The End of the Anthropocene: Ecocriticism, the Universal Ecosystem, and the Astropocene by Michael Gormley

Trees in Literatures and the Arts: Humanarboreal Perspectives in the Anthropocene edited by Carmelina Concilio and Daniela Fargione

Lupenga Mphande: Eco-critical Poet and Political Activist by Dike Okoro

Environmental Postcolonialism: A Literary Response edited by Shubhanku Kochar and M. Anjum Khan

Reading Aridity in Western American Literature edited by Jada Ach and Gary Reger

Reading Cats and Dogs: Companion Animals in World Literature edited by Françoise Besson, Zelia M. Bora, Marianne Marroum, and Scott Slovic

Turkish Ecocriticism: From Neolithic to Contemporary Timescapes edited by Sinan Akilli and Serpil Oppermann

Avenging Nature: The Role of Nature in Modern and Contemporary Art and Literature edited by Eduardo Valls Oyarzun, Rebeca Gualberto Valverde, Noelia Malla Garcia, María Colom Jiménez, and Rebeca Cordero Sánchez

Migrant Ecologies: Zheng Xiaoqiong's Women Migrant Workers by Zhou Xiaojing

Climate Consciousness and Environmental Activism in Composition: Writing to Save the World edited by Joseph R. Lease

Modernism and the Anthropocene

Material Ecologies of Twentieth-Century Literature

Edited by Jon Hegglund
and John McIntyre

LEXINGTON BOOKS
Lanham • Boulder • New York • London

Published by Lexington Books
An imprint of The Rowman & Littlefield Publishing Group, Inc.
4501 Forbes Boulevard, Suite 200, Lanham, Maryland 20706
www.rowman.com

86-90 Paul Street, London EC2A 4NE, United Kingdom

British Library Cataloguing in Publication Information Available

Library of Congress Cataloging-in-Publication Data

Names: Hegglund, Jon, editor. | McIntyre, John, 1966- editor.
Title: Modernism and the anthropocene : material ecologies of
    twentieth-century literature / edited by Jon Hegglund and John D.
    McIntyre.
Description: Lanham : Lexington Books, [2021] | Series: Ecocritical theory
    and practice | Includes bibliographical references and index. | Summary:
    "Bringing together work from twelve leading scholars in the field of
    ecocriticism, Modernism and the Anthropocene explores the diverse ways
    that early twentieth-century literature initiated far-reaching
    conversations about the material and non-human world"—Provided by
    publisher.
Identifiers: LCCN 2021027564 (print) | LCCN 2021027565 (ebook) | ISBN
    9781498555388 (cloth ; alk. paper) | ISBN 9781498555395 (ebook)
Subjects: LCSH: Human ecology in literature. | Literature, Modern—20th
    century—History and criticism. | Human ecology and the humanities. |
    Modernism (Literature) | LCGFT: Literary criticism.
Classification: LCC PN56.H76 M63 2021 (print) | LCC PN56.H76 (ebook) |
    DDC 809/.9353042—dc23
LC record available at https://lccn.loc.gov/2021027564
LC ebook record available at https://lccn.loc.gov/2021027565

Contents

Acknowledgments   vii

Introduction: Modernism and the Emergent Anthropocene   ix
Jon Hegglund and John McIntyre

PART I: MODERNISM-ANTHROPOCENE ENCOUNTERS

1   Revolt against the *Anthropos*: The Human-Environment
Conflicts in D. H. Lawrence   3
Joseph Anderton

2   Vorticism in an Age of Climate Change   21
Jessica Martell

3   Hart Crane: A Poet of Our Climate   39
Robert Savino Oventile

4   "What kind of creature uttered it . . . ?": A Stratigraphy of
Subjectivity in Samuel Beckett's *The Unnamable*   59
Emily Chester

PART II: PLANETARY TIME AND SPACE

5   The Modernist Cosmos: Olaf Stapledon, Pierre Teilhard
de Chardin, and the Crisis of Species   79
Timothy Wientzen

6   Modernist Planets and Planetary Modernism   97
Joshua Schuster

7   Early Ecology and Climate Change in the Future Histories
of H. G. Wells and Olaf Stapledon   115
Ted Howell

8   Second Modernism and the Aesthetics of Temporal Scale   133
Charles M. Tung

PART III: WRITING MATERIALS

9   Comics: Worldmaking in the Anthropocene   153
Glenn Willmott

10   Modernism on Ice: Marianne Moore and the Glacial Imagination   173
Julia E. Daniel

11   The Poetics of Modernism's Plastics   191
Michael D. Sloane

12   Sky and Smoke: Literary Atmospherics in Cary and Ibuse   209
Stuart Christie

Index   229

About the Editors and Contributors   243

Acknowledgments

Jon would like to thank colleagues at Washington State University for providing a supportive, encouraging, and congenial professional environment. Work on the volume was completed with the assistance of a Lewis G. and Stella E. Buchanan Distinguished Professorship award, along with a summer research stipend—both generously bestowed by the WSU Department of English. And thanks, of course, to Emily and Oscar for everything else.

John would like to thank the members of the Arts faculty at the University of Prince Edward Island for their friendship and collegiality. Thanks too to the research group at the UPEI Climate Lab, all of whom have been so welcoming to humanities-centered research on climate and the environment.

Thank you to all the contributors, who stuck with us over a long road from conception to publication. And, finally, to the editors at Lexington Books who have helped see this book through to completion: Lindsey Porambo, Michael Gibson, Kasey Beduhn, and Alexandra Rallo.

Grateful acknowledgment is made to the Estate of Shōmei Tōmatsu for permission to reproduce the images found in chapter 12. © Shomei Tomatsu-INTERFACE.

Modernism and the Emergent Anthropocene

Jon Hegglund and John McIntyre

Looking back on modernist literature and art from a century after its heyday, it is easy to see, in retrospect, new perspectives on the nonhuman world that foreshadow early twenty-first century discussions and debates about what we now know as the Anthropocene. In *Heart of Darkness*, Joseph Conrad's Marlow imputes a dreadful, inscrutable agency to the landscape of West Africa, in the process of being ravaged by the resource extraction and social repression of European empires. In Thomas Hardy's "Convergence of the Twain," the speaker takes a remarkably inhuman, cosmic view of the collision between the most extravagant expression of modern technological hubris, the *HMS Titanic*, and the insensible iceberg that found its way into the ocean liner's path. Paul Nash's stark, abstract 1918 painting, *We Are Making a New World*, depicts the shell-blasted landscapes after the Battle of Ypres but also, with its ironic title, suggests the more widespread ecological devastation wrought by modern technologies of warfare. On a less overtly tragic note, Virginia Woolf, in works such as "Kew Gardens," *To the Lighthouse*, and *The Waves*, gives narrative prominence to entities—a snail, a house, a beach—that exist independently of human action, intention, and perception. And finally, that looming monument of poetic modernism, T. S. Eliot's *Waste Land*, juxtaposes mythological stories of infertile, desiccated landscapes with their contemporary urbanized analogues, damaged by the practices of industrial technology, atomized society, and burgeoning mass cultures. These works represent but a thin slice of modernism's developing concern with the changing relations between humanity and nature, but they all speak to a skepticism and doubt about the superiority of the former over the latter. While it is difficult to generalize any one motif or theme from these diverse examples, they—along with many others—speak to human interventions in nature that have led to profound, disproportionate, and ungovernable consequences: landscapes that cannot be subdued, technologies that cannot be controlled, beings that cannot be understood.

These concerns were not limited to the literature and art of experimental, "high" modernism. Beyond the scope of self-consciously literary forms, writers in more popular fictional genres were likewise speculating on the wonder and dread of the nonhuman world. H. G. Wells famously imagined an alien species insensitive to human concerns in *The War of the Worlds*, and in *The Time Machine* he forecasts the evolutionary (or devolutionary) branching of the human species into the physically weak, decadent Eloi, and the monstrous, subterranean Morlocks (not to mention a flash-forward to a distant age when nothing even remotely resembling human life remains). Horror writer H. P. Lovecraft built an entire story universe around the myth of the "Old Ones," alien demigods residing eternally deep within the earth, utterly apathetic toward the infinitesimal human world, and whose contact with the human race often occurs through the destruction and terror wreaked by the gargantuan, tentacular, sea-monster Cthulhu. And in Thornton Wilder's best-selling novel from 1928, *The Bridge of San Luis Rey*, the repeated collapses of the eponymous bridge endow it with an indifferent agency that is entirely suited to its role as the novel's inhuman "antihero." Literature, in all spheres, was addressing a shifting relationship between human actors and the diverse agencies of the nonhuman world.

The emerging technology and cultural medium of film likewise projected the attractions of the nonhuman. The medium's affordances—the recording and reproduction of moving photographic images of the world—was an especially powerful vehicle in the representation of environments. Whether through the fanciful imagination of the moon in Georges Méliès's *Voyage à la Lune* (1905) or the dystopian vision of the robot Maria in Fritz Lang's *Metropolis* (1927), the emergent new genre of film threw a spotlight on the nonhuman even if it was framed in anthropocentric terms. The movie camera could also give prominence to the nonhuman in more everyday settings, and many filmmakers experimented with the camera's indifference to what appeared in its field, particularly in the early genre of the *actualité*, pioneered by the Lumière Brothers. The French duo opened the lens of their camera on the happenings of everyday life, be they workers leaving their factory shifts, coal being mined, or, most famously, a train arriving at a station. The unmoving camera, "passively" recording reality, had the effect of defamiliarizing everyday spaces, turning the unnoticed backgrounds of life into framed images calling for their own scrutiny and examination. The photo-documentary style of the Lumière eventually developed into the city symphony genre, which showed the thriving activity of different urban centers, such as Charles Sheeler and Paul Strand's *Manhatta* (1921), Walter Ruttmann's *Berlin:*

Symphony of a Metropolis (1927), and Dziga Vertov's *Man with a Movie Camera* (1929). This genre showed the city itself as a kind of ecological organism, highlighting the assemblages between humans, machines, and built environments. In a more literal instance, Charlie Chaplin's *Modern Times* (1936) takes place in an inhuman and mechanized workplace— at once futuristic and contemporary—whose triumph over humanity is both inevitable and largely unremarkable. While film still tended to focus, literally and figuratively, on the human form, its abilities to document and interrogate the nonhuman world were clearly in evidence in its earliest decades.

The apex of modernism falls within the spectrum of possible dates marking the onset of the Anthropocene, which observers have variously identified from the early modern era of European colonization to the latter half of the twentieth century. When Paul Crutzen and Eugene Stoermer joined efforts in 2000 to popularize the term as an official epoch in geological history, they initially settled on the latter part of the eighteenth century as the proverbial "golden spike" delimiting the transition from the Holocene to the Anthropocene, pointing to evidence of an increase in carbon dioxide and methane in the atmosphere, which happened to coincide with James Watt's invention of the steam engine in 1784 (Crutzen and Stoermer 2000, 17–18). Another recent study offers 1610 as the dawn of the Anthropocene, citing the environmental consequences of European colonization of the Americas as a decisive environmental impact (Lewis and Maslin 2018, 13). And the new, "official" dating offered in 2016 by the Anthropocene Working Group (AWG) has agreed upon 1950—based on the plutonium fallout from atomic bomb explosions—as the golden spike that confirms the new epoch (Anthropocene Working Group 2019, n.p.). The fuzzy dating of the onset of the Anthropocene epoch should not blind us to the fact that, whether we date it as far back as the dawn of agriculture, or as recently as the post-World War II "Great Acceleration" that has been decided by the AWG, the chronological period commonly associated with modernism—say, the first half of the twentieth century—is crucial to understanding the Anthropocene's emergence. This claim forms part of the rationale for the present volume.

It bears reminding that the Anthropocene is, fundamentally, a specific term used for the dating of geological strata. While any measure of time is to some degree arbitrary, there is an institutional force carried by the establishment of the Anthropocene that operates differently within the discourses of science than periodizations more common to the humanities. Because the concept of the Anthropocene has arisen within a particular history (as all scientific concepts do, of course), it is easy to see it within a human-centered historical scale, similar to those often used in Anglocentric literary histories. Geology reminds us that the term is not intended to be historical in the sense of human history, but *epochal* in the sense of a much longer planetary history. Thus, one of the constitutive, structural components of any cultural-historical reading of the Anthropocene is a tension between the "period" and the "epoch," between a human history measured in biographies, generations, decades, centuries, and a geo-history measured in millennia, strata, plate tectonics, and the evolution and extinction of species—our own included. *Modernism and the Anthropocene* does not attempt to resolve these scalar tensions; in fact, each of the chapters below finds precisely those points within different artistic forms—novels, poetry, comics, visual art, and others—at which the irreconcilable nature of these tensions is pushed to the foreground, becoming a thematized component within individual works. Pairing the terms "modernism" and "Anthropocene," therefore, is not meant to suggest any kind of conceptual or formal equivalence. In fact, we wish to point out how each term interrupts and contradicts the other: the designation of figures and works as "modernist" risks confining ecologically expansive artistic concerns into a well-contained stylistic and historical box, while, by contrast, the epochally-scaled Anthropocene can obscure the specific historical, social, and artistic contingencies that generated such environmentally, cosmically suggestive works. The chapters below shuttle between these two temporal frameworks, using one to critique and challenge the other.

One way to frame the scales of time addressed by the different chapters in this collection is through Robert Markley's tri-partite model of temporality in a post-climate-change world. The most individualized, small-scale register is what he calls "experiential or embodied time," which identifies the subjective, phenomenological flow of moment-to-moment experience. This register is particularly on display in many modernist works that foreground individual, perceptual experience—often named conventionally by the well-worn label, "stream of consciousness." The second register is what Markley calls "historical time," the successive generational sweep of human culture that outlasts individual lives but still remains within a longer narrative of human existence, often organized by concepts such as "period," "progress," and "development." Even as it tends to foreground experiential registers, modernist literature often implies its location with longer arcs of human history—whether through scattered or oblique references to colonial conquests, anticolonial struggles, ruling regimes, technological change, urbanization, or war. The broadest domain of time in Markley's model is what he calls the "climatological," though we might also use synonyms like "deep historical," "geological," or "planetary." This, according to Markley, "is a non-anthropogenic time that transcends both individual and historical experience," and "can be conceived only differentially, paradoxically, in its relation to phenomenological perceptions of time and existence" (Markley

2012, 51, 52). One of the features of a modernist Anthropocene, then, is the oblique expression of climatological, planetary time through tropes that find their way into conventional literary forms as deformations, disturbances, or formal ambiguities. The well-studied fascination with myth in *The Waste Land* is one such example; in inviting us to consider the juxtaposition of fragments of consciousness, early-twentieth-century European history, and various myths of fertility and ecology, Eliot puts experiential, historical, and climatological time in conversation. The fragmented form keeps one register from dominating the other, opening up a space for the consideration of planetary, ecological forces that cannot be contained within either an individual or historical framework.

This collection recognizes that evidence of the Anthropocene manifested in cultural productions long before it was definitively named as such in the early 2000s. We advance the notion of an "emergent" Anthropocene sensibility becoming more culturally foregrounded from the latter part of the nineteenth century through the middle of the twentieth. Our notion of an emergent Anthropocene borrows from Raymond Williams' ideas of dominant, residual, and emergent moments of culture in his 1977 book, *Marxism and Literature.* For Williams, emergent cultural formations embody "new meanings and values, new practices, [and] new relationships" that emerge as "substantially alternative or oppositional" to dominant culture (Williams 1977, 123). As we look back from the twenty-first century, we can identify strains of modernism that challenge dominant practices of resource-based capitalism—this hegemony often framing ideologies of nationalism, militarism, colonialism, racism, and class and gender oppression—as a way of giving voice to material agencies not fully accounted for nor contained by human intention. For us, the emergent Anthropocene does not indicate that the geological and ecological phenomena of the Anthropocene only come into view within the first half of the twentieth century, but rather that artistic practices that address the material conditions of the Anthropocene are contiguous with modernism, even if there is yet no such name with which to label this altered relationship between humans and the earth. What each of the chapters in this collection point out, within artifacts associated with modernism, is a growing awareness of a convergence between large-scale, nonhuman agents and a sense of an accelerated condition of modernity. In other words, we see a dynamic within modernity within which concerns that are not typically cast as "environmental" are still part of a recognition of the precarity of anthropocentrism and the agency of the nonhuman world, in its many forms.

The consideration of modernism and the Anthropocene is a logical step forward from the increased attention to ecological perspectives on modernism, which has slowly followed the lead of the "new modernist studies" that launched both the Modernist Studies Association and the journal *Modernism/Modernity* in the late 1990s. One reason for the relatively slow uptake of environmental and ecocritical concerns stems from the new modernism's antipathy toward nature as a sphere of inherent moral and ethical authenticity and value—a sensibility justified by many canonical modernists' suspicion and critique of the concept. As Anne Raine documented in 2014, however, a more ecologically-minded modernist studies nonetheless found its way into critical conversations in the late 1990s and early 2000s, whether through ecocritics who centered more on nineteenth-century literature and who occasionally edged into the twentieth, such as Jonathan Bate and Lawrence Buell, in omnibus collections such as *The Green Studies Reader* (Coupe 2000), or in Susan Stanford Friedman's notion of planetarity, which arises from a postcolonial, transnational approach to modernism (Raine 2014). Until the first part of the last decade, however, modernist studies "had largely ignored ecocriticism" (Raine 2014, 100).

The recent materialist wave of ecocriticism has begun to influence the course of modernist studies. Recent critical works have embraced and incorporated the perspectives of the materialist ecocriticism pioneered by writers including Donna Haraway, Karen Barad, Timothy Morton, and Jane Bennett. Jeffrey Mathes McCarthy's *Green Modernism: Nature and the English Novel, 1900–1930* (2015) addresses itself most clearly to a revision of ecocritical assumptions about "nature." For McCarthy, "nature defines green modernism by, on the one hand, empowering cultural interventions and, on the other hand, existing as a physical ground beyond language" (McCarthy 2015, 7). This is a bridge from a prior model of both modernist and ecocritical studies toward a more materialist, nonhuman framing of ecocritical interpretation. Drawing on Timothy Morton's "ecology without nature" to propose a "modernism without nature," Joshua Schuster's *The Ecology of Modernism: American Environments and Avant-Garde Poetics* (2015), reads ecology less as a green "elsewhere" and more as a feature intrinsic to American modernist poetics. Kelly Sultzbach, in *Ecocriticism in the Modernist Imagination: Forster, Woolf, and Auden* (2016), approaches a set of English modernist writers through a more rigorously eco-materialist lens. Sultzbach shifts critical focus toward the question of how writers engage the nonhuman world on fundamental, perceptual levels, "showing how modernist literature revises environment-as-object to acknowledge environment-as-being" (2016, 13). In this phrasing, we can see how a fundamental motif of modernism—across many different mediums—is the blurring of a clear distinction between subject and object, figure and ground. Sultzbach takes this logic to its ecocritical conclusion: the environment itself is full of nonhuman agencies and beings that trouble an anthropocentric view of the world.

OUTLINE OF BOOK

The chapters that follow begin from the shared premise that modernism, in some of its most recognizable forms and contours, is bound up with a non-human world that remains central yet, ultimately, inaccessible to human subjectivity. Part I, "Modernism-Anthropocene Encounters," is comprised of chapters that address the convergences between aesthetic modernism and nascent Anthropocene concerns. In "Revolt against the Anthropos: The Human-Environment Conflicts in D. H. Lawrence," Joseph Anderton connects some thematic currents in Lawrence's work with concerns animated by the current wave of Anthropocene-based ecocriticism. Anderton sees Lawrence's obsession with the vitality of nature as a critique of modernity's reification and ruination of ecologies and landscapes—nature's agency and power help envision a world that outlasts the depredations of industrial modernity. Jessica Martell similarly identifies a figure and movement—Wyndham Lewis and Vorticism—that call for an ecocritical reconsideration. In "Vorticism in the Age of Climate Change," Martell focuses on Lewis's attention to the relations between climate and culture within modernity. Even as Lewis can veer toward environmental determinism and ethnocentrism, Martell argues that the sustained attention to ecology reveals an "intricate and vivid environmental imagination" within a figure and movement often associated with an urbanized modernism.

Modernist poetry's engagement with deep-historical temporality of the planet is a central concern of Robert Savino Oventile's "Hart Crane: A Poet of Our Climate." Oventile contrasts sections from Crane's epic poem, *The Bridge* (1930), with an earlier verse, "O, Carib Isle!" (1927), arguing that the earlier, less well-known poem is an "*avant-la-lettre* example" of an Anthropocene lyric, achieving a "material sublime" that contextualizes human existence, and eventual extinction, within a deep history of the planet itself. In doing so, Oventile argues, Crane is a modernist particularly attuned to emergent Anthropocenic questions. The blurring of lines between the fleeting time of the human and the deep-historical scales of the material world are likewise highlighted in the work of Samuel Beckett by Emily Chester. In the section's closing chapter, "'What kind of creature uttered it. . .?': A Stratigraphy of Subjectivity in Samuel Beckett's *The Unnamable*," Chester reads the Irish author's 1958 novel as an attempt not merely to dismantle the boundary between human and the environment but to author a novel that denies the possibility of subjective human experience at every turn. Beckett's attempt to evacuate the human from narrative, Chester argues, is a precursor to the conceptual challenge of the Anthropocene: to name the epoch without collapsing

it into the *Anthropos*, the limiting frame of the human itself. The Anthropocene, even as it has been given a human name, is ultimately unnamable.

Part II, "Planetary Time and Space," takes up a developing planetary
consciousness as a signal trope of an emergent Anthropocene sensibility.
Timothy Wientzen's chapter, "The Modernist Cosmos: Olaf Stapledon,
Pierre Teilhard de Chardin, and the Crisis of Species," sees the idea of "scalar
thinking" as a common mode in both the Anthropocenic thinking of French
paleontologist Teilhard (with his notion of the "noosphere," similar to the
Anthropocene) and the speculative fiction of the English writer Stapledon.
Wientzen's chapter sees both thinkers focused on the "precarity of the spe-
cies, cosmopolitan politics, and the aesthetic modes appropriate to both."
Thinking cosmically, for Teilhard and Stapledon, means thinking critically
about human futures on planet Earth. In "Modernist Planets and Planetary
Modernism," Joshua Schuster approaches the question of planetarity more
explicitly. Schuster frames the work of Stapledon and Polish writer Stanislaw
Lem, within the work of the Russian geologist Vladimir Vernadsky. Instead
of viewing the Earth as an inert object of study, Vernadsky advanced a more
symbiotic theory of planetarity that anticipates the idea of the Anthropocene.
Schuster argues that both Stapledon, in the novel *Star-Maker* (1937), and
Lem, in *Solaris* (1961), forge narratives that exemplify Vernadsky's idea of a
planetary agency. Both Stapledon and Lem anticipate the Anthropocene idea
of "thinking like a planet."

Ted Howell and Charles M. Tung turn to questions of time as well
as space in their chapters. Howell's chapter , "Early Ecology and Climate Change in the Future Histories of H. G. Wells and Olaf Stapledon,"
also takes up Stapledon's work, comparing it to the speculative fiction
of H. G. Wells. Howell shows how both Wells and Stapledon were, in
the 1920s and '30s, grappling with many questions that animate discussions of the Anthropocene today: in particular, the problem that humanity was transforming its environment more quickly than it could adapt.
Both writers project a liberal, utopian hope onto their diagnosis of ecological challenges, but Howell argues that, in their insistence on a nonhuman, ecological agency, they should be seen as forerunners of contemporary expressions of the Anthropocene. In "Second Modernism and the
Aesthetics of Temporal Scale," Tung connects modernism's well-known
fascination with novelty and rupture with longer, deep-historical notions of
duration and epochal scale. After examining some examples of this "second
modernism," Tung focuses on more recent attempts to represent this time—
most notably the Clock of the Long Now, a contemporary project to expand
everyday notions of time to a geological scale (and in so doing, explicitly
bridging all three realms of time outlined by Markley). Both Howell's and

Tung's chapters show us that there is no shortage of resonance between modernist and contemporary understandings of planetary time and space.

The final section of the collection, "Writing Materials," engages more directly the physical matter that is both text and context, medium and message, in modernist Anthropocene writing. Glenn Willmott, in "Comics: Worldmaking in the Anthropocene," takes up the narrative form of the comic on a material, medial level, arguing that its very form is ecological, focusing as it does on "explicit worldmaking," a kind of in-built story ecology that exceeds the direct function of linear storytelling. Willmott turns to three examples from the first half of the twentieth century, showing how the medium of comics can figure its ecologies in ways that admit different types of "environmental" thinking into its narrative designs. "In Modernism on Ice," Julia E. Daniel also considers the materiality of form, turning to the poetry of Marianne Moore. Daniel draws on Timothy Morton's notion of the "hyperobject" to understand Moore's long poem, "The Octopus." Connecting the hyperobject to the "hyper-abundance" of verse, Daniel shows how the material complexity of the glacier on Mount Rainier in Washington leads to a proliferation of figures of forms in the poem, offering an example of modernism's experiments with form rooted in experiential encounters with the material world.

The final two chapters of this book examine those most Anthropocene of human-made materials: plastic and radioactive nuclear fallout. Michael Sloane's "The Poetics of Modernism's Plastics" takes a tour through the frequent modernist references to one of the ubiquitous new materials in the twentieth-century industrial world. Sloane analyzes both the content of plastic and the plasticity of form as they interact in the works of Italian Futurism, Gertrude Stein, Mina Loy, William Carlos Williams, The Baroness Elsa von Freytag-Loringhoven, and Abraham Lincoln Gillespie. The image and form of plastic shows up in modernism as a material and figural example of the spread of mass-produced culture and the transformation of both human and ecological natures. Plastic emerges as a material embodiment of many anxieties about modernity's "artificial ecology," but it also proves to be a generative trope for modernist poetics. Stuart Christie expands both the historical and geographical scope of an Anthropocenic modernism in "Sky and Smoke: Literary Atmospherics in Cary and Ibuse." Christie's focus on the role of atmosphere in narrative charts a contrast between Joyce Cary's use of sky in *The Horse's Mouth* (1944) as a vehicle for imaginative escape from the grimy material and economic conditions of modern London. Cary's protagonist, the failed painter Gulley Jimson, fixates on the sky as a figure of artistic freedom in a sullied world. Japanese novelist Masuji Ibuse, by contrast, understands the sky as a source of threat and death in the world of post-World War II Japan. Ibuse's novel *Black Rain* (1962) depicts the aftermath of the Hiroshima bombing, a world in which skies are not an empty space for the projection of human concerns but a radioactive, smoke-filled realm that signifies the ubiquitous, and lethal, agency of the environment. Christie's chapter ends the book on a refreshingly, if not disturbingly, material note.

Modernism and the Anthropocene is not intended to be an encyclopedic treatment of the conjunction of these two historically and geographically intractable terms. Instead, it offers a sample of scholarship that has taken this conjunction as a generative inspiration—both to reframe works and authors treated as canonically modernist, as well as to open up the definition of modernism to incorporate a wider range of texts and genres that take up questions of ecology, nature, and the role of the human on a rapidly changing planet. It is our hope that putting modernism in the context of an emergent Anthropocene will prompt an even more thoroughgoing reconsideration of a literary and artistic period that, in its ecological, planetary preoccupations, becomes more and more contemporary with each passing year.

WORKS CITED

Anthropocene Working Group. 2019. "What Is the Anthropocene? Current Definition and Status." http://quaternary.stratigraphy.org/working-groups/anthropocene/. Accessed March 21, 2021.

Coupe, Laurence, ed. 2000. *The Green Studies Reader: From Romanticism to Ecocriticism*. New York: Routledge.

Crutzen, Paul J., and Eugene F. Stoermer. 2000. *International Geosphere-Biosphere Programme Newsletter* 41: 17–18.

Lewis, Simon L., and Mark A. Maslin. 2018. *The Human Planet: How We Created the Anthropocene*. New Haven, CT: Yale University Press.

Markley, Robert. 2012. "Time, History, and Sustainability." In *Telemorphosis: Theory in the Era of Climate Change*, Vol. 1, edited by Tom Cohen, 43–64. Ann Arbor , MI: Open Humanities Press.

McCarthy, Jeffrey Mathes. 2015. *Green Modernism: Nature and the English Novel*. New York: Palgrave Macmillan.

Raine, Anne. 2014. "Ecocriticism and Modernism." In *The Oxford Handbook of Ecocriticism*, edited by Greg Garrard, 98–117. New York: Oxford University Press.

Schuster, Joshua. 2015. *The Ecology of Modernism: American Environments and Avant-Garde Poetics*. Tuscaloosa: University of Alabama Press.

Sultzbach, Kelly. 2016. *Ecocriticism in the Modernist Imagination: Forster, Woolf, and Auden*. New York: Cambridge University Press.

Williams, Raymond. 1977. *Marxism and Literature*. Oxford: Oxford University Press.

Part I

MODERNISM-ANTHROPOCENE ENCOUNTERS

Chapter One

Revolt against the *Anthropos*

The Human-Environment Conflicts in D. H. Lawrence

Joseph Anderton

D. H. Lawrence's acute sensitivity to the natural world is a celebrated feature of his writing. His contemporary, Ford Madox Ford, witnessed Lawrence's unusual affinity with nature, describing him as "a half-mad, woodland creature" (Ford 1981, 61). Through such environmental awareness, Lawrence understood the profoundly deleterious effects humans were having on the natural environment and its inhabitants in the early twentieth century. In a late fragment of poetry, he wrote most pointedly: "There are too many people on earth, / insipid, unsalted, rabbity, endlessly hopping. / They nibble the face of the earth to a desert" (Lawrence 1994, 500). Lawrence implies here that the world's resources are finite and that the human species' population and consumption, like an indiscriminately propagative and ravenous animal, is damaging the planet. Although Lawrence does not have the geological or climatic knowledge and vocabulary of the Anthropocene at his disposal, he is nevertheless conscious of humanity's impact on and changing relationship with nature and the environment owing to modernity's industrialism, mechanization, urbanization, and capitalist materialism.

Lawrence identifies the modern human as a problem, the cause of "a process in which nature recedes into the past or into the margins of modernity, destroyed or displaced by new technoscientific practices and by the large-scale changes to the material environment those practices enable" (Raine 2014, 101). In redressing this alienation from nature, Lawrence reflects his own version of "the characteristic anxiety of modernism, that civilisation has taken a wrong turn somewhere" (Norris 2011, 115), and by which evolutionary success, exponential growth, and material progress are bound up with visions of decline, depletion, and ultimately, destruction. In his poem "To Let Go or to Hold On," for example, Lawrence uses flood imagery to convey the plight of the human species, which is "ebbing" and "floating" on a "deep,"

3

"cold black wave" (Lawrence 1994, 336). He wonders if the twilight of civilization has occurred: "Are we nothing, already, but the lapsing of a great
dead past?" (Lawrence 1994, 347), and later asks whether it is time to accept
the failure of modern ways of life and set out a new beginning, "Have we got
to get down and clear away the debris / of a swamped civilisation, and start
a new world for man that will blossom forth the whole of human nature?"
(Lawrence 1994, 347). The poem intimates that modernity has been deluged
with material excess and ideological stricture, and that the aftermath might
give rise to a better, purer being.

In this chapter I argue that Lawrence's work presages key implications of
the Anthropocene through his attention to civilization's manifold ills, modernity's lasting impact on the natural environment and nonhuman world, and
humanity's prospects. By drawing on several of Lawrence's stories, poems,
and essays from the 1920s, particularly *St. Mawr* (1925), this chapter will
show that Lawrence's work is alive to the modern human's adverse effect on
and accountability for the environment. He condemns the humanizing and
denaturing forces of modern civilization, the same drivers that would later
require humankind to govern the environment, as if from an increasingly
discrete, godly position. Instead, Lawrence implores people to get back in
touch with nature—as something out in the material world and embedded
deep within the human—in order to preserve the natural environment but also
to salvage the vitality of the human and mitigate the two-way process that
damages the human subject in the course of harming the nonhuman world. It
is often through animals, as the "frontier between nature and humanity" (Sax
2012, 31), that Lawrence conveys modernity's deadening of the human spirit
and loss of immanence to the physicality, immediacy, instinct, and authenticity of nature. In an essay on Lawrence's zoopoetics, Andrew Keese suggests
that, "[b]ased on his observations of animals, Lawrence sees both a path to
destruction if humankind does not make changes in its behaviour and a way
toward redemption through a recognition and acceptance of its basic animal
nature" (Keese 2012, 137). To divert the course of humankind, Lawrence
seeks to recuperate nature, frequently through primitivism and biocentrism, to
fulfil his vision of the "new world" that will emerge after modernity.

However, considering Lawrence's work in the context of the Anthropocene
introduces an alternative angle to humankind's mastery over and mistreat-
ment of a predominantly vulnerable environment. He instead concentrates
on the natural world's immense power, impressive hostility, and incessant
conflict with people. While the human impingement on the environment is
clear from statements such as "the country is so lovely: man-made England
is so vile" (Lawrence 2004, 291), Lawrence accentuates nature's resistance
and resilience, not as an ecological sceptic, but as means to fully respect the

natural environment and reassert humanity's possible place within it. In his introduction to *Wildlife in the Anthropocene*, Jamie Lorrimer points out two responses to the human domination of nature that the new geological era implies. The first view, the "dream of mastery," which tallies with the 2015 "An Ecomodernist Manifesto," "presents the Anthropocene as an economic and scientific opportunity necessitating more modernization—more knowledge, more technology, and better (i.e., more rational) forms of social and environmental organization" (Lorrimer 2015, 2). More cognate with Lawrence's doctrine, however, is the "dream of naturalism" in which "the geology confirms the unnatural character of modern, urban, industrial society" and advocates "a return to a premodern or even prehistorical state revealed through a valorization of traditional/indigenous knowledge" (Lorrimer 2015, 2). This second response chimes with both Lawrence and his champion F. R. Leavis, who claims that the industrial era's "utter insensitiveness to humanity and the environment" inflicted "the loss of human naturalness or normality" and "the loss of organic community," resulting in the fact that "the current age of human life is, in the strictest sense, *abnormal*" (Leavis and Thompson 2000, 75). Whereas the "dream of mastery" maintains the human hierarchy over nonhuman nature, Lawrence, like Leavis, sees a kind of perverted "homesickness" at work in modernity, in which it seems that "the knowing animals are aware that we are not really at home in our interpreted world," as his contemporary Rainer Maria Rilke articulates it (Rilke 2009, 3). In Lawrence's writing, he supports a more lateral, horizontal relationship between humanity and the natural environment that would recognize the balance between life forces and distance the conquest over nature in favor of a dynamic of endless contest. As Lawrence explains in his 1924 essay "Pan in America": "life itself consists in a live relatedness between man and his universe: sun, moon, stars, earth, trees, flowers, birds, animals, men, everything and not in a 'conquest' of anything by anything" (Lawrence 2009, 164). In true Lawrentian style, though, he apparently contradicts this sentiment in the slightly later essay "Reflections on the Death of a Porcupine," arguing that "[a]s far as existence goes, that life-species is the highest which can devour, or destroy, or subjugate every other life-species against which it is pitted in contest" (Lawrence 1988, 358). In truth, Lawrence's approval of the nonhuman world and his thoughts on the human's uncoupling from the natural environment largely appear through these conflicts, whereby human arrogance is often humbled and ignorance edified. With echoes of Nietzschean striving, "contest" has a place in Lawrence's schema, although his depictions of landscapes, flora, and fauna reveal a sublime power and radical alterity that humans cannot "conquer."

LAWRENCE AND THE INTERRUPTION OF MODERNITY

Lawrence's response to modernity is akin to the "dream of naturalism" response to the Anthropocene, which is at odds with certain strands of modernism that celebrate aspects of modernity, such as Futurism and the machine. Like his novels *The Rainbow* (1915) and *Women in Love* (1920), which, in part, chart the transition from agriculture to industrialism over three generations, Lawrence's literature and philosophy mark the tension between tradition and the new: rural and urban, organic and mechanical, instinct and consciousness, Romantic and Modernist. His poem "The Triumph of the Machine"—the title of which recalls F. T. Marinetti's 1911 essay "Multiplied Man and the Reign of Machine"—certainly clarifies that nature and the modern age are warring. The poem states boldly: "the machine will never triumph" (Lawrence 1994, 517). Nonhuman animals will eventually strike back at their physical and spiritual displacement: "And at last / all these creatures that cannot die . . . / will send up the wild cry of despair" (Lawrence 1994, 517). The indomitable animals in Lawrence's poem reflect his own resistance to the passive acceptance or exaltation of all aspects of modernity, which constitutes a confrontational spirit more in accord with the sensibility of modernism itself. As Astradur Eysteinsson specifies in *The Concept of Modernism*, it is "more to the point to see modernism as an attempt to *interrupt* the modernity that we live and understand as a social, if not 'normal,' way of life" (Eysteinsson 1990, 6). The natural world, as a sphere of alterity contrary to the techno-scientific advances of modernity, is not merely a Romantic sanctuary from the developments of the early twentieth century but a means of interrupting the factors and exposing the consequences of the era.

In Lawrence's *St. Mawr* and *The Woman Who Ran Away* (1925), which were inspired by the author's two years in New Mexico, his protagonists interrupt their modern lives by physically breaking away from the environments and cultures that stifle them. Lawrence's own "savage pilgrimage" (Lawrence 2002, 375) to the magnificent scenery of Taos, and his manual work at the nearby Kiowa Ranch in Questa, was a supremely significant experience for the author as it immersed him in a vast, demanding landscape and afforded him firsthand knowledge of the local American Indians. In contrast to the rapidity and evanescence of modern urban life, Lawrence wrote about Taos as a place of permanence that "still retains its old nodality" (Lawrence 2009, 125) and the Pueblo people as having "a sense of the inalterable" (Lawrence 2009, 126). Del Ivan Janik goes as far as to suggest that the indigenous American Indians exemplified Lawrence's "belief in the superiority of the 'blood'—the irrational, sensual aspect of being—and in the importance of the 'dark' mysterious sources of vitality that lie beyond human reason" (Janik 1983, 366). Lawrence thought that such cultures "still knew and acted out of those deep sources" (Janik 1983, 366) and his short novel *St. Mawr* evinces his gravitation to these Native Peoples, their ancient customs and connections to the land and its nonhuman inhabitants, as an alternative to the sterility of life in Europe, particularly England.

In *St. Mawr*, witnessing the grief and recalcitrance of the eponymous stallion, as well as attempts to geld the superannuated horse, encourages Lou Witt to leave the ignoble, superficial gentry class of London and, after a brief return to Texas, settle in the Rocky Mountains of New Mexico. For Lou, the dulling and insincere existence in civilized society is diametrically opposed to the real vitality of nonhuman animals and the natural world: "The marvellous beauty and fascination of natural wild things! The horror of man's unnatural life, his heaped-up civilisation!" (Lawrence 2006b, 149). Despite this exaltation, she does not exactly desire to return to a state of primitiveness. Lou is more intent on assimilating the spiritedness of animality back into her humanity, which seems to run on stale fuel: "I don't want to be an animal like a horse or a cat or a lioness, though they all fascinate me, the way they get their life *straight*, not from a lot of old tanks, as we do. I don't admire the cave man, and that sort of thing. But think, mother, if we could get our lives from the source, as the animals do, and still be ourselves" (Lawrence 2006b, 81). The life-sapping existence Lou leads is further realized in the smallest encounters with nature, which act as the tonic to her staid, manufactured life: "It is terrible when the life-flow dies out of one, and everything is like cardboard, and oneself is like cardboard. I'm sure it is worse than being dead. . . . He found me some water-cresses, and they tasted so damp and alive, I knew how deadened I was" (Lawrence 2006b, 135). It appears that the quasi-Romantic outlook of Lawrence's characters, including the belief in the power of nature and disapproval of rationalism, is in fact a rally against the maladies of modernity. Crucially, the untamed spirit of landscapes, plants, and animals that has been repressed in humans counters the machinations of life in civilized European cities.

In a reification of the epiphany in *St. Mawr*, a horse acts as the literal vehicle of escape in *The Woman Who Rode Away*, in which an unfulfilled woman leaves the "invincible slavery" (Lawrence 2006b, 6) of her guarded domestic life after the closure of husband's silver mining enterprise in the Sierra Madre and seeks out raw, profound alternatives with an American Indian tribe. It is noticeable that *St. Mawr*'s movement from the horse's animal vitality to America's wilds extends in *The Woman Who Rode Away* to Indigenous Peoples and cultures. After a visitor's suggestion that adventure and distinctiveness are lacking in the metropolises, as *"everybody* lives in London or Paris or New York," the Chilchui tribe's "old religions and mysteries" are attractive to the woman, to the extent that "she was overcome by a foolish romanticism more unreal than a girl's" (Lawrence 2006b, 8). In the end, she prefers an actual death as the tribe's sacrifice to the apathetic death of her former life; such is her entrapment in mundanity and enchantment by the Indians. If, as Kenneth Inniss argues, Lawrence's work teaches that "[t]he animal kingdom . . . is within us" and "'Africa' or 'Mexico' are objective correlatives, correspondences, for a level of consciousness, for states of soul" (Inniss 1971, 23), here it is remarkable that other cultures activate that zoological level of being, therefore forging identification between certain Aboriginal human groups and the primitive natural world. The woman's impression that the Pueblo people are inhuman reaffirms this association, such as how "he would look at her with this strange soft glow of ecstasy that was not quite human, and terribly impersonal" (Lawrence 2006b, 22) and the description of "the strange uplifted savage sound of men singing round the drum, like wild creatures howling to the invisible gods of the moon and the vanished sun" (Lawrence 2006b, 26).

This kind of appropriation or inspiration of "primitive" cultures is arguably one of the few contracts modernism keeps with nature, or at least a productive human-nature interface. Admittedly, there is the suggestion that "modernist formal experimentation is ecological because it seeks to preserve the alterity of the nonhuman" (Raine 2014, 107), although, in Lawrence's case, he is against the "psychological minutiae" of modernist novels that would help to conjure such different epistemologies and ontologies. As his recent biographer Andrew Harrison points out, Lawrence instead pursued a combined fiction and philosophy to produce "modern kind of gospels, and modern myths" (Harrison 2016, 256). Yet Lawrence's use of primitivism to develop these modern myths is problematic if it does not support the idea that "modernism's resistance to romantic and realist nature discourse . . . reflects the sense that accepted forms of nature discourse relied on reductive or anthropocentric habits of thought that were inadequate to convey the world's 'multifarious otherness' and often complicit with the instrumental domination of nature" (Raine 2014, 103). Accordingly, in both *St. Mawr* and *The Woman Who Rode Away*, the received normality of the modern civilized world is disputed through profound experiences in other places and cultures. This primitivism, although arguably an index of controversial imperial legacies, is modernism's attempt to recover an older, more genuine, and ultimately positive relationship with the natural environment.

DETHRONING THE HUMAN:
MISANTHROPY AND BIOCENTRISM

Lawrence's interruption of modernity entails a reevaluation of human cultures, particularly in Western capitalist societies, and this critique frequently tips over into a misanthropic sensibility. Predominantly, the misanthropy in Lawrence's work originates from the resentment of humanity's denatured status and humans as a denaturing force. Inniss argues that, in Lawrence's "last period," he "appears to have had a vision of the Just City—a place in touch with the creative wild, where the animal principles in man are recognised, tiger balanced against deer" (Inniss 1971, 13). To achieve this vision of modernity, Lawrence urges humans to reject what he sees as the inorganic constrictions of individual consciousness, social propriety, and political establishment. In his poem "Wild Things in Captivity," for instance, Lawrence depicts humans as creatures trapped in "[t]he great cage of our domesticity" (Lawrence 1994, 399), while in "Escape," he implores people to "get into the forest again" away from "our own ego" (Lawrence 1994, 397). In doing so, "old things will fall down / we shall laugh, and institutions will curl up like burnt paper" (Lawrence 1994, 397). Crucially, capitalism and materialism are also major impediments to the liberation Lawrence associates with the wild: "Our last wall is the golden wall of money. This is a fatal wall. It cuts us off from life, from vitality, from the alive sun and alive earth, as nothing can" (Lawrence 1988, 363). These forms of psychological and institutional alienation from nature contribute to the hatred or shame directed toward the human species in Lawrence's work.

Jeff Wallace avers that nature is "an always-already 'managed' condition informed by human interests and priorities" as "human and non-human are locked into systems of conflict, dependency, but of necessary engagement and relationship" (Wallace 2005, 128). The Anthropocene is the apotheosis of this detached management and involved relationship. No longer is nature a "single, timeless, and pure domain untouched by Society," since "this world is hybrid—neither social nor natural" (Lorrimer 2015, 1–2). What is problematic in terms of Lawrence doctrine here is that the Anthropocene's "unsettlement of the entrenched binaries of modernity (nature and culture, object and subject)" (Macfarlane 2016, n.p.) has not occurred through a recovery or co-option of nature, but through a "humanization" of nature, making the natural environment beholden to the activities of human beings. Lawrence is aware that the presence of humans on Earth is becoming ubiquitous: "Not a space, not a speck of this country that wasn't humanized, occupied by human claim. Not even the sky" (Lawrence 2006b, 127). In response to this pervasive anthropomorphism, misanthropy in Lawrence's work can counteract the human bias to promote a progressive, critical objectivity and nonanthropocentric perspicacity toward the denaturing consequences of human interference.

In *St. Mawr*, misanthropy is one of the catalysts for the characters' migration from the city of London to the wilds of New Mexico. Lou is particularly scathing about people, although the use of free indirect discourse at times means the narrative voice shares partially in the dislike of humans. When the Vyners and the Witts discuss whether the "dangerous" St. Mawr should be euthanized, Lou is incensed: "These people almost roused her to hatred. Oh, these awful house-bred, house-inbred human-beings, how repulsive they were!" (Lawrence 2006b, 108). The obtuse treatment of the horse spurs Lou and her mother on to express repeatedly their desires to escape from contemptible people. Lou's artist husband, Rico, imagines her response to civilized London society: "No dear, I don't love it at all! I want to be away from these people" (Lawrence 2006b, 95), whereas for Mrs. Witt, the English countryside and the European continent only stoke her longing for the new world of America again: "she felt an almost savage desire to get away from Europe, from everything European. . . . Something just writhed inside her, all the time, against Europe" (Lawrence 2006b, 120). The male characters in the text have a similar aversion to the urban masses as to Phoenix: "the city was a sort of nightmare mirage, and to Lewis, it was a sort of prison. The presence of people he felt as a prison around him" (Lawrence 2006b, 57). The effect of these compulsions to disassociate from insensitive, false people and incarcerating crowds is a "biocentric displacement of human priority" (Granofsky 2003, 30) that deposes anthropocentrism to engender a more balanced attention to other forms of life. Lawrence equalizes the human and nonhuman by demoting people as much as elevating glorious elements of nature, such as St. Mawr's violent animal power or America's remote environments. Although Harrison asserts that, as part of Lawrence's critique of British imperialism in *St. Mawr*, "he turned away from people altogether, concentrating instead on the proud singleness of the horse named St. Mawr, and on the inhuman qualities of the New Mexican landscape" (Harrison 2016, 281), it is notable that Lawrence and his characters deliver several parting shots to humans in the turn to nonhuman animals and inhuman environs. The fact that the hatred of humans is intense is really a sign of the measures necessary to subvert entrenched human chauvinism.

Lawrence adds an ecological subtext to the negative portrayal of people in *St. Mawr* by associating the metropolitan masses with suffocating and polluting conditions. The congestion and depravity of the city is expressed as a lack of breathing space and poor air quality. The reader is told that "the English air: it was never quite free from the smell of smoke, coal-smoke" (Lawrence 2006b, 126), and Paris does not fare any better: "'Something unlucky is bound to happen to me in this sinister, unclean town,' she said. 'I feel it in the air. I feel *contagion* in the air of this place,'" (Lawrence 2006b, 43). The literal pollution of the fossil fuel links back to a figuratively toxic atmosphere in the diffusion of foreboding feelings and harmful circumstances. It is Mrs. Witt who affiliates the idea of contaminated air with oppressive overcrowding more concretely, however, when she says: "I'll start immediately after lunch, for I can't *breathe* in this place any longer" (Lawrence 2006b, 119). With Lawrence, then, the stifling environmental conditions have a corresponding spiritual repercussion, meaning the damage done to the material world affects the holistic well-being of the human subject. Yet, not all groups of people are causes of such contamination. Late in the text, the ancient rituals of the Indigenous People are supposedly purifying, "That's what the moon people do: they wash the air clean with moonlight" (Lawrence 2006b, 128), which positions their reverent wisdom gleaned from pantheism, animism, and pagan nature religions as the antidote to modern excess.

The dislike for a sullying humanity is even more apparent in *Women in Love* when Rupert Birkin expresses a posthumanist desire for Earth to be "cleaned of all people" as they are "a mistake" (Lawrence 1987, 127) and "a defilement" of the world (Lawrence 1987, 128). He says to Ursula, "don't you find it a beautiful clean thought, a world empty of people, just uninterrupted grass, and a hare sitting up? . . . I much prefer to think of the lark rising up in the morning upon a human-less world" (Lawrence 1987, 127–28). Rupert believes that conserving nature involves removing humans, and his vocabulary of cleansing and spoiling identifies the *anthropos* as a corrupting force, indicating both an environmental and ethical responsibility; he evokes the idea of preserving the virtue of nature as well as its material conditions. Foreseeing the co-dependency between human and environment implied in the Anthropocene, Ursula argues that Earth is bound to humankind and if man dies out "the world will go with him" (Lawrence 1987, 128). The misanthrope Rupert disagrees, claiming that life will be refreshed with the end of the human species; it will be a "new start, non-human" (Lawrence 1987, 128). This conversation in *Women in Love* shows Lawrence posing an extreme measure to secure the future of the environment, in which survival appears to boil down to one or the other: humans or nature. Ronald Granofsky observes that on such occasions, misanthropy in Lawrence's work exceeds the shift from anthropocentrism to biocentrism: "In such radical ecologist moods, Lawrence is not content to engage in what [Margot] Norris calls 'the dismantling of an anthropocentric ontology'; he is happy to contemplate the extinction of the human species as an improvement, on the whole, for the planet" (Granofsky 2003, 30). Whereas the Anthropocene identifies humankind as the perpetrator of long-term environmental change as well as the potential savior of the planet, Lawrence broaches the idea of human absence being the best contribution to the survival of life.

The dislike of humans in Lawrence's stories corresponds with a possible self-critical reaction to the Anthropocene's impact on the environment. Academics such as Ian Angus (2016) and Raj Patel (2013) have noted the satirical term "misanthropocene" to describe the deprecation of humanity and its dystopian world resulting from anthropogenic climate change. Whereas this "Hateful Human Age" is despondent, misanthropy in Lawrence's work mainly serves to avoid value and perspective types of anthropocentrism to develop a more clear-eyed view of the impacts of humanity and therefore develop sensitivity to nature and others. In an essay on Nietzsche, Elizabeth Kuhn suggests that "an alternative anti-humanist modernism dethrones ego, consciousness, and interiority with an eye to the furthering of life rather than life's cancellation; life as a force capable, at its best, of taking the human beyond itself into unthinkable modes of alterity" (Kuhn 2011, 2). Extreme negativity toward humans seems capable of the type of expansion Kuhn identifies, redirecting attention to other nonhuman life, for example. It also raises the possibility that Lawrence is not against the *anthropos* wholesale but against the current form of humanity, or particular groups of humans, and that the species could be renewed, as the "horse was an improvement on the ichthyosaurus" (Lawrence 1994, 429), resulting in a better incarnation. Receptivity to alterity and the homogeneous substrate of life that underpins the diversity of the biosphere is a step toward this self-discovery.

An anthropocentric, humanized environment is highly contrary to the trajectory Lawrence envisions repeatedly in his literature, in which there remains the promise of humans absconding from the "conquest" over nature to partake in a more mutual "contest," closer to adjacent involvement than estranged management. He wrote in "Him with His Tail in His Mouth" that "too much *anthropos* makes the world a dull hole" (Lawrence 1988, 315), and it is this overwhelming domination that might recede into a proper equilibrium, competitive but balanced, which would be spiritually nurturing for humanity, as well as a sign of respect for and reciprocation with the natural world and the animal kingdom. In this way, Lawrence appears to circumvent an oversight in ecocriticism, which, according to Adam Trexler, is a field in which "the preoccupation with life sciences led ecocritics to diagnose climate change as a human incursion on ecosystems or Nature writ large, rather than a process that inextricably binds human and nonhuman systems" (Trexler 2015, 17). For Lawrence, at least, modernity's impact on the environment and the human's changing relationship with nature caused the acute severance from, and prescribed the confluence with, the nonhuman.

"ANIMOSITY": THE NONHUMAN REVOLT

If the Anthropocene names the human corruption of the wildness of the natural environment, Lawrence's preemptive thought was to promote the correspondences and relationships between the human and nonhuman, while observing the fundamental differences or otherness. Indeed, "cut off from [nature] by his 'civilised consciousness,' Lawrence continually sought places and people whom he could imagine had a more authentic, 'primal' relationship to animal Others" (Garrard 2011, 167). Although the ontological disparity between human civilization and the natural world enforces a veritable distance, Lawrence conveys a more intimate relationship with nature, often through the oppositional, conflicting dynamic between humans and other nonhuman species and environments. Landscapes, plants, and animals are invariably resistant to humans in epistemological, spiritual, and physical senses, which ensure that humans and nonhumans coincide but are not conflated. The ennui that Lawrence finds in a disproportionately humanized world leads him to convey the alterity of nonhuman animals in *St. Mawr*, for example, by drawing attention repeatedly to the fact that animals occupy "another world." He writes: "The wild, brilliant, alert head of St. Mawr seemed to look at her out of another world" (Lawrence 2006b, 50), and, later, "in his dark eye, that looked, with its cloudy brown pupil, a cloud within a dark fire, like a world beyond our world, there was a dark vitality glowing, and within the fire, another sort of wisdom" (Lawrence 2006b, 61). The horse's gaze confronts humans with an obscure energy that is not easily overcome or manipulated; it confounds human reason and interpretation until, as Carrie Rohman supposes, in *Stalking the Subject*, "the fact that St. Mawr cannot be encompassed by a totalizing meaning in the text points to the fullness, if you will, the plenitude of his meaning as animal other, as unknowable quantity, as a being radically different from the human" (Rohman 2009, 131). Even when humans can apparently learn something about the self from the animal or topographical other, to the extent of incorporating aspects of its life, it is without negating the uniqueness of their respective identities. Lawrence's recommendations for engaging with indigenous worldviews could equally apply to animals here: "to take up an old dark thread from their vision, and see again as they see, without forgetting we are ourselves" (Lawrence 2009, 110). Through these appeals to primitivism, it seems Lawrence reinforces the civilized/savage binary, yet he inverts the typical derogatory value of the latter term, imploring people to eschew the limitations of anthropocentric societies and embrace repressed primal qualities, which would effectively re-wild the human rather than humanize nature.

It is appropriate that the animal's alterity should be embodied as "another world," as the environmental conditions, terrains, plants, and animals that his characters encounter are often physically imposing, as well as psychologically intimidating. Nonhuman beings and inhuman environments appear antagonistic and formidable, unseating the conception of them as merely passive victims or pliable objects. The agitated St. Mawr seems to harbor indignation toward people, such as when Lou infers that "somewhere deep in his animal consciousness lived a dangerous, half-revealed resentment, a diffused sense of hostility. She realised that he was sensitive, in spite of his flaming, healthy strength, and nervous with a touchy uneasiness that might make him vindictive" (Lawrence 2006b, 48). Even the words "sensitive" and "nervous," in this context, suggest volatility. St. Mawr is alert to his surroundings and responsive to the human actions, yet he will react with unpredictable violence and furious vengeance. He is also a mulish animal, indisposed to yield to human will: "The devil was in him. He would turn down every turning where he was not meant to go . . . St. Mawr flew on, in a sort of *élan*. Marvellous the power and life in the creature" (Lawrence 2006b, 69). Lawrence's depiction imbues the animal with the vibrancy that constitutes modernity ostensibly, in the velocity of activity and volume of production, but that it is devoid of qualitatively, owing to numbing superficiality and artificiality. As "a precursory agent of some deeper nonhuman state of being that looms near the end of the story" (Gutierrez 1981, 190), the horse's forcefulness actually connects to the power and profundity of the wider natural world, indicating that Lawrence advocates a new reverence for nature as a result of the hostile reactions to the antibiotic relationship with modern pressures, rather than solely conveying the fragility of the nonhuman. As a strand in Lawrence's gamut of the primitive, nonhuman beings can act as a barometer of human interference, environmental change included, with each hostile conflict betraying the human's alienation from and subsequent impingement on the natural world. However, the animal's reactive spirit draws humans back into a more primitive confrontation in Lawrence's writing, reactivating a seemingly favorable condition of contest, while simultaneously revealing modernity's real spiritual exclusion from the vitality of nature.

The other world that nonhuman animals occupy is arguably immanent to the unmediated experience of nature known as the "Open" that Rilke expresses in his *Duino Elegies*. In "The Eighth Elegy," in contrast to the outward gaze of the natural world, human eyes are turned "backward, and surround plant, animal, child / like traps, as they emerge into their freedom. / We know what is really out there only from the animal's gaze" (Rilke 2009, 49). The animal's membership in the pure space of the Open means that the life force in animals, or rather "animosity," is one that also flows through the features of natural environments. Like St. Mawr, the New Mexican flora and fauna are combative as they struggle for survival with all other living things: "The wild life, even the life of the trees and flowers, seemed one bristling, hair-raising tussle. The very flowers came up bristly, and many of them were fang-mouthed, like the dead-nettle: and none had any real scent. But they were very fascinating, too, in their very fierceness" (Lawrence 2006b, 168). Typically delicate and beautiful wildlife has an aggressive, resilient side, and although this aids its continuation in the biosphere generally, Lawrence ensures that a specifically anti-human angle is prevalent: "the ash-trees are mad, they want to kill all these people" (Lawrence 2006b, 128). Nature's uprising might seem like a precursor to a fantastically speculative post-apocalyptic novel such as John Wyndham's *The Day of the Triffids* (1951), but Lawrence is actually nostalgic for the survival dynamics of the evolutionary past, in which regression is paradoxically a means of developing a more positive image of the future, both ecologically sustainable and anthropologically enriching.

In the pathetic fallacy of attributing motivations to the nonhuman, it is possible that Lawrence contributes to the anthropomorphism that he finds tedious. This is particularly noticeable in his treatment of the New Mexican landscape and the recurrent terms "malevolent" and "invidious" in *St. Mawr* to describe the mountainous environment. The narrator expands on the difficult conditions at length: "At one time no water. At another a poison-weed. Then a sickness. Always some mysterious malevolence fighting, fighting against the will of man. . . . A curious disintegration working all the time, a sort of malevolent breath, like a stupefying, irritant gas, coming out of the unfathomed mountains" (Lawrence 2006b, 163). In this suggestion of evil doing, Lawrence injects agency into the environment, as if the harsh conditions are intentionally to wear humans down. An epistemological resistance also accompanies the environment's physical difficulty, as the mountains are "stupefying" and "unfathomed," beyond the intellectual comprehension conducive to human mastery. These two aspects together generate a power struggle in which the material environment is unusually campaigning and potent while the human is toothless and trivial. In effect, Lawrence's projection of motivations and mysteries onto the nonhuman explodes the inertness of the natural world, highlighting an animistic liveliness that reflects human guilt over the treatment of the environment and grief over the loss of nature.

As the examples of active force against humans accumulate in *St. Mawr*, Lawrence indicates that nature is revolting against an anthropocentric mentality and seeking retribution for humanity's insolence. Nature is not only reacting, it is attacking: "At the same time, the invisible attack was being made upon her. While she revelled in the beauty of the luminous world that wheeled around and below her, the grey rat-like spirit of the inner mountains was attacking her from behind" (Lawrence 2006b, 167). Lawrence conjures the environment's sublime quality here in the juxtaposition of the mountain's splendorous scale and its fearsome, animal-like determination. More than a surface aesthetic to be observed, though, nature is a penetrating presence to be felt; it is a spirit as much as a sight: "the animosity of the spirit of the place: the crude, half-created spirit of the place, like some serpent-bird forever at-tacking man, in a hatred of man's onward-struggle towards further creation" (Lawrence 2006b, 170). Lawrence ensures that the human-environment conflicts surpass a simple antagonistic relationship to evoke a nonhuman au-tonomy that commands attention and respect. Far from claiming that hostile nonhuman animals and inhuman environments can endure an anthropogenic assault without change, however, the implication is that the massive extent to which life struggles to remain, and remain itself, in light of human opposition, renders life precious. Lawrence's ecological message is deferential to the sheer wilfulness of life in its multiple forms, especially after the anthropo-centrism of humanist traditions, aspects of which underpin the Anthropocene. His recourse to a resilient natural world implies humans should re-engage with the urgency of contest in the wild to recapture the vitality of nature and, in doing so, environmental conservation will occur through integration rather than top-down management. The removed, human-constructed perspective should therefore dissolve into the immanence of being, as Granofsky ac-knowledges apropos of Lawrence's vitalism: "The Nietzsche in Lawrence drives him to imagine an abolition of the old hierarchies for a new vitalistic one, so that ultimately the hierarchies of class and race become subsumed to the hierarchy of existence and survival" (Granofsky 2003, 28). In the shared arena of power, hostility, conflict, and survival, then, Lawrence validates applying the related actions, motivations and emotions to the nonhuman, without resorting to anthropomorphism exactly, as these dynamics are less exclusively human than first assumed.

Malevolent agency is also prevalent in Lawrence's depiction of the envi-ronment in the ironically titled 1927 story, "The Man Who Loved Islands." The story follows an unnamed man as he moves between three islands, start-ing with an ambition for a utopian society and ending as a hate-filled hermit. On the third and final island, the narrator describes how "[o]ut of the very air came a stony, heavy malevolence. The island itself seemed malicious. It would go on being hurtful and evil for weeks at a time" (Lawrence 2006a, 295). As with the animal St. Mawr, the virulent island assumes a subjectivity of its own, seemingly showing spiteful intent. The indecipherability of the place is also a challenge, albeit double edged, at once intriguing and repellent; it enchants and assails its human inhabitant: "The island was still mysterious and fascinating. But it was also treacherous and cruel, secretly, fathomlessly malevolent" (Lawrence 2006a, 297). The curiosity it inspires is primarily because the man's self-conceit causes him to seek mastery over his surroundings, first in a social-communal regard, and, when that fails or disappoints, in a solitary, pastoral way. As Harrison notes, this text eventually discloses the man's "horror and madness as the desire for integrity and control bring him into conflict with Nature itself" (Harrison 2016, 323). Yet, unlike *St. Mawr*, there is a genuinely apocalyptic resolution to this conflict that evokes the human's catastrophic fate in environmental and climatic terms. As the story concludes, the island slips into "a dull, deathly cold" (Lawrence 2006a, 309) and, when several birds die, it appears that vitality is receding from the place: "It was as if all life were drawing away, contracting away from the north, contracting southwards" (Lawrence 2006a, 310). Death reigns over the "corpse-like land" (2006a: 310) and only incongruous traces of nature remain. The narrator notices how "Curiously natural the pebbles looked, in a world gone uncanny. The sun shone no more" (Lawrence 2006a, 311). The human and the nonhuman appear to endure an antibiotic relationship in this narrative, resulting in a decline in organic life and the increase in extreme weather conditions, including lightning, thunder, and snowstorms. The earth itself "fumed like volcanoes" (Lawrence 2006a, 312) and in the final words of the story comes the ominous "[y]ou can't win against the elements" (Lawrence 2006a, 312). "The Man Who Loved Islands" is therefore a microcosm of the human species' influence on and subjection to its surroundings, and while it is suggested that the man is an active participant in his own demise, the inhospitable environment also shows that, in the end, he is the disposable, losing party in the human-environment conflict. As humanity, wildlife and habitable conditions disappear, it is notable that Lawrence touches on an ecological staple, namely "a congruence of environmental themes and apocalyptic rhetoric" (Garrard 2011, 97). This endgame revolves around the biosphere's dependency on the ecosphere, and the incompatibility of the two domains results in the absence of life and the aggravated wrath of the elements. In an eschatological twist, it is the environment that casts the final judgement on the man, condemning his arrogant ambitions and ecological failings.

However, apocalyptic narratives are prophetic, indicative of *potential* futures and therefore implicitly appeal for change. Whereas the recent "An Ecomodernist Manifesto" rejects the notion "that human societies must harmonize with nature to avoid economic and ecological collapse" ("Ecomodernist" 2015, 6) in favor of an essentially more educated, efficient form of modernity, this "harmony" is precisely what Lawrence advocates, at least where harmony means the joining together of human and nonhuman, albeit into a balance that comprises competition and conflict from the natural will to survive. Lawrence's ecology, which finds its greatest need in the context of the Anthropocene, apprehends the human's friction with a resilient, defensive but ultimately mutable environment, but also diminishes anthropocentric values in an effort to revive the naturalness of human beings and thereby produce the posthuman. For Lawrence, the current human trajectory is owing to the selfish apathy of the species: "They know civilisation has got to smash, sooner or later. So they say: 'Let it! But let me live my life first,'" (Lawrence 1994, 206). In contrast, realising the organic interconnectedness of life could remedy this miserable self-centredness, as he says in the final section of his last major work, *Apocalypse*: "I am a part of the great whole, and I can never escape. But I can deny my connections, break them, and become a fragment, then I am wretched" (Lawrence 1974, 126). Although Lawrence preceded the term "Anthropocene," he nevertheless recognised the indelible impact of human activity on the environment in the past and yet would have doubted the humanness of the prospective solution, at least in its current modern guise.

WORKS CITED

"An Ecomodernist Manifesto." 2015. Accessed 6 November 2015. http://www.eco modernism.org.

Angus, Ian. 2016. *Facing the Anthropocene: Fossil Capitalism and the Crisis of the Earth System*. New York: New York University Press.

Eysteinsson, Astadur. 1990. *The Concept of Modernism*. Ithaca: Cornell University Press.

Ford, Ford Madox. 1981. *An Editor's Impression, D.H. Lawrence, Interviews and Recollections*, Vol. 1. Edited by Norman Page. London and Basingstoke: Macmillan.

Garrard, Greg. 2011. *Ecocriticism*. London: Routledge.

Granofsky, Ronald. 2003. *D. H. Lawrence and Survival: Darwinism in the Fiction of the Transitional Period*. Montreal: McGill-Queen's University Press.

Gutierrez, Donald. 1981. "The Ancient Imagination of D. H. Lawrence." *Twentieth Century Literature* 27 (2): 178–96.

Harrison, Andrew. 2016. *The Life of D. H. Lawrence*. Oxford: Wiley-Blackwell.

Inniss, Kenneth. 1971. *D. H. Lawrence's Bestiary: A Study of His Use of Animal Trope and Symbol*. Paris: Mouton.

Janik, Del Ivan. 1983. "D. H. Lawrence and Environmental Consciousness." *Environmental Review: ER* 7 (4): 359–72.

Keese, Andrew. 2012. "Pansies: Lawrence's Search for the Animal Other in Humans." *D. H. Lawrence Studies* 20 (2): 135–52.

Kuhn, Elizabeth. 2011. "Toward an Anti-Humanism of Life: The Modernism of Nietzsche, Hulme and Yeats." *Journal of Modern Literature* 34 (4): 1–20.

Lawrence, D. H. 1974. *Apocalypse*. London: Penguin.

———. 1987. *Women in Love.* Edited by David Farmer, Lindeth Vasey, and John Worthen. Cambridge: Cambridge University Press.

———. 1988. *Reflections on the Death of a Porcupine and Other Essays.* Edited by Michael Herbert. Cambridge: Cambridge University Press.

———. 1994. *The Complete Poems of D. H. Lawrence.* London: Wordsworth.

———. 2002. *The Letters of D. H. Lawrence*, Vol. 4. Edited by Warren Roberts, James T. Boulton, and Elizabeth Mansfield. Cambridge: Cambridge University Press.

———. 2004. *Late Essays and Articles.* Edited by James T. Boulton. Cambridge: Cambridge University Press.

———. 2006a. *Selected Stories.* London: Penguin.

———. 2006b. *The Woman Who Rode Away / St. Mawr / The Princess.* London: Penguin.

———. 2009. *Mornings in Mexico and Other Essays.* Cambridge: Cambridge University Press.

Leavis, F. R. and Denys Thompson, 2000. "The Organic Community." In *The Green Studies Reader: From Romanticism to Ecocriticism*, edited by Laurence Coupe, 73–76. London and New York: Routledge.

Lorrimer, Jamie. 2015. *Wildlife in the Anthropocene: Conservation after Nature.* Minneapolis: University of Minnesota.

Macfarlane, Robert. 2016. "Generation Anthropocene: How Humans Have Altered the Planet Forever." *The Guardian*, April 1, 2016.

Norris, Trevor. 2011. "Martin Heidegger, D. H. Lawrence, and Poetic Attention to Being." In *Ecocritical Theory: New European Approaches*, edited by Axel Goodbody and Kate Rigby, 113–25. Charlottesville: University of Virginia Press.

Patel, Raj. 2013. "Misanthropocene?" *Earth Island Journal* 28 (1). Accessed December 20, 2019. https://www.earthisland.org/journal/index.php/magazine /entry/ misanthropocene.

Raine, Anne. 2014. "Ecocriticism and Modernism" In *The Oxford Handbook of Ecocriticism*, edited by Greg Garrard, 98–117. New York and Oxford: Oxford University Press.

Rilke, Rainer Maria. 2009. *Duino Elegies and The Sonnets to Orpheus.* Edited and translated by Stephen Mitchell. New York: Vintage.

Rohman, Carrie. 2009. *Stalking the Subject: Modernism and the Animal.* New York and Chichester: Columbia University Press.

Sax, Boria. 2012. "What is this Quintessence of Dust? The Concept of the 'Human' and its Origins." In *Anthropocentrism: Humans, Animals, Environments*, edited by Rob Boddice, 21–36. Leiden: Brill.

Trexler, Adam. 2015. *Anthropocene Fictions: The Novel in a Time of Climate Change.* Charlottesville and London: University of Virginia Press.

Wallace, Jeff. 2005. *D. H. Lawrence, Science and the Posthuman.* Basingstoke: Palgrave.

Chapter Two

Vorticism in the Age of Climate Change

Jessica Martell

We assert that the art for these climates . . . must be a northern flower.

—Wyndham Lewis, *Blast 1* (36)

Vorticism was a short-lived but influential avant-garde movement that made a splash on both sides of the Atlantic just before the First World War. Founding member Ezra Pound is credited with introducing the term *vortex* to describe the sense of controlled chaos that fueled the group's aesthetic and to capture the artists' intentions to stir up the public with "maximum energy" and controversy (Lewis 1914, 153).[1] In 1914, the publication of *Blast*, an electric pink volume of manifestos, poems, and drawings edited by the artist and author Wyndham Lewis, announced the Vorticists' aggressive arrival onto the international art scene.

One of many manifestos that accompanied the emergence of modernism, the first volume of *Blast* was in part an Anglo-American response to F. T. Marinetti's "Futurist Manifesto," which was printed in *Le Figaro* in 1909. Like Cubism, Futurism challenged the public's placid devotion to realist landscapes and pastoral themes. For instance, Marinetti called for the celebration of machines and speed as new wells of creativity for modern artists. With its love of aeroplanes, roaring locomotives, and high wire bridges, Futurism epitomizes anthropocentric attitudes toward nature and celebrates the possibility of a future in which industrial growth, accompanied by technological innovation, would eliminate nature's constraints upon human potential. *Blast 1* suggests that the Vorticists regarded the industrial age with greater skepticism, refusing to applaud the triumph of human designs with the same unbridled optimism. Though equally inspired by machine-age forms, the Vorticists' manifestos denounce "Marinetteism" as simple-minded "automobilism" and attribute its "undigested" style to its "melodramatic" embrace of technology (*B1*, 8, 143–44). Instead, it advises the artists of the future to avoid such sentimental fetishism, cultivating a cool, detached aesthetic in its place.

I use the word "cool" deliberately because the rationale for *Blast*'s rejection of Futurism is based largely upon climate. This chapter explores how *Blast* enlists the language of climate, along with other physical systems like weather and geography, to formulate its unique vision for artistic revolution. The manifestos of the Vorticist project pivot upon the premise "that what is actual and vital for the South is ineffectual and unactual in the North" (*B1*, 34), asserting that artistic genius is subject to regional variation. Futurism's "sentimental" gushing is spurned as a non-native species, a product of immoderate Southern warmth that cannot remedy Britain's cultural inertia (*B1*, 8, 42–43). Instead, the text demands that Vorticists develop their style into a "necessary native art" by embracing the archipelago's own physical attributes. The new movement "must be a northern flower" if its revolution is to take root (*B1*, 37, 36).

The Vorticist fusion of the aesthetic with the climatic imports crucial environmental concerns into modernist studies. I argue that *Blast*'s preoccupation with ecological distinctiveness opens the possibility of a "responsible" connection to nature where its avant-garde contemporaries, like the Futurists, do not.[2] Its climatic schema for avant-gardism may justly be regarded as chauvinist and ethnocentric, but it also aims to cultivate an artistic vision that is derived from the uniqueness of an indigenous ecology. For all its regressive tendencies, *Blast* is equally energized by what Bonnie Costello terms an "entanglement of nature and culture" and unmistakably finds creative vitality within this entanglement (Costello 1998, 574). This is to read *Blast* somewhat against its intended purpose as a manifesto designed to administer cures for social and cultural, rather than ecological, ills. But the text is nevertheless oriented toward the environment, if unconsciously so. By amplifying its ecological content, even against its own tendency to relegate it to the backdrop of cultural drama, I want to reveal an intricate and vivid environmental imagination in *Blast* that illustrates what we now understand conceptually as the Anthropocene long before this term existed.

While *Blast* presents neither a "good" nor "bad" Anthropocene, it does weave a hybrid mesh between nature and industry from which Vorticism will emerge. The text refrains from fetishizing technology in the absence of humanity, as many of Marinetti's writings do; in the initial manifestos, Lewis as primary author seems indifferent to the machine except as a reflection of human will and desire. There are, of course, plenty of problematic possibilities in this stance should these desires prove destructive. But what is intriguing about *Blast*'s glorification of industry, from an environmental perspective, is how Lewis must resort to images from nature in order to represent industrial triumph and its infinite potential for artistic inspiration. By examining the activity of natural forces as they weave their way into *Blast*'s manifestos, this chapter contends that *Blast* should still be read as an environmental text even if it cannot easily be reconciled with what many critics would understand as a progressive environmental praxis. Rather, its contribution is to grant equal agency to physical systems as they interact with human designs. Its insistence that Vorticism be an aesthetic counterpart to its native latitude and geography encourages a fluidity between artist and environment that explores the integrative challenges of the Anthropocene.

TOWARD AN AESTHETIC OF ENTANGLEMENT

In the words of some its most distinguished theorists, the Anthropocene is "a new phase in the history of both humankind and the Earth, when natural forces and human forces become intertwined, so that the fate of one determines the fate of the other" (Zalasiewicz et al. 2010, 2231). As this formulation suggests, the Anthropocene is an essentially dialectical concept, requiring us to think together what have usually been understood as distinct orders of being (Ford 2013, 65). Its unprecedented conflations of natural processes with human history challenge existing forms of historical understanding, encouraging scholars to blend capital and species histories, as Dipesh Chakrabarty argues; to collapse shallow into deep timescales, as in the work of geologist Jan Zalasiewicz; and to subvert notions of agency and causality, as Bruno Latour suggests. While the concept of the Anthropocene has taken root in the critical imagination across the disciplines, literary studies as a field has been slower to adopt this new awareness, which assumes a nexus that includes both humanity and nature as continuous entities.

Part of this sluggishness has been a perceived divide between ecocriticism and work under the interdisciplinary banner of the Anthropocene. The former has been faulted for early critical trends that, it is alleged, romanticized literary works that engaged in pastoral retreat, idolized pure nature, or cast human involvement in nature as contamination—all habits of thinking that reinforce nature and culture as fundamentally separate categories. In the past, ecocriticism's focus upon ahistorical figurations of nature in literature has been blamed for its failure to engage current environmental concerns.[3] This framing problem persists; recently, for instance, Trexler indicts the "preoccupation with the life sciences," which has "led ecocritics to diagnose climate change as a human incursion into ecosystems or Nature writ large, rather than a process that inextricably binds together human and nonhuman systems" (Trexler 2015, 17). As an interdisciplinary concept, the Anthropocene renders untenable any desire for the separation of human society from nature because each is fully woven into the other's designs.

Yet literary studies remains poised to expand our capacity to comprehend this nexus of influence, as the field has long worked to provide specific nodes of cultural work that evince broad historical formations. If the Anthropocene enables the Earth to once more become "an agent of history" in the human imagination, then Latour reminds us of the literary foundation of this awareness: "storytelling is not just a property of human language, but one of the many consequences of being thrown in a world that is, by itself, fully articulated and active" (Latour 2014, 13). Understanding the Anthropocene involves mining literature for evidence of dynamic collaboration between human societies and the natural world as the former has reckoned with the incomprehensible yet uncompromising agency of the latter. Second- and third-wave ecocritical work has encouraged this direction. For a literary text to be understood as environmental, it no longer needs to advocate for an escape from the modern world. Nor does it need to conform to preservationist tenets like Aldo Leopold's land ethic, which defines a "thing"—and, we could posit, a text—as "right . . . when it tends to preserve the integrity, stability, and beauty of the biotic community" and "wrong" when it does not (Leopold [1949] 1987, 224–25). Robert Kern expands the idea of "environment" beyond a landscape or setting, arguing that, for critics, "all texts are at least potentially environmental (and therefore susceptible to ecocriticism or ecologically informed readings) in the sense that all texts are literally or imaginatively situated in a place, and in the sense that their authors, consciously or not, inscribe within them a certain relation to their place" (Kern 2003, 259). The loosening of prior categories like these "dissolves the idea of unitary selfhood, and rigid dualistic separations between culture and nature, subject and object, and human and nonhuman" (Kerridge 2012, 597), and scholars are increasingly examining human interactions with nature without defaulting to an isolationist stance.[4] New trends encourage us to imagine ourselves as alive in what David Abram has called a "more-than-human world" (qtd. in Kern 2003, 258) as opposed to one that must be tamed or else segregated as pristine. Furthermore, ecocritical readings value the literary text as being able to construct such a world and to stretch the human capacity for reimagining our role within it. Increasingly we have at our disposal the language of "co-evolution, shared ancestry, the fluidity of species, hybridity, system, process, energy flow, symbiosis, biosemiotics, the mesh" (Kerridge 2012, 597). As our critical vocabulary expands, so does our ability to describe and comprehend the reality that we share our narratives with a "fully articulated and active" world.

By and large, modernist texts have yet to be drafted in support of this endeavor, and even the most comprehensive studies of the environmental imagination in modern Anglophone literatures tend to omit the early decades of the twentieth century or else betray a casual but entrenched view that, in a modernist ethos, nature is somehow inarticulate, unimportant, or presented only as abstraction.[5] Yet many early twentieth-century texts like *Blast,* poised as they are at the cusp of great social transformations from agrarian to industrial economies, provide access to what Bonnie Costello calls a state of "entanglement," a condition of interrelatedness between natural and human forces that does not simply imply contamination or mess but also testifies to the creative potential of concrete and generative connections, inviting us to combine what critics should no longer habitually separate.

Costello's analysis of the poetics of "superfluity" in the American tradition, when brought to bear upon the manifestos of *Blast*, reveals the productive enmeshing of nature into an avant-garde program that has come to occupy a prominent place in modernist studies. Her pivotal 1998 essay, "'What to Make of a Diminished Thing': Modern Nature and Poetic Response," places Richard Poirier's analysis of Ralph Waldo Emerson in opposition to Lawrence Buell's study of Henry David Thoreau in order to privilege the Emersonian qualities of profligacy and ecstatic communion with nature over Thoreau's monastic, self-denying, embarrassed retreat from it. Costello's essay encourages ecocritics to equally engage with writers whose "fecund imaginations" and stylistic extravagance are not content with the ethic of restraint that doctrinaire conservation (and by implication some strains of ecocriticism) often seem to require (Costello 1998, 569–70).

Costello's directive enables *Blast* to be integrated into an environmental literary project because she advocates for an understanding of nature as something which "may be sensed . . . in the margins or between the seams of or even as a force within our world, rather than as a place alternative to it, a retreat or respite from the agitation of the social condition, or even as a superseding content in which we operate" (Costello 1998, 572). Texts that display this tendency arguably have more to tell us about our own possibilities for living in relation with nature than works which have been celebrated for their idealization of wilderness, beauty, and escape. Such a model attests to the value of *Blast*'s own fecund use of nature, a stylistic profligacy that offers us, not the displacement of nature with art, but a vision for artistic genius that delights in the productiveness of their entanglement.

BLAST AS MESH

While recent critics have contributed work on its form, medium, and politics,[6] my interest in *Blast* stems from Lewis's reliance upon climate, geography, and other physical systems as he formulates Vorticism's revolutionary framework. The following close reading of *Blast*'s manifestos demonstrates the text's pivotal position in the historical formation of the Anthropocene. Far before its time, *Blast* presents a fusion of natural with human systems at the threshold of the first technological world war, which was the culmination of decades of social transformations, from urbanization and factory farming to Taylorism and mass production; and which is commonly perceived as the final retreat of nature from modern, metropolitan life. Yet images of nature and the environment seep up through the stitches of *Blast*'s programmatic assemblage, evincing an "indissoluble mixture of gray and green" (Costello 1998, 571) that characterized the prewar era.

To define a fleeting movement like Vorticism presents a critical challenge. Its foundation is contested ground, both for its founding members and later for scholars who have tried to piece together its narrative in retrospect. *Blast*, a two-issue periodical, makes the task even more fraught, as the volumes themselves consist of bits and pieces that were composed by several people and in several stages, with multiple revisions in evidence. Paul Edwards suggests that, perhaps in an echo of its totem symbol of the vortex, the "chaos" of the volume exhibits "a trace of improvisatory energy—and not only Lewis's—that moved too fast to tidy up in its wake" (Edwards 2013, 210).[7] At least the first volume, his account suggests, lacked a central doctrine until very late in the composition process and attempted to assemble a framework after many of the artists' contributions had already been composed.

But one certain feature of *Blast*'s emergence is the impact of Italian Futurism and its charismatic leader F. T. Marinetti upon Lewis's designs for *Blast 1*, which announced the arrival of Vorticism and sketched out its core tenants. Edwards posits that, in its earliest form, *Blast 1* was likely conceived of as "an English Futurist publication" (Edwards 2013, 201). Lewis's interest in Futurism is well documented,[8] but as 1914 progresses, Lewis distances his revolutionary efforts from Marinetti's. His growing impatience with Futurism is evinced in the witheringly entitled article "A Man of the Week: Marinetti," in the *New Weekly* in May 1914, published one month before *Blast 1* appeared in print. In it, Lewis questions the centrality of the Italians to the future of European art and begins his quest to generate an English response to the Futurist movement rather than midwife an organic outgrowth of it. While "Futurism" often seems to function as a catch-all term for Continental movements in articles like these, Lewis confounds that assumption by announcing that "a Futurism of Place is as important as a temporal one" (Lewis 1989, 32). This latent preoccupation with locality would soon form the basis of the Vorticist aesthetic program. Lewis concludes his article with a challenge to an as-yet-unformed English avant-garde: "As modern life is the invention of the English, they should have something profounder to say about it than anybody else" (Lewis 1989, 32). This polemic registers Lewis's growing skepticism of Marinetti's magnetic influence and foreshadows *Blast's* much more forceful insistence upon place-based aesthetics.[9]

Taking "Man of the Week" as his cue, Edwards suggests that Vorticism situated itself within the crowded avant-garde milieu by "[making] the case that everything the Futurists wished to celebrate about modernity was actually of 'anglo-saxon' origin and was hence the proper province of English rather than Italian art" (Edwards 2013, 205–6). Such a relocation reveals the interface between nation, ecology, and technology that Vorticism later relies upon. While Lewis's early conception of a "Futurism of Place" suggests that England is the wellspring of "modern life," his contributions to *Blast*, especially its first three manifestos, clarify and develop this premise. Here he makes clear that England's advanced industrial culture is a product of human interaction with an island geography and maritime climate. Distilling this essence is the Vorticist symbol warning of a "storm from the North"[10]—a vortex, in word and image, to supplant the ecstatic Futurist brand with colder, more austere forces.

MANIFESTO.

Figure 2.1. This nautical symbol, which warns of a "storm from the North," appears three times in *Blast 1*.

The celebration of the meteorological emblem is also a celebration of natural forces as agents of change which stimulate human ingenuity.

Ursula Heise has cataloged the fallacies which result from assuming that ecology and human culture will interact in predictable ways. To rely upon a simple, formative link between them does not, for instance, consider "how different cultural frameworks . . . might condition quite divergent perceptions of what the local ecology consists of, what it requires from humans, or what an appropriate way of responding to it might be" (Heise 2008, 44). Nevertheless, Lewis's impulse to source his artistic project from the particular weather, climate, and geography of England is worth considering as a radical strategy of disruption, unsettling the intellectual sterility that he perceived as being imposed upon the public by a powerful cultural elite. His anti-Futurist stance targets the perceived consensus among Edwardian intellectual and artistic circles that British arts and literature were less sophisticated—and "less modern"—than Continental production. "Many agreed with Matthew Arnold that English culture was fundamentally provincial," explains Paul Peppis (2000, 84), and the collective belief that English artists had much to learn from their European counterparts demoted the attachment to England as a place to an indication of quaint or folk status. Lewis's polemics against cosmopolitanism in *Blast 1* are not solely chauvinist blustering but also substantiate his desire to challenge the commonplace assumptions of the educated English set, who seemed to disdain England as a habitable place for world-class modern arts. By turning to what he terms "Anglo-Saxon" industry, Lewis is attempting to theorize a basis for a movement that would challenge the assumption of Continental prestige by asserting the primacy of the "province" as worldly and avant-garde in its own right. "We whisper in your ear a great secret. LONDON IS <u>NOT</u> A PROVINCIAL TOWN," declares the manifesto (*B1*, 19), betraying a gleeful delight in exposing the faulty wisdom of the cultured elite, who have not deigned to notice the revolutionary potential of, quite literally, their own backyard.

The first three sections of *Blast 1* lay the groundwork for a native art revolution and, though the prose is often difficult and ambiguous, attempt to prescribe both a philosophy and an aesthetic that reject the homogenous internationalism lauded by the educated establishment. "Long Live the Vortex!" (*B1*, 7–8) is a two-page mission statement of sorts; the first section of the manifesto (*B1*, 11–30) "BLASTS" and "BLESSES" lists of people, places, objects, and ideas that Vorticists laud and loathe (some of which, like "England" and "France," receive both treatments); and finally, a second extension of the manifesto (*B1*, 30–43) elaborates upon the reasoning behind its classificatory schema, expounding upon the qualities of Englishness that, contrary to assumptions about its provincial scope, are summoned to under-gird a world-class movement.

"Long Live the Vortex!" opens the volume by aggressively demarcating Vorticism from its Continental counterparts. Scorning both the "sentimental Future" and the "sacripant Past,"[11] the artists who occupy London's "great art vortex" are dedicated to the "the Reality of the Present" and seek "an art of Individuals" who enable "THE WORLD TO LIVE." While its indi-vidualist bent jabs at social reformers like the Fabians, the primary target is Marinetti: "AUTOMOBILISM (Marinetteism) bores us. We don't want to go about making a hullo-bulloo about motor cars, any more than about knives and forks, elephants or gas-pipes. Elephants are VERY BIG," the text smirks. "Motor cars go quickly" (*B1*, 7–8). This patriotic sarcasm inaugurates Lewis's extended comparison between the Italian and English movements, which finds the former lacking. By "mimicking Marinetti's polemical enthu-siasm," Lewis emphasizes "the familiarity—for the English—of everything Italians find so amazingly new," and therefore implies that "nothing about modern life, be it exotic animals or automobiles, can surprise the inhabit-ants of a nation so industrially developed" (Peppis 2000, 86). It becomes clear throughout the manifestos that Lewis, as "A Man of the Week" had anticipated, will position industrialism as England's formative contribution to European modernity, which artists from other nations can only marvel at from a belated position. The Italian Futurists, he implies, may have made a splash in the public's imagination with their lectures, paintings, and literature, but their contributions to the history of letters and art owe their innovative energy to Anglo-Saxon ingenuity, in the form of industry.

The gap in the lived experiences of industrial modernity between England and Italy is developed in the two sections that follow, which are both labeled "Manifesto." The first appearance of the Vortex symbol predicting "storms from the North" provides the segue, and then the blasting commences. After the nationalist fervor of the opening remarks, it seems surprising that Eng-land is first under attack—but the excoriation begins, counterintuitively, by targeting its climate rather than its culture.[12] In giant black letters, the blasting "curse[s]" the Gulf Stream, that "1000 MILE LONG, 2 KILOMETER DEEP BODY OF WATER . . . pushed against us from the Floridas, TO MAKE US MILD" (*B1*, 11). In this early passage, England's climate becomes a "DISMAL SYMBOL, SET round our bodies, of effeminate lout within" (*B1*, 11). Extending the bodily metaphor of unfitness to the atmosphere, the text laments the "the flabby sky that can manufacture no snow" before saddling it with responsibility for the mediocrity of British letters—the Gulf Stream can only "drop the sea on us in a drizzle like a poem by Mr. Robert Bridges," the recently appointed poet laureate (*B1*, 11–12). Yet if it aims to be an aggressive critique of the arts, the section feels misdirected, even diluted; and the exaggerated tone eventually gives way to a note of hopeful prophecy, also about the weather: "Ten years ago, we saw distinctly both snow and ice here. May some vulgarly inventive, but useful person, arise, and restore to us the necessary BLIZZARDS. LET US ONCE MORE WEAR THE ERMINE OF THE NORTH" (*B1*, 12). The gist of the extended meteorological metaphor is clear: mildness "produces only weaklings and waverers," while "Nordic blizzards build character" (Orchard 2000, 18), establishing the link between a frigid climate and genius, although it takes the rest of the manifesto to cash out the significance of climate to the measure of artistic success.

The meteorological language allows Lewis to resolve what Peppis has identified as a fundamental contradiction in Vorticism's platform. On the one hand, *Blast*'s individualist political ambitions sought to undermine the British establishment, as the subsequent catalog of the "Blasted" clearly demonstrates. The list curses over fifty writers, thinkers, and institutions that were perceived to support the political and cultural status quo, from the National Portrait Gallery director to the Post Office. But the text is also saturated with competitive anxiety over the perception of superior Continental culture, and the Vorticists, although many (like Pound) were intellectually anti-provincial, also sought to elevate Britain's national prestige. Peppis cannily identifies Lewis's solution to this quandary: "*Blast* practices a long-standing technique of nationalist polemic: it recasts the modes of state power it praises as national characteristics." Certain features of England's global reputation become "expressions of national genius," traits of a national character that are included to recruit support for the fledgling movement (Peppis 2000, 89). But these national traits, in turn, are grafted onto the ecological features of the British Isles. In effect, *Blast* invents a revolutionary and aesthetic nationalism that it means to install in place of any official state message; and it does so by shifting its illustration of "natural" supremacy from England's human institutions to its climatic and geographical systems. For the rest of my reading, I will focus on two alleged English attributes, naval power and industrial prowess, in order to understand why environmental features undergird Lewis's project of revolution—we should not take for granted the fact that climate, weather, and geography surround, and give rise to, his nationalist rhetoric.

England's moderate climate bears responsibility for the mediocre mainstream culture that has lingered on after the "hirsute" Victorians (the "years 1837–1900" receive particularly virulent blasting [*B1*, 13–20]); but when England is Blessed, the text celebrates the ocean as the source of its true cultural and literary genius, from Shakespeare to the present. The ocean is an inextricable part of the physical system, which includes the "flabby" Gulf Stream, but *Blast* nevertheless exalts England's island status: "Bless England <u>FOR ITS SHIPS</u> which switchback on Blue, Green, and Red SEAS all around the PINK EARTH-BALL, BIG BETS ON EACH" (*B1*, 22). To bless English "seafarers" is partly an ironic recapitulation of imperial propaganda (recalling "Britannia rules the waves"), a campaign which had, by 1914, been ramping up in the face of foreign, especially German, competition. But as the manifesto continues, the vividness of its environmental imagination becomes equally apparent: "BLESS ALL SEAFARERS. They exchange not one LAND for another but one ELEMENT for another. The MORE against the LESS ABSTRACT. BLESS the vast planetary abstraction of the OCEAN. BLESS the ARABS of the ATLANTIC. This island must be contrasted with the bleak waves" (*B1*, 22). The navy and other industries of the sea provide national might, but the sea itself provides the basis for the abstract aesthetic that Vorticism promotes. Critics from Fredric Jameson onward have analyzed Lewis's celebration of "coldness" and "abstraction."[13] But this style has yet to be understood as sourced from northern latitudes and "the vast planetary abstraction" that the sea provides. The latter is particularly important in distinguishing England from its southern neighbors. "The English Character is based on the sea," the manifesto continues, and its greatest artists communicate an "unexpected universality" (*B1*, 35). This is perhaps because its ports, ships, and sailors maintain international ties, although the text also asserts that England's harbors and fleets are the most technically advanced. An image of the island-as-workshop ends the section: "BLESS ENGLAND, industrial island machine, pyramidal workshop, its apex at Shetland, discharging itself on the sea" (*B1*, 23–24). Like the sea, the factory is England's domain, which Lewis graphs onto the archipelagic whole in this image. The "island machine" has become an intriguing "mesh," to employ Kerridge's term—a seamless fusion of human with natural activity, and an intriguing image for the Anthropocene.

The next manifesto develops the interface of nature and culture that it had begun to assemble by alleging the existence of a fundamental divide between the characteristics of Northern and Southern art. The Vorticist program calls for the return of a "northern flower" to England's shores (*B1*, 36). While it recognizes that complacent England, with "its heavy pools of stagnant Saxon blood," deserves its mediocre, "anti-artistic" reputation, *Blast* still kindles hope that a world-class movement might "burst up" out of such a "lump of compressed life" (*B1*, 32). Here, England's repressed culture becomes a coal-like substance waiting for the right spark, which only "a necessary native art" (*B1*, 37) will be able to ignite. The text then provides an extensive rationale for why a "native art" is required to ignite the revolution. "The Art-instinct is permanently primitive" and finds "the same stimulus" in "the chaos of imperfection, discord, etc." of modern life as it would "in Nature." Thus, the

modern artist is akin to a "savage" at home in "this enormous, jangling, jour-
nalistic, fairy desert of modern life," which "serves him as Nature did more
technically primitive man" (*B1*, 33).[14] It is England that, through industrial
supremacy, has made this "jangling . . . desert" of modern life, and English
artists are most at home in this new 'kind' of environment that industrialism
has manufactured. This is the evidence that *Blast* presents for Lewis's earlier
claim that, since England was the true author of the Industrial Revolution—
"Machinery, trains, steam-ships, all that distinguishes externally our time,
came far more from here than anywhere else" (*B1*, 39)—then the celebration
of modernity is the proper province of English artists above all others.

The modern world is shaped by industry, which is the subject of Vorticist
art. But Vorticists, unlike Futurists, seem cognizant that industrial growth has
made its own kind of ecosystem, one that the manifesto implies exists beyond
human control. As it describes art's new milieu, the manifesto provides as
compelling an effort to represent what we now imagine as the Anthropocene
as any other I have found in the early twentieth century. In its effort to prove
that the "northern flower" of English art is destined for superiority, the text
must first clarify that it does not always confine the word "climate" to its
literal meaning:

> It is not a question of the characterless material climate around us. Were that
> so the complication of the Jungle, dramatic Tropic growth, the vastness of
> the American trees, would not be for us. But our industries, and the Will that
> determined, face to face with its needs, the direction of the modern world, has
> reared up steel trees where the green ones were lacking; has exploded in useful
> growths, and found wilder intricacies than those of Nature. (*B1*, 36)

Because England lacks the steamy jungles and severe weather patterns that
Lewis clearly adores, its "material climate" has to become a state of mind.
English industry has created its own "vast" trees and "Tropic" growth which,
for the Vorticist artist, generate encounters with the unruliness of nature that
their own rolling landscapes and mild weather do not provide. Facing a deprivation of ecological extremes, a temperate nation has had to manufacture
its own experiences of nature using steel, concrete, and machinery—and
because England can conjure the "wild intricacies" of any climate zone, its
artists are more poised than any group for explosive growth in the modern
era. This kind of creation is described as superior to nature's own "Realist"
systems of production:

> Machinery is the greatest Earth-medium: incidentally it sweeps away the doc-
> trines of a narrow and pedantic Realism at one stroke. By mechanical inventive-
> ness, too, just as Englishmen have spread themselves all over the Earth, they

have brought all the hemispheres about them in their original island. It cannot be said that the complication of the Jungle, dramatic tropical growths, the vastness of the American trees, is not for us. For in the forms of machinery, Factories, new and vaster buildings, bridges, and works, we have all that, naturally, around us. (*B1*, 39–40)

What strikes me as remarkable about this (admittedly anthropocentric) depiction of modernity is its unconscious reliance upon the forms of nature, such as the jungle, to communicate its potential. Lewis's account of English industrial superiority, exhilarated though it is by factories and bridges, is still composed of derivative steel copies of Nature's "wilder intricacies." His language is trapped in the condition of the mesh, revealing a hybrid beauty in its acts of creation.

"The Futurist individual of Mr. Marinetti's limited imagination" (*B1*, 33) is unfit to navigate modernity's hybrid wilderness, which is the province of the Northern artist. Throughout *Blast*, the categories of North and South are ambiguous and shifting. Englishness can produce "a Northern flower," a designation that sometimes shares characteristics with the French, the Germans, the Russians, and the Slavs. Italian Futurism, however, is consistently regarded as a disturbance from the South, a category that overlaps frequently with "Latin" (which is also pitted in opposition to "Anglo-Saxon"). What is consistent about Lewis's ethnic formulation is his critique that Futurists are "Romantic peoples" who "gush over machines, aeroplanes, etc." and are "the most romantic and sentimental 'moderns' to be found" (*B1*, 41).[15] From the opening passage, which complains that "Marinetteism bores us," Lewis characterizes the Futurists as simple, mocking their delight with motion, speed, and machinery as unsophisticated machine-worship. English artists, in contrast, are soon to discover their position as the legitimate heirs to industrial modernity and will then become "the inventors of [a] bareness and hardness" of style that will position them as the "great enemies of Romance" (*B1*, 41–42). The implication is that the Vorticists have this machine world "naturally" around them. The "jangling . . . fairy jungle" of modernity began as their province, and it has overtaken the Continent. "Technology has created a new Nature surrounding humanity," the text challenges. "Now it is up to Art to keep up" (Orchard 2000, 19), and the Vorticists are poised to answer.

These passages of *Blast*, then, can be viewed as a confident declaration that England has authored the age of the Anthropocene—and that it has been at home in it for longer than its European rivals. *Blast*'s program posits the grandiose claim that its nation invented, and then exported, the technologies that allow humanity access to a fully mediated, fully enmeshed state in which human industry generates a new Nature.

CONCLUSION: AGAINST RETREAT

Towards the end of *Blast*'s first volume, in a section entitled "Life is the Important Thing!," Lewis lambasts Impressionist painters for romanticizing nature and encouraging ecological ignorance. This rationale echoes his polemics against Marinetti's unexamined infatuation with machinery, reinforcing Continental perceptions of environment as unsophisticated and sentimental—a feeble imitation of a real, vital relationship with the external world. The rage for Impressionism, writes Lewis, is the source of a ridiculous but "wide-spread notion" that nature provides "inexhaustible freshness of material." In characteristic style, he counters: "NATURE IS NO MORE INEXHAUSTIBLE, FRESH, WELLING UP WITH INVENTION, ETC., THAN LIFE IS TO THE AVERAGE MAN OF FORTY, WITH HIS GROOVE, HIS DISSILLUSION, AND HIS LITTLE ROUND OF HABITUAL DISTRACTIONS" (*B1*, 179). The primary purpose of this bathos is to reinforce the aging torpor of the passé Continental movement, but it also returns some agency to the natural world, acknowledging its resistance to anthropomorphism. Furthermore, it evinces the responsible assumption of ecological carrying capacity. Continuing, Lewis guts ecophilic trendiness with delight:

> Nature is a blessed retreat, in art, for those artists whose imagination is mean and feeble, whose vocation and instinct are unrobust. When they find themselves in front of Infinite Nature with their little paint-box, they squint their eyes at her professionally, and coo with lazy contentment and excitement to just so much effort as if hygienic and desirable. She does their thinking and seeing for them. (*B1*, 180)

This withering critique anticipates the contemporary summons for a rejection of hyper-Romantic solipsism as the primary figuration of human responsibility for nature. Only flaccid, mediocre artists with no inner resources marvel at the external world in a state of passivity, returning in their weakness to be refreshed. Again, a personified Nature is granted agency. It is not posing for an artistic likeness but contributing thought and vision to the scene in order to compensate for human deficiencies in both.

Blast offers an exploration of human culture as it clashes and meshes with nature, and it finds opportunities to celebrate the overlapping of human with natural processes. Its insistence upon regional distinctiveness, especially in its climatic schema, carries with it the undesirable burden of overwrought nationalism. But it also encourages artists to sift through their mass of influences and separate the native from the derivative. There are multiple routes to ecological awareness, and, by opening the possibility for sustained interest in provincial intricacies, *Blast* provides an early instance of the equally constitutive exchanges between artist and environment that undergird the narrative of the Anthropocene.

NOTES

1. Wyndham Lewis edited two volumes of *Blast*. *BLAST: Review of the Great English Vortex* appeared in June 1914, while the second volume, known as "The War Number," appeared in June 1915. Future references to the two volumes appear parenthetically in the text as *B1* and *B2*.

2. In an environmental context, Wendell Berry's term "responsible" denotes the potential for a permanent connection to place (Berry 1998, 937).

3. This lineage is arguably grounded in Lawrence Buell's foundational study of Thoreau in *The Environmental Imagination* (1995), although his later work engages this criticism; Timothy Morton's *Ecology Without Nature* (2007), among others, critiques ahistorical representations of the natural world in first-wave ecocriticism.

4. Even Thoreau has received this attention. Purdy (2013), for example, points out (among other details) that the bean fields of *Walden* already have trash in them.

5. The assumption that "modernism" is synonymous with "technology," and functions to displace nature, is widespread. For instance, Carruth contrasts the "pastoral sensibilities" of the texts she examines with "the modernist veneration of industrial agriculture," which provides "a vision of an engineered system with technological fixes that save populations from the unpredictability of nature" (Carruth 2013, 12–13). Even Costello, whose work inspired this chapter, remarks that Robert Frost "refused the modernist displacement of nature with art" (Costello 1998, 572). This is not just an Americanist view. The language used by the international Ecomodernist movement, which published its own manifesto in 2015, indicates the persistence of this habit of thinking across disciplines and oceans.

6. The global tour in 2011 of Vorticist works at Duke University's Nasher Museum, the Tate Britain Gallery in London, and the Peggy Guggenheim Collection in Venice, has contributed to the resurgence of interest in the movement as an international phenomenon. For recent contributions to literary studies, see Antliff and Klein (2013) and Waddell (2012).

7. Edwards also chronicles later statements by Lewis, Pound, and William Roberts that confirm this lack of cohesion (Edwards 2013, 199–210).

8. For accounts of Marinetti's impact on Lewis, see Edwards (2000); Orchard (2000); and Puchner (2010).

9. Additionally, Lewis's relationship with C. R. W. Nevinson, an English disciple of Marinetti, was initially close, but Nevinson's contribution was later edited out of *Blast 1*, further substantiating Lewis's desire to discard the Futurist label (Edwards 2013, 204).

10. Paul O'Keeffe is credited with discerning this meaning (Edwards 2013, 202).

11. Both phrases insult Italian literary culture, with "sentimental" appearing elsewhere to critique Futurism and "sacripant" referring to medieval Italian romances.

12. Sections 3 through 6, however, make short work of British cultural institutions, from Bloomsbury and beards to humor and sport.

13. For analysis of the masculinist "coldness" celebrated by Vorticism, see Tickner (1994).

14. Gasiorek discusses of the rhetoric of primitivism that circulated in prewar artistic circles and notes its presence in both Futurist and Vorticist texts (Gasiorek 2013, 54–56).

15. Peppis analyzes Lewis's anti-Futurist rhetoric, steeped as it is in ethnocentric generalities, as "aggressively nationalistic cultural doctrine." He aligns Vorticism with the British state's "official nationalism" as it attempts to "[fortify] . . . Britain's increasingly contested imperial, military, and economic power" against the threat of Italy's imperial forays into north and east Africa (Peppis 2000, 84–85).

WORKS CITED

Antliff, Mark, and Scott W. Klein, eds. 2013. *Vorticism: New Perspectives*. Oxford and New York: Oxford University Press.

Berry, Wendell. 1998. "The Regional Motive." In *The Literature of the American South: A Norton Anthology*, edited by William L. Andrews, Minrose Gwin, Trudier Harris, and Fred Hobson, 934–37. New York: W. W. Norton & Company.

Buell, Lawrence. 1995. *The Environmental Imagination: Thoreau, Nature Writing, and the Formation of American Culture*. Cambridge and London: Harvard University Press.

Carruth, Allison. 2013. *Global Appetites: American Power and the Literature of Food*. Cambridge and New York: Cambridge University Press.

Chakrabarty, Dipesh. 2009. "The Climate of History: Four Theses." *Critical Inquiry* 35 (2): 197–222.

Costello, Bonnie. 1998. "'What to Make of a Diminished Thing': Modern Nature and Poetic Response." *American Literary History* 10: 569–605.

Edwards, Paul. 2013. "*Blast* and the Revolutionary Mood of Wyndham Lewis's Vorticism." In *Vorticism: New Perspectives*, edited by Mark Antliff and Scott W. Klein, 199–219. Oxford and New York: Oxford University Press.

———. 2000. *Wyndham Lewis: Painter and Writer*. New Haven, CT: Yale University Press.

Ford, Thomas H. 2013. "Aura in the Anthropocene." *symploke* 21 (1–2): 65–82.

Gasiorek, Andrzej. 2013. "Modern Art in England Circa 1914: Hulme and Lewis." In *Vorticism: New Perspectives*, edited by Mark Antliff and Scott W. Klein, 199–219. Oxford and New York: Oxford University Press.

Heise, Ursula K. 2008. *Sense of Place and Sense of Planet: The Environmental Imagination of the Global*. Oxford and New York: Oxford University Press.

Latour, Bruno. 2014. "Agency at the Time of the Anthropocene." *New Literary History* 45 (1): 1–18.

Leopold, Aldo. (1949) 1987. *A Sand County Almanac and Sketches Here and There*. Oxford and New York: Oxford University Press.

Lewis, Wyndham, ed. 1914. *Blast 1*. https://modjourn.org/issue/bdr430555/. Accessed September 10, 2020.

———. ed. 1915. *Blast 2*. https://modjourn.org/issue/bdr430768/. Accessed September 10, 2020.

———. 1989. "A Man of the Week: Marinetti." In *Creatures of Habit and Creatures of Change: Essays on Art, Literature and Society, 1914–1956*, edited by Paul Edwards, 29–32. Santa Rosa, CA: Black Sparrow Press.

Kern, Robert. 2003. "Ecocriticism: What is it Good For?" In *The ISLE Reader: Ecocriticism 1993–2003*, edited by Michael P. Branch and Scott Slovic, 258–81. Athens: University of Georgia Press.

Kerridge, Richard. 2012. "Review." *Interdisciplinary Studies in Literature and Environment* 19 (3): 595–98

Morton, Timothy. 2007. *Ecology Without Nature: Rethinking Environmental Aesthetics*. Cambridge and London: Harvard University Press.

O'Keeffe, Paul. 1986. "Vortex: Pound and Lewis." *Enemy News* 22: 21.

Orchard, Karin. 2000. "'A Laugh Like a Bomb': The History and Ideas of the Vorticists." In *BLAST: Vorticism 1914–1918*, edited by Paul Edwards, 14–23. Burlington, VT: Ashgate.

Peppis, Paul. 2000. *Literature, Politics, and the English Avant-Garde: Nation and Empire, 1901–1918*. Cambridge and New York: Cambridge University Press.

Puchner, Martin. 2010. "The Aftershocks of *Blast*." In *Bad Modernisms*, edited by Douglas Mao and Rebecca Walkowitz, 44–67. Durham, NC: Duke University Press.

Purdy, Jedediah. 2013. "In the Shit with Thoreau: A Walden for the Anthropocene." *Huffington Post*. https://www.huffpost.com/entry/in-the-shit-with-thoreau_b_3526416. Accessed January 10, 2016.

Tickner, Lisa. 1994. "Men's Work? Masculinity and Modernism." *Visual Culture: Images and Interpretations*, edited by Norman Bryson, Michael Ann Holly, and Keith Moxey, 42–82. Hanover, NH: Wesleyan University Press.

Trexler, Adam. 2015. *Anthropocene Fictions: The Novel in a Time of Climate Change*. Charlottesville and London: University of Virginia Press.

Waddell, Nathan. 2012. *Modernist Nowheres: Politics and Utopias in Early Modernist Writing 1900–1920*. New York: Palgrave Macmillan.

Zalasiewicz, Jan, Mark Williams, Will Steffen, and Paul Crutzen. 2010. "The New World of the Anthropocene." *Environmental Science and Technology* 44: 2228–31.

Chapter Three

Hart Crane

A Poet of Our Climate

Robert Savino Oventile

The American modernist poet Hart Crane (1899–1932) lived during three booms—car, oil, and population—that laid the foundation for the Anthropocene's "Great Acceleration." In the first three decades of the twentieth century, the number of automobiles in America grew from 8,000 to 26.5 million (Schuster 2015, 162). In 1899, the US produced 57,071 thousand barrels of crude oil; in 1929, the US produced 1,007,323 thousand barrels ("US Field Production" 2015, n.p.). In 1900, the US population was approximately 76,094,000 and in 1932 approximately 124,840,471. Crane wrote as increasing population, emerging technologies, and spreading industrialization in the US and abroad were establishing the conditions for the Great Acceleration, the period starting about 1950 marked by data spikes testifying to the earth system's anthropogenic modification and thus to the Anthropocene. While readers link Crane's work to the technological sublime, or to "The American Sublime," Crane engages further ranges of sublimity newly readable given the contexts, themes, and logics the Anthropocene underscores.

Crane described himself as a *"Pindar* for the dawn of the machine age" (Crane 2006, 328). Crane's essay "Modern Poetry" argues that to achieve its "contemporary function," poetry must "absorb the machine, i.e., *acclimatize* it as naturally and casually as trees, cattle, galleons, castles and all other human associations of the past" (Crane 2006, 171). Machines must become elements of the poet's climate. Rather than as spectacles appreciated from a distance ("the wonderment experienced in watching nose dives"), machines hold "creative promise" as absorbed into habitual everydayness, the unconsciously ready-to-hand, Crane citing "the familiar gesture of a motorist in the modest act of shifting gears" (Crane 2006, 171–72). With "its connotations emanat[ing] from within" the poet, the machine allows for "as spontaneous a terminology of poetic reference as the bucolic world of pasture, plow, and

barn" (Crane 2006, 172). To fuse in imagination the pastoral world traditional
to poetry with the petro-chemical world of modern machines: Crane purses
this goal in *The Bridge* (1930), which he called an "epic of the modern consciousness" treating "the Myth of America" (Crane 2006, 554, 557).

With the Great Acceleration, the motorist's "modest act of shifting gears"
acquires new "connotations." *The Bridge* stages poetic transport in terms
of fossil-fueled transportation. Crane's poetry gives the sublime a double
cast appropriate to *Homo sapiens*, paradoxical situation transitioning to
the Anthropocene: vulnerable because triumphant. *The Bridge* celebrates
the species' technologically mediated triumph. Nostalgically eternizing the
Holocene, *The Bridge*'s recuperative sublime seeks "Nature's" return. Crane
drafted much of *The Bridge* during his 1926 May to October stay at the cot-
tage his maternal grandmother owned, the Villa Casa on the Isle of Pines
(adjacent Cuba). During this stay, Crane also wrote "O Carib Isle!" (1927,
2006). This poem's *ekstasis* registers a thrownness in vulnerability amidst the
biosphere. Pondering extinction, "O Carib Isle!" sojourns into what Claire
Colebrook calls the "geological sublime" (Colebrook 2016, 124).

"O Carib Isle!" reads as an *avant-la-lettre* example of the "Anthropocene
lyric" Tom Bristow theorizes in his book of the same name (Bristow 2015,
4). Anthropocene lyrics articulate poetry, person, and place as inseparable
yet depart from ideologies of holism and aesthetics of organic unity. The
speakers find themselves thrown into a "more-than-human world" (Bristow
2015, 5). Rather than existing at a distance from a landscape contemplated as
a backdrop to humanity's drama, and rather than absorbed within an eternal
Nature taken as an organic whole standing against the human world, an Anthropocene lyric's speaker, bereft of anthropocentric status, walks a "destitute
planet" and encounters a specific multi-specied place inviting the speaker to
"rethink . . . personhood within a larger domain of life" (Bristow 2015, 3, 6).

Bristow's Anthropocene lyric resembles the eighteenth- and nineteenth-
century topographical poems Angus Fletcher resurrects in *A New Theory
for American Poetry: Democracy, the Environment, and the Future of
Imagination*. Fletcher's topographical poems attend to given environments
to incorporate the dynamics of those "surrounds" (Fletcher 2004, 127).
Fletcher praises these poems as enfolding the daemonic within the sublunary
and fitting the human holistically into an organically unified "surround."
Bristow keeps pace with Fletcher in terms of the lyric channeling a "surround." The Anthropocene lyric works with "Attunement to—and confine-
ment by—place" and fosters "a new Anthropocene paradigm of place-based
personhood" (Bristow 2015, 14). Bristow explores the new ranges of affect
and personhood lyric speakers attain in the Anthropocene. While the daemon

goes quiescent in Fletcher's "environment-poem" (Fletcher 2004, 127), Bristow allows for the daemonic sublimity "O Carib Isle!" sparks in anticipating the Anthropocene lyric.

Among the Greeks, daemons, intermediaries between immortals and mortals, inspired mortals toward their fates. Did Kenneth Burke speak with Crane about the Christian evil/good binary demonizing the daemon? Crane spoke of being demonically possessed and wrote of his "demon-heroes" (Mariani 1999, 213; Crane 2006, 567). Crane's friend Charmion von Wiegand testified to Crane's "daemonic side": "I mean, sweetness and light alone does not make poetry. I mean, it's the dual aspect of the nature of the unconscious that really fused. . . . The ancients called it the daemon, didn't they?—And he had that" (Unterecker 1987, 770). For McKenzie Wark, the "Anthropocene calls attention not to the psychic unconscious or the political unconscious but to the *infrastructural unconscious*" that registers "climate change as an unintended consequence of collective human labor" (Wark 2015, 180). Timothy Clark ties the "environmental 'unconscious' to the "material infrastructure" of fossil-fueled existence (Clark 2015, 104). Freud argues the unconscious may register events prior to their impingement on consciousness. Revising Freud, Harold Bloom insists, "The daemon knows" (Bloom 2015, 156). What did Crane's daemon know?

Consider Heraclitus's fragment *ethos anthropoi daimon*: "A man's character is his fate." The *Iliad*'s Athena, Achilles's daemon, draws the hero out from his brooding stasis in the Achaean camp and down to his ecstatic dispatching of Hector. In the act, Achilles realizes his warrior character and accepts his fate: immanent demise. For Timothy Morton, in the Anthropocene "art becomes an attunement to the demonic" (Morton 2013, 175). Daemonic inspiration returns via hyperobjects, objects like the human species "that are massively distributed in time and space relative to humans" (Morton 2013, 1). Uncannily familiar and unfamiliar, the human species newly looms as a hyperobject for each human and for all the humans. Disbanding the Holocene's relative stasis, this hyperobject draws humans ecstatically out and down to their singular fates in the Anthropocene. The human species as daemon prompts a weird revision of Heraclitus: *anthropos anthropoi daimon*. Attunement to the uncanny hyperobject "human species" may trigger sublimity. Traversing extinction anxiety, "O Carib Isle!" attains such daemonic sublimity. Crane's daemon draws the poet into a multi-specied arena evoking ecological catastrophe. In contrast, *The Bridge* exhibits a Platonic-Christian containment of the daemon, a nostalgic hypostatization of "Nature," and a proto-accelerationist exaltation of fossil fuels.

ON *THE BRIDGE*

The Bridge dreams of retrieving the timeless pastoral existence Crane imagines pre-Columbian Native American life to have been and celebrates the fossil-fueled transportation of the decades prepping the Great Acceleration. Crane would fuse "the pure nature-world" Native Americans inhabited with a Platonically ideal city, an Atlantis subsuming the America of cars, trains, planes, steamships, and subways (Crane 2006, 643). *The Bridge* reaches the pre-Columbian in "The Dance," which exhorts a Native American chieftain, Maquokeeta, to "dance us back the tribal morn!" (Crane 2006, 57, 59–60). As Maquokeeta glimpses Pocahontas, he sees a pre-Columbian past that stands outside of historical time: "Lo, through what infinite seasons dost thou gaze— / ... And see'st thy bride immortal in the maize!" (Crane 2006, 82, 84). Echoing the "trillions of winters and summers" rhapsodized by Whitman's "Song of Myself" (Whitman 2002, 1138-39), Crane hyperbolizes Holocene seasonal cycles as "infinite." The temporally finite seasons embody their temporally limitless return, each winter being the *ekphrasis* of an infinite series of winters, et cetera. Crane figures Pocahontas as "the mythological nature-symbol chosen to represent the physical body of the continent" (Crane 2006, 554). In "The Dance," she personifies timeless "Nature": "She is the torrent and the singing tree" and will remain "virgin to the last of men" (Crane 2006, 91, 92). "The Dance" imagines "Nature" as what *The Bridge*'s finale "Atlantis" calls an "Everpresence, beyond time" (Crane 2006, 89).

Crane posits Holocene conditions as eternal. This hypostatization's flipside, *The Bridge*'s proto-accelerationism, surfaces when "Cape Hatteras" develops a recuperative petro-chemical sublime. Encompassing Kill Devil Hills, where the Wright brothers flew, North Carolina's Cape Hatteras becomes a locale for meditating on fossil fuels as what time promised humanity and as the energy to accelerate humanity beyond time into the eternity of "Nature" retrieved in a city of the imagination, "Atlantis." "Cape Hatteras" invokes the inaccurate notion that oil derives primarily from dinosaurs. (Oil derives primarily from "ocean plankton, algae, and other forms of simple marine life" [Nersesian 2010, 181].) In "Cape Hatteras," problems of scale make petroleum's derivation from dinosaurs virtually imponderable.

The opening reads as the perspective of a pilot flying over Cape Hatteras. The line arrangement parallels the arrangement later in the poem of lines offering a visual analogy of a plane circling out from the sky to crash down at the Cape. A "geologic framing" (Berthoff 1989, 105), the opening also mimics the movement of expired dinosaurs sinking beneath accumulating geologic strata:

> Imponderable the dinosaur
> sinks slow,
> the mammoth saurian
> ghoul . . .
>
> (Crane 2006, 1–3)

The dinosaurs went extinct millions of years ago. The disjunction of scale between the time span of human lives and the time span since that extinction is "Imponderable," a Kantian sublimity: a gap opens between the imagination's capacity and the temporal vastness the imagination attempts to exhibit. Crane references the lay understanding: dinosaur corpses under sedimentary layers' pressure became oil. Crane notes this process's solar precondition: "Combustion at the astral core—the dorsal change / Of energy—convulsive shift of sand" (Crane 2006, 8–9). Solar combustion's heat and light allowed for the life forms that went under to become fossil fuels, transformed solar energy. This transformation's time scale staggers the imagination: during the untold millennia over which corpses became oil, silence reigned ("slowly the hushed land" [Crane 2006, 7]): an imponderable stretch of time without poetry. How is a dinosaur a "ghoul"? "Ghoul": "An evil spirit supposed (in Muslim countries) to rob graves and prey on human corpses" (*OED*). An *Allosaurus* scavenging *Stegosaurus* corpses counts as ghoulish. Unearthing fossil fuels, humans rob graves to feed steam and internal combustion engines. For Crane, fossil fuels entail something ghoulishly demonic.

After emphasizing the rift between human and geologic temporal scales, Crane moves to the human scale: "But we . . . / . . . return home to our own / Hearths" by "round[ing] the capes" (Crane 2006, 10, 13–14, 10). Sailors rounding Cape Hatteras risk joining the ocean floor's decaying biotic matter, the cape's waters being "The Graveyard of the Atlantic." The dinosaurs' sinking (geological time scale) prefigures ships' sinking (human time scale). Crews sunk off Cape Hatteras may eventually become oil.

Hearth: the place to burn coal. Hearth, heart, Hart: another association of Crane's name and the heart with fossil fuels appears in the poem's next lines. The speaker returns to hearth and home to reminisce about overseas trips:

> Those continental folded aeons, surcharged
> With sweetness below derricks, chimneys, tunnels—
> Is veined by all that time has really pledged us . . .
>
> (Crane 2006, 20–22)

To determine quality, nineteenth-century oil prospectors tasted their discoveries. Oil low in sulfur, tasting sweet, was called "sweet crude oil." Whitman and Crane are "in thrall" to their "native clay" (Crane 2006, 17, 18),

"Those continental folded aeons": the geologic strata that, accumulating over "aeons," are now "surcharged" with sweet crude oil that rests "below" oil "derricks," factory "chimneys," and car and subway "tunnels." Pocahontas's "red, eternal flesh" (Crane 2006, 19) is "veined" with "all that time has really pledged us": oil as blood. The oil time promised drives the "machine age" Crane would fuse with Pocahontas's timeless "nature-world."

The "machine age" includes mechanized warfare. Crane imagines a bullet-riddled warplane spiraling "down gravitation's / vortex into crashed / . . . dispersion . . . into mashed and shapeless debris..." (Crane 2006, 153–55). The pilot's plane and corpse are "bunched" into a ghoulish "heap" or mound. This corpse beached at Cape Hatteras then associates with the corpses America's Civil War and Europe's Great War produced. One of Whitman's hands, holding a baton, "[h]as beat a song" (Crane 2006, 174). The other rests on Crane's heart like a plummet, a plumb line's lead weight:

> And this, thine other hand, upon my heart
> Is plummet ushered of those tears that star
> What memories of vigils, bloody, by that Cape,
>
> (Crane 2006, 175–77)

Whitman's lively baton-holding hand associates with the covenant he offers: "O, upward from the dead / Thou bringest tally, and a pact, new bound / Of living brotherhood!" (165–67). Resting leaden, dead, on Crane's heart, Whitman's "other hand" associates with the tears that come as Whitman recalls the nightlong battlefield vigils he kept over corpses during the Civil War. Crane connects Civil and Great War battlefields with Cape Hatteras, where the pilot's corpse rests:

> Thou, pallid there as chalk
> Hast kept of wounds, O Mourner, all that sum
> That then from Appomattox stretched to Somme!
>
> (Crane 2006, 179–81)

At Appomattox, the Civil War's final battle occurred. The war left approximately six hundred thousand soldiers dead. "The same casualty figure attaches *on each side* of the battle of the Somme (July–November 1916)" (Kramer 2011, 82n63). Whitman tallies those corpses, "all that sum." The "tally [. . .] / Of living brotherhood" entangles with the tally of "fraternal massacre" (Crane 2006, 179) via oil figured as blood.

Time's promise of oil informs the covenant with Whitman. Whitman's "Open Road" becomes a path driven or, here, flown, in vehicles' gasoline powers:

> . . . Easters of speeding light —
> Vast engines outward veering with seraphic grace
> On clarion cylinders pass out of sight . . .

> (Crane 2006, 217–19)

In "Cape Hatteras," aircraft first associate with the dinosaurs' extinction and
then with "fraternal massacre." Here, the fantastic craft's light-speed acceleration figures resurrection, Easter. With "seraphic grace" these craft speed,
"out of sight"

> To course that span of consciousness thou'st named
> The Open Road—thy vision is reclaimed!
> What heritage thou'st signalled to our hands!

> (Crane 2006, 220–22)

The flight of the "Wright windwrestlers" prefigures interplanetary travel:
"The soul, by naphtha fledged into new reaches / Already knows the closer
clasp of Mars" (Crane 2006, 84, 88–89). "[F]ledged" rhymes with "pledged."
The fossil fuels time pledges fledge the soul as an arrow speeding to Mars, the
red planet's soil recalling Pocahontas's eternal red flesh. As Plato's *Phaedrus*
explains, fallen souls require millennia to attain the wings allowing them to
leave the temporal realm below to return home to the timeless realm above
(Plato 1973, 54, 51). "Cape Hatteras" accelerates this process: petroleum,
"naphtha," gives the soul feathers like an arrow's, and the craft that "course
that span of consciousness [Whitman] named / The Open Road" seem angelic
vehicles fit for wish-fulfilling *Interstellar*-type cli-fi.

With the promise of aircraft or spacecraft, Crane reclaims Whitman's "vision," the "heritage" Whitman bequeaths to Crane: "And see! the rainbow's
arch—how shimmeringly stands / Above the Cape's ghoul-mound, O joyous
seer!" (Crane 2006, 223–24). Humans and oil have a covenant: humans use
and may become oil. The crews sunk at Cape Hatteras join the sedimentation
process, as do the corpses the Civil War and the Great War produced. By
association with the pilot's body, these bodies belong to the "Ghoul-mound
of man's perversity at balk / And fraternal massacre" (Crane 2006, 178-79)
over which arches what Thomas Pynchon might call gravity's rainbow: because of gravity, biotic material under sedimentary pressure becomes the oil
allowing for the industrialized warfare that produces corpses that eventually
may become oil.

Crane superimposes geological and biblical histories. In Genesis, God
places his "bow in the cloud" as "a token of a covenant between [him] and
the earth" (9:13). The rainbow signals a promise: "the waters shall no more

become a flood to destroy all flesh" (9:15). Seeing a rainbow, God will remember his promise never again to trigger a mass extinction via a flood. The Genesis flood would have drowned untold numbers of creatures that would become fossil fuels. God's promissory rainbow arches over a postdiluvian creation gestating oil. As if recalling the ghoulishly carrion-eating raven Noah released before sending out the dove (8:7), Crane takes the flood-induced oil deposits to be covenantal.

Time promised humans oil in layering sediments over extinct creatures. The rainbow over the "ghoul-mound" images this promise. Crane and Whitman will join this mound: the lines describing their walk sink, visually echoing the lines sinking to evoke the plane sinking earthward and the lines sinking to evoke the dinosaur sinking below sedimentary layers. The oil "veined" in Pocahontas's "red flesh" echoes in the blood in the "veins" of the "Recorders" (Crane 2006, 225), whose pulse echoes Whitman's tread. The oil figured as blood and as promised at the poem's start morphs into the blood pulses figuring the covenantal footsteps of Whitman, at the poem's end, treading the Open Road with Crane: covenant of oil, of blood.

ON "O CARIB ISLE!"

Crane drafted "O Carib Isle!" in June or July, 1926, during or following his visit to Grand Cayman Island (Crane sailed there from the Isle of Pines) and before he began intensive work on *The Bridge* (Brunner 1985, 250). In his October 8, 1926 letter to Crane, Malcolm Cowley stated he was seeking poems for Eugene Jolas, who, in Paris, was compiling an anthology of American poems to appear in French translation (250). Crane submitted "O Carib Isle!" On October 19, 1926, a hurricane struck the Isle of Pines, wrecking the Villa Casa and prompting Crane's departure for New York City, where he arrived on October 28 (Fisher 2002, 317, 321).

In a November 28, 1926 letter, Crane mentions that "O Carib Isle!" had been accepted for publication by *Poetry* (Crane 2006, 500). Seeking another non-US venue, Crane submitted the poem to the British journal *Calendar* in January 1927. In February 1927, Jolas, by then coeditor of *transition*, notified Crane that "O Carib Isle!" would appear in the journal's first issue (April 1927). The poem appeared with the subscription "*Grand Cayman, West Indies*" (Crane 1927, 102). Months after *Poetry* had accepted the poem, Crane submitted an extensively revised version to the journal. Crane revised the poem during "the spring and even summer of 1927" (Brunner 1985, 253). *Calendar* folded before the poem (the initial version) could appear in it. In October 1927, *Poetry* published the initial version, not the revised version.

The version that appeared in *transition* and, with minor changes, in *Poetry*, gives readers the poem substantially as Crane wrote it prior to undergoing the hurricane on the Isle of Pines. In the final version, readers confront the poem as recrafted by Crane after undergoing the hurricane.

Crane's November 28, 1926 letter describes "O Carib Isle!" as "a rather violent lyric urging the hurricane on the Isle of Pines, which, of course, *came*" (Crane 2006, 500). The hurricane that reached the island on October 19, 1926, was among "the most severe late-season hurricanes ever observed in the Caribbean Sea" (Longshore 2008, 230). "An incipient Category 4 hurricane of extreme destructiveness," the storm took "650 lives in Cuba and another 88 in Bermuda" (Longshore 2008, 230). Soon after dawn on October 20, with winds reaching 130 miles per hour, the storm raked the Isle of Pines' northern extremity, devastating the island's principal city, Nueva Gerona (Longshore 2008, 230). An October 26, 1926 United Press report titled "Isle of Pines Storm" calls the tempest "the most devastating hurricane in the history of the island" ("Isle" 1926, 3). The storm killed at least twenty-five residents ("Isle" 1926, 3). Of Nueva Gerona's five hundred buildings, the storm "completely demolished" one hundred and fifty and "badly damaged" the remainder ("Isle" 1926, 3). A witness stated, "The force of the wind was such that buildings appeared to dissolve rather than crash to earth" ("Isle" 1926, 3).

The Villa Casa's caretaker, Mrs. Sally Simpson, directed Crane in their preparations to meet the approaching storm. The pair decided to "shelter . . . beneath the biggest bed in the house" (Fisher 2002, 317). When the storm receded, the pair "walked into Nueva Gerona, unprepared for the destruction that greeted them: the streets were chaotic with damaged vehicles, uprooted wires and trees, dead animals, injured survivors, and miscellaneous debris" (Fisher 2002, 318).

The revisions distinguishing the pre- and post-hurricane versions of "O Carib Isle!" evidence the storm's impact. The pre-hurricane version declares, "The wind / . . . is almost kind," words absent from the post-hurricane version (Crane 1927, 12–13). Crane replaces them with: "The wind that knots itself in one great death— / Coils and withdraws" (Crane 2006, 15–16). In the pre-hurricane version, the poet voices the melancholy of the unmarked shell-bordered graves he encounters: "This pity can be told . . . ," the kind wind allowing for the poet's voice (Crane 1927, 9). In the post-hurricane version, the hurricane as noose mutes the poet's voice. The pre-hurricane version, voicing pity, touches on mourning. The post-hurricane version depicts a pitiless realm void of mourning.

The post-hurricane version begins with the speaker meditating on a graveyard adjacent a coral beach. Observing the shadows, pondering "the dead" buried in the "white sand / Near the coral beach," the speaker notes the

absence of mourning amongst the tarantulas and crabs scampering across
sands betokening their fate:

> . . . —No, nothing here
> Below the palsy that one eucalyptus lifts
> In wrinkled shadows—mourns.

(Crane 2006, 5–7)

The exoskeletons of the beach dwellers will become sand, the wave-ground
grains mixing with the virtually uncountable grains that make up the beach,
tarantula-, crab-, and coral-derived grains sifting together. This fate, dying
into indistinction, troubles neither the tarantulas nor the crabs. The feet of the
tarantulas, the crabs, the lily, the dead, and the poet all rest on or in the sand.

The speaker also notes how the crabs "anagrammatize your name"
(Crane 2006, 5). As humans do on blank, inscribable surfaces, the speaker
had traced his name in the sand; the scuttling crabs reshape and rearrange
the letters. The names of the sand-buried dead are unknown, the graves
being unmarked. Shells demarcate the nameless graves' boundaries. A
hurricane would scatter the shells and exhume the bodies, the surf eventually grinding the shells and bones into white grains to join the white sand.
Numberless grains from ground-up skeletons, whether of coral, crabs, tarantulas, or humans: this beach realizes yet cancels the promise Yahweh
made to Abraham: "That in blessing I will bless thee, and in multiplying
I will multiply thy seed as the stars of the heaven, and as the sand which
is upon the sea shore" (Genesis 22:17). In Genesis, to invite the creatures
to participate in the creation's differential burgeoning, the god who later
promises to bless Abraham blesses the creatures: "And God blessed them,
saying, Be fruitful, and multiply," a blessing he then grants the creatures he
made in his image (1:22, 28). To figure offspring's boundless multiplication, God says Abraham's progeny will be as numerous "as the sand . . .
upon the sea shore." Virtually innumerable, the sand Crane evokes derives
from countless skeletal remains, human and nonhuman, mixed indistinguish-
ably. In Genesis, the blessing of fruitful multiplication becomes what the
Abrahamic covenant promises, Yahweh promising to "multiply" Abraham's
offspring as numerously as "sand." In "O Carib Isle!," doubting any deity
captains the island, Crane exclaims of this inexistent god, "His Carib mathematics web the eyes' baked lenses!" (Crane 2006, 22). This absent deity's
unpromising "mathematics" multiply only blindingly white sand.

Crane reverses Genesis's sand trope. In figuring the offspring he promises
Abraham as innumerable sand grains, Yahweh ties the sand to the beginning
when the creatures, including the humans, burgeoned out into their differentiation to receive the blessing: "Be fruitful and multiply." The Genesis

sand figures more life burgeoning into the future, fulfilling the promise. In "O Carib Isle!," various creatures, including humans, lose their future and their differentiation in becoming sand, cancelling the promise. Crane's sands betoken extinction.

The poet had attempted to sign the white sand. Crane titled his first collection *White Buildings*. Crane's poetry collections each attempt to sign a whiteness deriving in part from Percy Bysshe Shelley's "Adonais":

> Life, like a dome of many-coloured glass,
> Stains the white radiance of Eternity,
> Until Death tramples it to fragments. . . .
>
> (Shelley 1977, 462–64)

To join this "white radiance," Shelley imagines sailing his "spirit's bark" into a storm-wracked ocean, steering by Adonais's soul, that, "like a star, / Beacons from the abode where the Eternal are" (Shelley 1977, 488, 494–95). Shelley giving himself to the sea in voyaging toward the "white radiance of Eternity" returns in *The Bridge*'s finale, "Atlantis." Following an epigraph Crane takes from Shelley's translation of Plato's *Symposium* ("Music is then the knowledge of that which relates to love in harmony and system" [Plato 1880, 184]), in "Atlantis" the poet cries out, "O Love, thy white pervasive Paradigm . . . !" and then addresses the Brooklyn Bridge ("Thou") to imagine sailing through death to join the eternal: "And like an organ, Thou, with sound of doom— / Sight, sound and flesh Thou leadest from time's realm / As love strikes clear direction for the helm" (Crane 2006, 48, 62–64). In Shelley's *Symposium* translation, Diotima explains that "Love . . . is a great daemon" who conveys to mortals the gods' "commands and directions" (Plato 1880, 208–9). Thus, in "Atlantis," when personified love "strikes clear direction for the helm," Crane imagines Love as a daemon at the ship's bow beckoning the poet at the helm to steer his bark into the fatal storm, give over his mortality, and break into an immortal realm.

Crane frames Love as a Platonic-Christian "Word." In the poem preceding "Atlantis," "The Tunnel," Crane describes the subway tunnel as hell and the train as "the Daemon" who, with "hideous laughter" "Or the muffled slaughter of a day in birth," "pack[s] / The conscience navelled in the plunging wind, / Umbilical to call—and straightaway die!" (Crane 2006, 100, 107, 108, 112–14). Like the *Iliad*'s Athena, this daemon brings an epiphany tied to immanent demise. Crane contrasts this perishing to undergoing a resurrection "like Lazarus" toward "A sound of waters bending astride the sky / Unceasing with some Word that will not die . . .!" (Crane 2006, 119, 121–22). This immortal "Word" or quasi-Johannine Logos becomes the Platonic "Love"

"Atlantis" evokes. For *The Bridge*'s epigraph Crane takes words of Satan (*"From going to and fro in the earth, and from walking up and down in it."* [Crane 2006, 31; Job 1:7]), but Crane ends *The Bridge* by turning from the daemon as Christianity demonizes it and toward the daemon "Love" recuperated as a "Word" of Platonic-Christian provenance.

Crane's quest to sign eternity's white radiance founders in "O Carib Isle!" The graves are unmarked. When Crane signs the white sands, he attempts to overcome this namelessness and anticipates the sands becoming his own grave. To sign his own grave would mark death as the poet's own, as appropriated to the poet's will-to-inscription. This appropriation would bring the poet's death within the poet's will. But the crabs "anagrammatize" his name, displacing death from authentically being the poet's own. Death remains yet entirely without mournful commemoration in a monument to the poet's name.

Rather than remaining a proper noun signing whiteness, "Crane" becomes "nacre," a common noun referring to mother of pearl or white shells, the common noun within the adjective "nacreous" (Mariani 1999, 240):

> I count these nacreous frames of tropic death,
> Brutal necklaces of shells around each grave
> Squared off so carefully . . .
>
> (Crane 2006, 9–11)

Confronting a mourning-void surround, the poet would count the shells framing the graves, shells hurricane-driven waves will scatter. In this imagined enumeration, with the adjective "nacreous," the crabs' rearranging of "Crane" disperses the poet's signature. His written name's scrambling foreshadows the muting of his attempt to "speak a name" to the "white sand." This speaking effort ends with the hurricane's noose ("The wind that knots itself in one great death") asphyxiating the "syllables" the poet would speak. The poet's "syllables" desire yet lack ("want") "breath." The naming effort would speak against "death's brittle crypt": death's crumbly tomb and enigmatic yet friable cipher that the spoken tree and flower names would decrypt ("Deliberate") and refute ("gainsay"). Like the writing effort, the speaking effort founders.

Balking the attempt to write or to speak a name, the sands and hurricane winds resist appropriation via prosopopoeia, the trope positing a voice, a face, a name. The poet finds only the mute, the anonymous, the faceless:

> But where is the Captain of this doubloon isle
> Without a turnstile? Who but catchword crabs
> Patrols the dry groins of the underbrush?
>
> (Crane 2006, 17–19)

After noting the presence of the scavenging crabs on the island, the poet turns to the absence of human life:

> What man, or What
> Is Commissioner of mildew throughout the ambushed senses?
> His Carib mathematics web the eyes' baked lenses!

(Crane 2006, 20–22)

A "what," the "crabs," associate with "who" ("Who but catchword crabs"), and "man," a "who," associates with "what" ("What man"). This crossing of who and what, following the second "What['s]" enjambment, opens an expansive white space, like a coral beach, blank (without writing) and silent (without voice).

The poet's blocked effort to write or to speak a name, and doubts about the island having any captain, lead to the poet wishing his ghost would be drawn up from his sand-buried corpse through the roots of a poinciana whose red flowers canopy the tree:

> Let fiery blossoms clot the light, render my ghost
> Sieved upward, white and black along the air
> Until it meets the blue's comedian host.

(Crane 2006, 24–26)

From the roots, up the trunk, through the branches, and to the flowers: "Sieved upward" from his corpse, Crane's "ghost" would reach the air to encounter whatever humorous entity resides in the sky. Here, the opening lines' anxiety goes missing. Giving up the ghost becomes laconic, as if the poet need only recline beneath the tree and allow the sieving gently to proceed. The word "render" disturbs this tranquil vision. "To render" means to deliver. The blossoms deliver to the sky the ghost that has been "Sieved upward," "white and black," like ethereal white paper bearing black letters, as if "n," "a," "c," "r," and "e" were to recombine as a ghostly "Crane," the balked signing effort somehow realized above and beyond inscription. This outcome remains a wish.

"To render" can refer to the abstraction from a body of oil, fat, or another substance. The poet hopes his ghost will be rendered skyward via benign sieving. He would "Let" this happen, as if he could use the word "Let" as the Genesis god does. The stanza following the sieving stanza describes what the poet hopes will not happen, a far from gentle rendering. He imagines his own being as a terrapin nailed to the wharf, slowly dying:

> Each daybreak on the wharf, their brine caked eyes;
> —Spiked, overturned; such thunder in their strain!
> And clenched beaks coughing for the surge again!

(Crane 2006, 29–31)

Absent from the sieving vision, the anxiety of being-toward-death returns forcefully in the description of the sea turtles' "slow evisceration," their rendering. The creatures' agonized panic tests readers' resolve to follow the poet's imaginings. Turned on their backs with their flippers nailed to the wharf, the turtles' crucifixion involves no gentle giving up of the ghost but only a desperate effort and yearning to return to the sea. Remaining sound without articulation, their "coughing" fails to overcome the balking of voice.

From an anxiety-free, tree-facilitated human ghosting to the sharpest anxiety of turtles undergoing a human-imposed crucifixion: Crane articulates these options as in prayer. To whom or to what does the poem's human speaker plead? Prior to the stanzas contrasting dying options, the poet ran up against who-versus-what conundrums opening a silent, anonymous, faceless blank.

Nonhumans dismantle the name "Crane" into the adjective "nacreous": "Pearly or iridescent like nacre" or "Consisting of [. . .] nacre" (*OED*). Nacre is mother of pearl or the smooth, whitish lining of shells. The shells outlining the graves are "nacreous frames of tropic death" also because, to reveal the satiny nacre, the organism inhabiting the shell must be gone, eviscerated, dead. At the poem's end, the speaker rests on the shore like a corpse reducing to a skeleton, void of flesh, displaying its smooth nacre. He imagines that he will

> Congeal by afternoons here, satin and vacant.
> You have given me the shell, Satan,—carbonic amulet
> Sere of the sun exploded in the sea.

(Crane 2006, 33–35)

The name "Crane" undergoes anagrammatization to inhabit an adjective, "nacreous," and then the lyric "I" ends up "satin and vacant," adjectives describing a shell with its nacre exposed. Transformation continues: elements of the adjectives "*sat*in" and "vac*ant*" morph into a name: "Satan." Satin, Satan—the near homonym prompts readers to follow out the anagrammatization. The long vowel in \ˈvā-kənt\ scuttles to trade places with the short vowel in \ˈsa-tᵊn\, resulting in \ˈsā-tᵊn\. Pronounced the same, satin's "i" becomes Satan's second "a."

An early typescript of the pre-hurricane version of "O Carib Isle!" includes the phrase, "the lyric play of eucalypti" (Crane n.d., 5). The letters "p," "l," "a," and "y" inhabit "eucalypti." An emendation in Crane's hand changes "play" to "palsy," yielding the phrase in the poem's first published version: "the lyric palsy of eucalypti" (Crane 1927, 5). As do all the variants of the pre-hurricane version, the *transition* variant describes how "the small and ruddy crabs /. . . reverse your name" (Crane 1927, 3–4). However, in the typescript, Crane's emendation enacts anagrammatization, with a satanic "s" intruding to facilitate the transition from "play" to "palsy." The phrase "lyric play of eucalypti" suggests branches swaying in wind. The phrase "lyric palsy of eucalypti" reverses limber bending into paralytic rigidity, pre-echoing the skeletal "I" of the poem's close. The early typescript and the pre-hurricane variants include the anagrammatical relation between "satin," "vacant," and "Satan." Rewriting the poem post-hurricane, Crane attends to the letter's play and palsy in his text and adds the term "anagrammatize."

Carbonic: "of or relating to carbon or its compounds" or "to carbon dioxide" (*OED*). Seashells include carbon, so the shell Satan proffers is a "carbonic amulet." But why would Satan provide a luck charm that wards off evil, an "amulet"? An "amulet Quran" is a pendant inscribed with, or a neck-worn pouch holding, Quranic verses. The amulet Satan hands the poet enters "O Carib Isle!" via Wordsworth's "Dream of the Arab" in *The Prelude*. This episode begins with the poet recalling a day spent reading *Don Quixote* "in a rocky cave / By the sea-side" (Wordsworth 1979, 5.58–59). Falling asleep, the poet "passed into a dream": "I saw before me stretched a boundless plain / Of sandy wilderness, all black and void" (Wordsworth 1979, 5.70, 71–72). Overwhelmed by "distress and fear," the poet sees "Upon a dromedary . . . an Arab of the Bedouin tribes" (Wordsworth 1979, 5.73, 76, 77). This Arab carries "underneath one arm / A stone, and in the opposite hand, a shell / Of surpassing brightness" (Wordsworth 1979, 5.78–80). The stone and shell are "both . . . books" (Wordsworth 1979, 5.113). A "semi-Quixote," the "Arab phantom" tells the poet the stone is "Euclid's Elements" (Wordsworth 1979, 5.143, 142, 88). As the Arab hands the poet the shell, the Arab's words and the narrating poet's evoke a name: "'This,' said [the Arab], / 'Is something of more worth'; and at the word / Stretched forth the shell" (Wordsworth 1979, 5.88–90). Worth, word, plus a satanic "s": Wordsworth. Satin, vacant: Satan. Holding the shell to his ear, the poet hears "articulate sounds" "in an unknown tongue" (Wordsworth 1979, 5.94, 93). In "O Carib Isle!," having contemplated the shells, the poet "may speak . . . / Albeit in a stranger tongue" (Crane 2006, 12–13). In *The Prelude*, the dreaming poet hears from the shell a "prophetic blast of harmony; / An Ode, in passion uttered, which foretold / Destruction to the children of the earth," that is, an immanent ecological catastrophe

(Wordsworth 1979, 5.95–98). Tracking the Arab's backward glance, the poet sees a "bed of glittering light," which the Arab tells him is "the waters of the deep / Gathering upon us" (Wordsworth 1979, 5.129, 130–31). The poet follows the Arab, "In chase of him; whereat I waked in terror, / And saw the sea before me, and the book, / In which I had been reading, at my side" (Wordsworth 1979, 5.136–40). In the dream, the shell seems a book of poetry. Meditating on the dream, and on "the approach / Of an event so dire" as humanity's demise in an ecological catastrophe, Wordsworth feels he could become another apparently mad Quixote and "go / Upon like errand" to warn of an extinction already in progress (Wordsworth 1979, 5.157–58, 160–61): "Me hath such strong entrancement overcome, / When I had held a volume in my hand, / Poor earthly casket of immortal verse" (Wordsworth 1979, 5.161–64).

Weaving the theme of ecological catastrophe into Crane's poem, the Wordsworth allusion implies that, in handing over a shell, Satan hands over a text. As the Arab hands the shell/book to Wordsworth, the poet's name sounds. In "O Carib Isle!," the poet's name undergoes an anagrammatization from which emerges the name Satan. An uncanny guest, Satan hands the poet a shell, a poem ("O Carib Isle!") leveling human with nonhuman extinction. Only by the poet, his name, breaking up and going under, only by this *sparagmos*, does Satan manifest to deliver the lucky amulet. Why lucky? The poet attains sublimity: a daemonic moment on a shore decentered from anthropocentric horizons.

CONCLUSION

In "What is the Anthropo-Political?," Colebrook distinguishes in the Anthropocene between a "recuperative sublime" and a "material sublime," this last phrase citing Paul de Man (Colebrook 2016, 105). Crane anticipates both, the recuperative in "Cape Hatteras," the material in "O Carib Isle!" A *"Pindar* for the dawn of the machine age," Crane wrote odes for the decades preparing the Great Acceleration. Crane called "Cape Hatteras" an "ode to Whitman" (Crane 2006, 557). To the strong ode "O Carib Isle!" "Cape Hatteras" stands as the weak palinode. Satan handing the poet the shell overmatches Crane taking Whitman by the hand.

In the Anthropocene sublime's recuperative mode, "[s]ome matters—geological inscription—open the thought, anticipation or promise of the 'not yet.' In the very mark of our defeat and limit we are given a time to come; we are given a 'we', a 'humanity to come'" (Colebrook 2016, 105). "Cape

Hatteras" exhibits this mode. The apparition of humans' "geological inscription," of humans going under to become fossil fuel, occasions a covenant with Whitman, forming a "we" and opening a promise of an America to come, the Atlantis, with covenantal oil fueling a flight in return to eternal "Nature," whether that be Mars's colonization or a flight across "that span of consciousness [Whitman] named / The Open Road" to the timeless pastoral destination Whitman's halo of "pasture-shine" (Crane 2006, 228) intimates. Colebrook could be writing of "Cape Hatteras" when she links the recuperative sublime to such a mirage of "Nature" and follows Timothy Morton in seeking an "ecology *without nature*," without "the notion of nature as eternal and everlasting—a nature that would provide some ground for our nostalgia and yearning" (Morton 2013, 118). In efforts to name the current geologic epoch the "Corporatocene" or the "Capitalocene," efforts implying narratives good/evil binaries structure, Colebrook finds recuperative evasions attempting to look away from what the Anthropocene may imply: the suspension of any promise of salvational futurity (Colebrook 2016, 99). These evasions' denialism finds promise in an epoch climate science predicts could be blankly unpromising: "What the future promises us, at least from one mode of the Anthropocene, is the impossibility of promise: this is not definitely the case, for it is not certain that promising will be impossible, but it is certainly one possibility" (Colebrook 2016, 105).

"O Carib Isle!" achieves the "material sublime," with anagrammatic play enacting material inscription as promise-void geological inscription. "By contrast [with the recuperative sublime], de Man's material, non-recuperative, tropological, sublime would not allow some matters—such as geological inscription. . . —to promise or open any other register" (Colebrook 2016, 106). Adjourning the promise God offered his creatures, "O Carib Isle!" dissipates visions of a world to come while, via Wordsworth's dream of the Arab, dramatizing an implicitly eco-catastrophic now. "Cape Hatteras" evokes dinosaurs' and humans' demise, yet that poem and *The Bridge* push away the thought of extinction. Letting extinction edge into thought, "O Carib Isle!" relinquishes mourning, salvational futurity, and any covenantal "we." The "material sublime" conjures a mourning-free "*impersonality*," delivering readers to the pragmatics of questioning: "what calls to be saved? Is saving, surviving, and living on a prima facie value?" (Colebrook 2016, 120, 121). This transport Colebrook calls "the geological sublime," evaded in "Cape Hatteras," emergent in "O Carib Isle!": "The geological sublime is . . . the challenge of looking at the entire archive of the earth—including human script—as one might look at the marks left on buildings by the forces of weathering" (Colebrook 2016, 124).

WORKS CITED

Berthoff, Warner. 1989. *Hart Crane: A Re-Introduction*. Minneapolis: University of Minnesota Press.

The Bible: Authorized King James Version with Apocrypha. 1997. Oxford: Oxford University Press.

Bloom, Harold. 2015. *The Daemon Knows: Literary Greatness and the American Sublime*. New York: Spiegel & Grau.

Bristow, Tom. 2015. *The Anthropocene Lyric: An Affective Geography of Poetry, Person, Place*. New York: Palgrave.

Brunner, Edward. 1985. *Splendid Failure: Hart Crane and the Making of* The Bridge. Urbana: University of Illinois Press.

Clark, Timothy. 2015. *Ecocriticism on the Edge: The Anthropocene as a Threshold Concept*. London: Bloomsbury.

Colebrook, Claire. 2016. "What is the Anthropo-Political?" In *Twilight of the Anthropocene Idols*, by Tom Cohen, Claire Colebrook, and J. Hillis Miller, 81–125. London: Open Humanities Press.

Crane, Hart. 2006. *Complete Poems and Selected Letters*. Edited by Langdon Hammer. New York: Library of America.

———. n.d. "O Carib Isle!" *Harry Ransom Center Digital Collections*. Accessed January 5, 2016. https://hrc.contentdm.oclc.org/digital/collection/p15878coll32.

———. 1927. "O Carib Isle!" *transition* 1: 101–2.

Fisher, Clive. 2002. *Hart Crane: A Life*. New Haven, CT: Yale University Press.

Fletcher, Angus. 2004. *A New Theory for American Poetry: Democracy, the Environment, and the Future of Imagination*. Cambridge, MA: Harvard University Press.

"Isle of Pines Storm." 1926. *Chicago Daily Tribune*, October 26, 1926.

Kramer, Lawrence. 2011. *Hart Crane's* The Bridge*: An Annotated Edition*. New York: Fordham University Press.

Longshore, David. 2008. *Encyclopedia of Hurricanes, Typhoons, and Cyclones*. New York: Facts on File.

Mariani, Paul. 1999. *The Broken Tower: A Life of Hart Crane*. New York: Norton.

Morton, Timothy. 2013. *Hyperobjects: Philosophy and Ecology after the End of the World*. Minneapolis: University of Minnesota Press.

Nersesian, Roy L. 2010. *Energy for the 21st Century: A Comprehensive Guide to Conventional and Alternative Sources*. 2nd ed. Armonk, NY: M.E. Sharpe.

Plato. 1880. *The Banquet*. Translated by Percy Bysshe Shelley. In *The Works of Percy Bysshe Shelley*, Vol. 7, edited by Harry Buxton Forman, 160–235. London: Reeves and Turner.

———. 1973. *Phaedrus and Letters VII and VIII*. Translated by Walter Hamilton. New York: Penguin.

Schuster, Joshua. 2015. *The Ecology of Modernism: American Environments and Avant-Garde Poetics*. Tuscaloosa: University of Alabama Press.

Shelley, Percy Bysshe. 1977. "Adonais." In *Shelley's Poetry and Prose*, edited by Donald H. Reiman and Sharon B. Powers, 388–406. New York: Norton.

United States Census Bureau. 2000. "Historical National Population Estimates: July 1, 1900 to July 1, 1999." Accessed January 2, 2016. https://www2.census.gov / programs-surveys/popest/tables/1900-1980/national/totals/popclockest.txt.

United States Energy Information Administration. 2015. "US Field Production of Crude Oil." Accessed January 2, 2016. https://www.eia.gov/dnav/pet/hist/Leaf Handler.ashx?n=PET&s=MCRFPUS2&f=M.

Unterecker, John. 1987. *Voyager: A Life of Hart Crane.* New York: Liveright.

Wark, McKenzie. 2015. *Molecular Red: Theory for the Anthropocene.* London: Verso.

Whitman, Walt. 2002. *Leaves of Grass and Other Writings.* Edited by Michael Moon. New York: Norton.

Wordsworth, William. 1979. *The Prelude: 1799, 1805, 1850.* Edited by Jonathan Wordsworth, M. H. Abrams, and Stephen Gill. New York: Norton.

Chapter Four

"What kind of creature uttered it . . . ?"

A Stratigraphy of Subjectivity in Samuel Beckett's The Unnamable

Emily Chester

READING BECKETT IN THE ANTHROPOCENE

In 2014, S. E. Gontarski wrote that the current "apposite question" for Beckett scholars is how Beckett was "decreating worlds we thought we knew" (Gontarski 2014, 3). This extends a compelling invitation to examine how Beckett's writing engages with the "decreat[ed] worlds" that emerge from the act of naming the Anthropocene. As a self-standing term, the Anthropocene specifically refers to "the era of geological time during which human activity is considered to be the dominant influence on the environment, climate, and ecology of the earth" (*OED*). Fundamental to this definition is the emergent status of the human as a geological force acting upon a putatively passive and discrete nonhuman environment. In this sense, humans are active subjective agents, whose impact is borne out evidentially in terms of the material stratigraphic markers detectable on planet Earth.[1]

In recent years, however, scholars outside of the natural sciences have recommended the refinement and expansion of this definition. For instance, Maslin and Lewis (2015) advocate the inclusion of a range of definitions that extend beyond the field of geology, and, in a similar vein, Malm and Hornborg (2014) state their concerns that the natural sciences (as opposed to other scholarly disciplines) dominate, and thereby dictate, our understanding of the Anthropocene. Certainly, a crucial implication of the current definition of the Anthropocene is its implicit reference to a divide between the "human" and the "nonhuman." Richard Kerridge traces this split to "Enlightenment humanism, [in which] the separation of humanity from nature is at its most systematic in the philosophy of René Descartes. Reason, including understanding, self-awareness, and choice is for Descartes the quality that distinguishes humankind from non-human nature. Nature . . . is mechanical"

(Kerridge 2006, 539). Indeed, certain critics have viewed the act of naming the Anthropocene as a reinforcement of this divide. For example, Timothy James LeCain, who cautions against the assumption of implicit neutrality, argues that "the term itself is unapologetically anthropocentric" (LeCain 2015, 3). Considering the claim that this anthropocentrism might motivate humans to become responsible for their impact on the natural world, LeCain still concludes that, "[a]t base, both optimistic and pessimistic views of the Anthropocene often share the conventional modernist belief that powerful humans and their cultures are distinct from the natural material world" (LeCain 2015, 8). The worry here, therefore, is that rather than acting as an impetus for changed environmental attitudes, the definition of the Anthropocene in its current conception might instead reinforce the perceived separateness of "humans" and "the natural world."

In positioning Beckett's late modernist novel, *The Unnamable* (1953), alongside this critique, I have two broad aims. The first is to reinstate the value of modernist literature in giving nuance to current ecological issues. In light of this, I adopt Anne Raine's claim that "modernist scholars have largely ignored ecocriticism" as a rallying cry to acknowledge the value of modernist texts in Anthropocene discourses (Raine 2014, 100). Within this framework, my second aim is to reevaluate Samuel Beckett's engagement with the categories of the human and nonhuman. I consider Chris Ackerley's statement that "Beckett rejected what he called 'the impulse to anthropomorphism' by defining landscape as something ultimately unintelligible, and by making that absence of rapport between himself and the natural world his working principle" (Ackerley 2010, 149). Throughout, I demonstrate that, in *The Unnamable*, Beckett in fact resists the definition of "landscape," instead gesturing toward the inefficacy of binary oppositions between human self and natural world.[2] In relation to the figures of "the human" and "nature," we might thus identify Beckett's "working principle" with a less polarized model of subjectivity. In *The Unnamable*, this "principle" chimes with LeCain's critique of the act of naming the Anthropocene: anthropocentrism in the novel does not hold. However, the novel also considers how we might conceive of a qualitative subject beyond the human/nonhuman divide, recognizing the impasse we, as humans, face in achieving this. The text therefore intersects with the question: How might we meaningfully move beyond the modernist divide between the human and nonhuman?

Translated by Beckett from its French counterpart, *L'Innomable* (1953), *The Unnamable* is a verbally dense monologue that traces the narrator's attempts to categorize and place their[3] subjective identity, as the opening establishes the aporetic textual environs: "Where now? Who now? When now?" (Beckett [1953] 2010, 1).[4] Despite Ruby Cohn's observation that the novel "pulverizes plot" throughout, the narrator refers to, and, to some extent, identifies with the various figures of Basil, Mahoo, and, finally, Worm (Cohn 2001, 185). However, in spite of this, the narrator never achieves any concrete identity. As Dirk Van Hulle and Shane Weller suggest of Worm, each of these figures emerges as merely "the narrator's latest avatar" (Van Hulle and Weller 2014, 145). Beckett, therefore, presents us with a textual world that staunchly denies subjective definition and categorisation: Beckett himself stated of *L'Innomable* that "there's complete disintegration. No 'I', no 'have', no 'being'. No nominative, no accusative, no verb. There's no way to go on" (qtd. in Hutchings 1981, 111). In spite of this denial, I argue, the novel displays an obsessive-compulsive preoccupation with categorisation and placement of subjective identity, which is present on both thematic and formal levels, as the narrator documents "the mad need to speak, think [and] to know where one is" (*TU* 61).

Indeed, this "mad need" can be viewed alongside the obsessive-compulsive texture of the novel, which has been remarked upon by various critics. Deirdre Bair comments on "the obsessive-compulsive need for words" (Bair 1990, 423) in the text and Ruby Cohn asserts that "[t]he unnamable narrator's unparagraphed monologue drives on compulsively and self-consciously" (Cohn 2001, 189). I suggest that the obsessive-compulsive form of the text has direct parallels with the narrator's attempt to name the qualitative nature of their subjectivity. This "need of succour" (*TU* 10) leads the narrator to refer to "the compulsion [they are] under to speak of" those things that appertain "to the place where I am, to me who am there" (*TU* 12). Subsequently, this act of delineating subjective identity becomes figured as compulsive and necessary, rather than volitional. Indeed, the narrator claims that "all these questions [they] ask [themselves]" are not posited "in a spirit of curiosity", but because they "cannot be silent" (*TU* 4). Questioning and rumination thus permeate the text as the narrator embarks on the quest to pin down the qualitative form of their existence.

How, then, does the recognition of this obsessive-compulsive quest feed into the act of naming the Anthropocene? Throughout the novel, the quest for subjective placement is enacted through the narrator's attempted identification with three different qualitative agencies: 1) human, 2) nonhuman and 3) a hybrid agency that exists beyond the dichotomy of the rationalist human/nonhuman divide.[5] Interestingly, the narrator's identification with human and nonhuman forms of agency happens concurrently throughout the text, and, subsequently, the qualitative nature of the narrator morphs, back and forth, as we witness an intermittent layering or stratigraphy of human and non-human subjectivity. The intermingling of these different agencies throughout refutes the narrator's obsessive-compulsive attempt to identify concretely with either one.

In depicting the inadequacy of locating a concretely human or nonhuman subjective agency, Beckett's novel moves us away from the viability of an anthropocentric position, chiming with LeCain's critique of naming the Anthropocene. But as well as this, I suggest, Beckett's portrayal of a third elusive hybrid agency in the novel also alerts us to the difficulty of conceptualizing what kind of subjectivity might stand beyond the rationalist divide. In line with this, my analysis strives to avoid "an ecocritical cliché—that the subject/object binary, which radical ecologists identify as the root of modern ecological calamity, must be dissolved" (Saunders 2011, 68). Instead, Beckett's novel draws our attention to the fact that that which we cannot conceptualize, must, by default, remain unnameable.

This conceptual aporia recalls Dipesh Chakrabarty's suggestion that "[e]ven if we were to emotionally identify with a word like *mankind*, we would not know what being a species is, for in species history, humans are only an instance of the concept species as indeed would be any other life form. But one never experiences being a concept" (Chakrabarty 2009, 220). If one is never able to experience even the concept of being human, the question arises as to how we might conceptualize an integrated human/nonhuman entity that could enable a reframing of the Anthropocene era. Beckett's narrator, therefore, cannot fully align themselves with a human, nonhuman, or hybrid agency, as the text bears out the narrator's claim that "this cursed first person . . . is really too red a herring" (*TU* 56).

HUMAN AND NONHUMAN AGENCY

Throughout the text we apprehend instances of discrete human and nonhuman narrative agency. Inge E. Boer has written that *The Unnamable* is "a narrative seemingly devoid of humanity," but, rather than starting off as a blanket absence in the text, I argue, we instead witness the decline of both human and nonhuman agency throughout (Boer 2006, 62). Certainly, the narrator's attempts to affirm their selfhood in terms of either of these two binary forms of agency fail; human and nonhuman spheres are partial and deteriorating, morphing into each other concurrently. We learn that, in this textual world, "it's entirely a matter of voices" (*TU* 37), and it is this multiplicity of voices that frames the entire novel. The narrator begins by acknowledging "a feeble cry," and goes on to ask, "What kind of creature uttered it and, if it is the same, still does, from time to time?" (*TU* 6) In spite of the suggestion that the cry emanates from another entity, we can read it as uttered by the narrator themselves as they ask of the sound: "Is Malone the culprit? Am I?" (*TU* 6) From the outset, then, there is a preoccupation with pinning down "[w] hat kind" (*TU* 6) of qualities we can ascribe to subjectivity in the text, but there is also the suggestion that the answer to such a question would depend on the condition of that subject remaining "the same" (*TU* 6). Consequently, we are confronted with a narrative subject prone to assuming new qualitative forms and shifting between them. The instability of the qualitative form of the subject is displayed when the narrator suggests the answer to the original question is "[i]mpossible to say," but asserts that it is "[n]ot a human one in any case, there are no human creatures here, or if there are, they have done with crying" (*TU* 6). In spite of this initial denial that the cry is human, the conditional clause that follows reasserts the possibility of human agency. In this way, Beckett establishes conditionality, rather than certainty, as the framework for subjective definition, and we subsequently apprehend only partial or ailing human agency from the beginning.

Nevertheless, the narrator's identity again seems to possess human qualities. Shortly after the suggestion that "there are no human creatures here," the narrator asks whether "this place . . . wait[ed] for me to come and people it" (*TU* 6), which suggests renewed identification with the figure of the human, and, moreover, some pages later, the narrator also asserts, "I alone am man" (*TU* 10). However, it is a deteriorating human agency that persists throughout. The narrator claims that they are "just barely a man, sufficiently a man to have hopes one day of being one, my avatars behind me" (*TU* 27). Here, humanity is only present in a minimal sense, and, ironically, only to the extent that the narrator can experience hope for eventual human wholeness that will, ultimately, be denied by the end of the text.

Alongside this ailing human agency, we also witness a distinctly nonhuman agency. At first, we might characterize this agency as planetary as the narrator states they are "a big talking ball, talking about things" (*TU* 16), which is corroborated by the subsequent need to ask, "am I in equilibrium somewhere, on one of my numberless poles?" (*TU* 16) The presence of a material nonhuman agency is also affirmed when the narrator claims they are "tired of being matter, matter, pawed and pummelled endlessly in vain" (*TU* 62). Significantly, the narrator points here to the passivity of this material agency, as it seems destined to be violently abused by a qualitatively different force or agency. Further on, the narrator also ponders "am I to suppose I am inhabited" (*TU* 121), thereby reiterating the possibility of a planetary agency that questions the anthropocentric assumption that humans live "on" a material Earth, rather than "with" or "alongside" it. The concurrence of these different layers of subjective agency becomes more pronounced when we consider this material agency alongside the narrator's initial consideration of whether they might "people" "this place" (*TU* 6). Significantly, the repeated questioning and passivity demonstrated by the nonhuman agency here also places it in a position of decline. In this sense, we might term the human and non-human agencies in the text as co-deteriorating, rather than coexisting. This, in turn, challenges the anthropocentric stance implied by the definition of the Anthropocene as human agency in the novel is portrayed as too frail to be any kind of "dominant influence" (*OED*).

DETERIORATION OF HUMAN AND NON-HUMAN AGENCY

As the novel progresses, we see human agency deteriorating more and more, as the figure of the human is held up as untenable. For example, the narrator recalls Mahood's "lesson," during which they "couldn't" repeat that "Man is a higher mammal" (*TU* 50). Here, we are not only party to Mahood's inability to assert human preeminence, but also to the suggestion that the very question of the hierarchical status of the human subject is, in itself, uninteresting as the narrator states: "Frankly, between ourselves, what the hell could it matter to pupil Mahood, that man was this rather than that?" (*TU* 50). "[F]rankly" and "what the hell" convey a flippant disregard for the significance of the status of the human, which becomes even more overt when we consider Cohn's identification of Mahood with the very concept of "manhood" itself, and, in this sense, we witness a human recognition of its own conceptual insignificance. Moreover, the narrator's previous allusion to "the great life torrent streaming from the earliest protozoa to the very latest humans" (*TU* 34) locates the concept of "the human" as a temporary and dependent one, simply a component of "the great life torrent," as opposed to the essential natural kind that, according to Enlightenment humanism, is its status.

Moreover, the limitations of human agency are depicted through the narrator's awareness of their lack of knowledge of "the earth" as they state: "I was under the impression I spent my life in spirals round the earth. Wrong, it's on the island I wind my endless ways. The island, that's all the earth I know" (*TU* 39). In addition, the narrator's tendency to "wind [their] endless ways . . . [in] a succession of irregular loops" (*TU* 39) further suggests the futility of their existence on the island. That their movements are "invariably unpredictable in direction, that is to say determined by the panic of the moment" (*TU* 39) also tells of the arbitrary nature of this iteration. This is significant because these movements constitute the method of trying to gain knowledge of the island. Subsequently, the human method of attempting to acquire knowledge does not occur through a reasoning process but instead through reactions to "panic." Furthermore, "the endless" ways that the narrator "wind[s]" also gesture toward a compulsive quest without meaningful endpoint: instead of expanding the narrator's awareness, their cyclical "irregular loops" merely shut it down. In this way, we witness more than just Ackerley's "absence of rapport" (Ackerley 2010, 149) between the human and nonhuman as an a priori state of affairs; the problem, in fact, lies in the inability of the human agency in the text to accurately identify the nonhuman in the first place, thereby also casting doubt on the very reasoning faculties associated with human agency. Accordingly, the categories on which the Enlightenment notion of human reason and acquisition of self-awareness depend become futile and meaningless as the narrator asserts that "God and man, nature and the light of day, the heart's outpourings and the means of understanding, [are] all invented . . . by me alone" (*TU* 14). That such categories and concepts are positioned as mere constructs resonates with the sense of an ailing human agency in the novel as we no longer view the category of the human as a given.

Despite this portrayal of an ailing human agency, however, there is still a compulsion to continue seeking knowledge via the act of questioning in a seeming last-ditch attempt to cling onto the human categories that appear so arbitrary. Indeed, the narrator exclaims: "But fie these are questions again . . . I know no more questions and they keep on pouring out of my mouth. I think I know what it is, it's to prevent the discourse from coming to an end, this futile discourse" (*TU* 18). Here, the questions adopt a fluidity of their own as the narrator is rendered passive in their ability to control them. The capacity for language, which "Descartes identifies . . . as one of two features distinguishing people from 'machines' or 'beasts'" (Cowie 2008), becomes automatic and superfluous, as the questions are actively "pouring out of [the narrator's] mouth" (*TU* 18). In this sense, Beckett configures human agency as compulsively bound to seek knowledge, even in the recognition of the futility of such a quest. At first, this compulsive pursuit of knowledge-seeking seems to tire the narrator as they exclaim, "[e]nough questions, enough reasoning" (*TU* 19). However, any hiatus from attempting to discover the objects of knowledge is temporary as they experience the urge to "set about the truth again, with redoubled vigour" (*TU* 20). So pervasive is this cyclical pursuit of knowledge that it becomes emblematic of madness in the novel: the pursuit of rationality, intrinsic to Enlightenment humanism, ironically, becomes figured as irrational and dangerous.

Certainly, the language associated with the act of reasoning in the text also stunts the physical scale of the human figure, thereby further accentuating the motif of deteriorating human agency. We find the narrator "reduced to reason" (*TU* 51), which implies that, rather than facilitating subjective awareness or placement, reason actually narrows the subject, as opposed to confirming humanity's superior position as per Enlightenment humanism. Moreover, the narrator speaks of "the blessed pus of reason" (*TU* 68). Here, the irony is pronounced: for Descartes, reason is the opposite of the physical, but is depicted here, not only as material, but as a material waste product. In this way, Beckett depicts the anticipated fruits of human reason (knowledge and self-awareness) as the oozing remnants of a decidedly infected concept, which is then revered and, ignorantly, held up as "blessed" (*TU* 68).

Indeed, the obsessive-compulsive form of the novel can be read as a textual performance of a type of hyper-reasoning that is, ultimately, apprehended as irrational. For example, the narrator refers to the process of

> finding the cause, losing it again, finding it again, not finding it again, seeking no longer, seeking again, finding again, losing again, finding nothing, finding at last, losing again, talking without ceasing, thirstier than ever, seeking as usual, losing as usual, blathering away, wondering what it's all about, seeking what it can be you are seeking. (*TU* 102–3)

Here, the pursuit of seeking some explanatory origin in "the cause" is rendered cyclical and fruitless as each of the many clauses in the extract begins with a present continuous verb that establishes a cycle in which the subject is "finding," "losing," "seeking," and "wondering," only to continue this cycle without arriving at any correlate of knowledge. As the narrator continues, we learn, more specifically, what is being sought. The narrator refers to the act of

> seeking incessantly, in yourself, outside yourself, cursing man, cursing God, stopping cursing, past bearing it, going on bearing it, seeking indefatigably, in the world of nature, the world of man, where is nature, where is man, where are you, what are you seeking, who is seeking, seeking who you are, supreme aberration. (*TU* 103)

The convoluted syntax of this extract reflects the elusiveness of accessing the object of knowledge sought. Eventually, though, we learn that what is sought is the placement of subjectivity: "who you are." Significantly, however, the narrator delineates this as a "supreme aberration." This superlative denunciation of the pursuit of the placement of subjectivity is bolstered by the list of five questions, minus any question marks. This absent punctuation lends the extract a more urgent and sinister tone as the questions become akin to expressionless incantations rather than the trigger for concrete self-knowledge; this denial of their status as questions also presupposes that, despite the obsessive-compulsive "seeking," neither the place of "nature" nor "man" will be found, further reinforcing the deteriorating stability of both human and nonhuman agency.

Moreover, obsessive-compulsive attempts at reasoning are expressed as a form of madness that is then transferred to nonhuman agency in the novel, thereby also causing its degeneration. This is borne out by the way in which nonhuman agency appears to be tormented by the obsessive-compulsive voices to which it is, unwillingly, subject. For instance, the narrator claims, "I alone am immortal, what can you expect, I can't get born, perhaps that's their big idea, to keep on saying the same old thing, generation after generation, till I go mad and begin to scream" (*TU* 100). The reference to "generation[s]" suggests that the "they" of the quotation are human; the opposing "immortality" of the "I" is at odds with the generational and, therefore, temporally-bound, human agency.

When we examine the cause of the madness endured in this example, we notice that it is the persistent repetition, via linguistic utterance, of "that same old thing" (*TU* 100) that provokes the experience of madness. This relates to the previous quotation in which a seemingly human agency was described as "talking without ceasing" and "blathering away" (*TU* 103), suggesting that it is the human voices that are responsible for the accrued madness. Indeed, the narrator fantasizes, "if only they'd stop committing reason, on them, on me" (*TU* 102). Here, the very act of reasoning becomes akin to a crime, which further positions nonhuman agency as a victim of a human concept. This sense of nonhuman agency being forced to endure human concepts is corroborated by the narrator's accusation that "they've inflicted the notion of time on me too" (*TU* 37). This implies that the "mad[ness]" (*TU* 100) of the nonhuman agency is caused by a qualitatively different agency, compulsively imposing these human concepts. Indeed, the narrator denounces the efficacy of reason, claiming that "they build up hypotheses that collapse on top of each other, it's human, a lobster couldn't do it" (*TU* 88). In this formulation, then, the function of Cartesian reason is inverted as it is still depicted as a human differential, but in a wholly negative way: the "lobster" in this quotation has had a lucky escape from this compulsive tendency to reason.

Moreover, we see the inefficacy of human agency corresponding with a weakening of nonhuman agency. The narrator refers to "these maniacs let loose on me from on high for what they call my good" (*TU* 39) and also to "[t]he dirty pack of fake maniacs" who "know I don't know, they know I forget all they say as fast as they say it" (*TU* 84). These quotations recall LeCain's conception of a "'Good Anthropocene,' in which our human framing of the Anthropocene epoch is justified by considering those human actions that might be undertaken for the good of a discrete 'Earth-entity'" (LeCain 2015, 1). Indeed, this sense of enforcing distinctly human projects onto a nonhuman agency is reinforced through the motif of voice in the novel. We can read the nonhuman agency of the novel as demonstrating an

obsessive-compulsive preoccupation with an inability to speak, and, therefore, an inevitable inability to linguistically place and name their subjective
identity. This deprivation of voice characterizes the nonhuman agency's dete-
rioration. Indeed, at the beginning of the novel the narrator finds themselves
with "[n]othing then but me, of which I know nothing, except that I have
never uttered" (*TU* 14). This assertion, in itself, creates its own type of madness or unreason, as we are confronted with a narrator whose words form the
story on the page, but who states that they "have never uttered." This tension
is reinforced as the narrator goes on to claim of "[t]his voice" (*TU* 17) that

> [i]t issues from me, it fills me, it clamours against my walls, it is not mine, I
> can't stop it, I can't prevent it, from tearing me, racking me, assailing me. It is
> not mine, I have none, I have no voice and must speak, that is all I know, it's
> round that I must revolve, of that I must speak, with this voice that is not mine,
> but can only be mine. (*TU* 18)

Here, Beckett depicts a voice that is physically contained and embodied
within the "walls" of the subject but, on a phenomenological level, is experienced as alien. The voice possesses its own violent agency as it "tear[s],"
"rack[s]," and "assail[s]" the narrator. The ensuing lack of control that they
have over the voice that seems, tentatively, to belong to them, thus creates
a curious lack of synchronicity between the narrator and their very mode of
expression.

The suppression of the nonhuman agent's self-expression also leads
towards a shift from their victimization to the enactment of a veritable re-
venge. Indeed, we now witness the compulsion to avenge what has been lost
to "those who took away nature," which, again, positions an active agent,
"they," against a different agent that might embody "nature" (*TU* 113). At
one point, the narrator even aligns themselves with the air, claiming, "I'm the
air, the walls, the walled-in one" (*TU* 104). It is interesting to note here the
narrator's tendency to morph between different types of agency: previously,
the narrator spoke of an alien voice that "clamours against my walls" (*TU* 18)
but is now "the walls, the walled-in one," as well as "the air." But air, in the
novel, is not a life-giving force. Instead, the narrator informs us that "air is to
make you choke" (*TU* 80) and speaks of taking "[a] great gulp of stinking air"
(*TU* 84). Indeed, the textual world is one where "real little terrestrial[s]" (by
implication, humans) can be found "[c]hoking in the chlorophyll" (*TU* 27);
this threatening nonhuman agency is, as before, manifest in multiple forms of
materiality, here extending into material plant life.

We then shift back into a sense of planetary threat as we learn that even
"the ozone," normally associated with the protective function of blocking
harmful radiation from entering the Earth's atmosphere, "in the end too, it

sterilizes" (*TU* 82). "[S]terilizes" creates the image of a vengeful or merciless nonhuman agency, as planet Earth becomes associated with the eradication of life as opposed to fecundity. Moreover, the narrator also admits that "[they] listen, and . . . seek, like a caged beast born of caged beasts born of caged beasts born of caged beasts . . . with nothing of its species left but fear and fury" (*TU* 104). This identification of the narrator with a beast also places them, according to a Cartesian hierarchy, on a level beneath humans, due to a "beast's" lack of linguistic or reasoning faculties. In addition, the nonhuman agency's desire for self-definition is accentuated when they state, "I wanted myself, in my own land for a brief space, I didn't want to die a stranger in the midst of strangers, a stranger in my own midst, surrounded by invaders, no" (*TU* 115). Here, the motif of being "inhabited" resurfaces, as nonhuman subjectivity is, again, mediated by the "strangers" who seem to prevent even the apprehension of qualitative subjectivity beyond their influence; indeed, the narrator describes the opposing agency as "strangers", but also, tellingly, themselves as they appear unable to construct any qualitative subjectivity beyond this framework.

We might be tempted to view this aggrieved nonhuman threat as Beckett's ascription of a voice to nonhuman agency; in depicting a victimized and then vengeful nonhuman subjectivity, Beckett redresses the balance as nonhuman agency is, at last, able to name the qualitative limitations of their subjectivity. Reading the text in this way, however, through the lens of first-wave ecocriticism, where one "listen[s] to the 'voice' of nature," feels reductive (Wheeler and Dunkerley 2008, 8). Rather, in *The Unnamable*, Beckett challenges the very possibility of meaningfully giving a voice to nonhuman agency. The narrator ponders, "perhaps it's not a voice at all, perhaps it's the air, ascending, descending, flowing, eddying, seeking exit, finding none" (*TU* 99). Here, the narrator mistakes the air's kinetic movements for human utterance. In this way, Beckett points toward a human inability to accurately conceptualize the qualitative nature of nonhuman subjectivity. Certainly, the notion that we cannot simply ascribe a human voice to a nonhuman subject is implied later in the novel when the narrator says, "that's all words they taught me, without making their meaning clear to me, that's how I learnt to reason, I use them all, all the words they showed me, there were columns of them, oh the strange glow all of a sudden, they were on lists . . . (*TU* 127). In this example, language is presented as other to the narrating subject, who doesn't understand the words' meaning. Even though the narrator "learn[s] to reason" and "use[s]" these words, such use appears as a compulsive pursuit that can never lead to any practical gain. Authentic expression of selfhood cannot occur as the narrator does not understand the connotations of the language they use; learning language is configured here as a futile venture. Furthermore, these words have been taught by the "they" of the quotation, which, again, points to a human agency imposing a human construct (language) onto a nonhuman agency.

TOWARD A HYBRID AGENCY

Finally, I want to suggest how "Beckett's working principle" might move beyond the dichotomy of human and nonhuman agency (Ackerley 2010, 149). In *The Unnamable* we witness the desire to transcend this dichotomy, but, at the same time, the recognition of the conceptual difficulty of the qualitative expression of such transcendence. But, despite this recognition, Beckett still gestures toward the possibility of a hybrid subject that is qualitatively neither human nor nonhuman. We can view the emergence of this new type of agency as coinciding with the introduction of Worm. Rather than being just another of the narrator's arbitrary "avatars," (*TU* 27) we are told that "Worm is the first of his kind" (*TU* 51). Shortly after this, the narrator also informs us that "[i]t is obvious we have here a principle of change pregnant with possibilities" (*TU* 55), which implies that we are apprehending a new qualitative form of subject in the novel, and, what's more, that such a qualitative subject might be a decidedly positive phenomenon as the word "pregnant" implies the imminent manifestation of such "a principle of change."

In fact, this third agency is not bound by, or, indeed, even able to access the categories of "knowledge," "reason," "human," or "non-human." Of Worm we learn that "to say he does not know what he is, where he is, what is happening, is to underestimate him. What he does not know is that there is anything to know. His senses tell him nothing, nothing about himself, nothing about the rest, and the distinction is beyond him" (*TU* 60). In this example, the subject's awareness of dichotomies, of "himself" and "the rest," is denied, precisely because the apprehension of such differences is "beyond him." Here, Beckett depicts Worm as unable to grasp the concept of binaries, which is emphasized, when, just before the introduction of Worm, the narrator hypothesizes that "[p]erhaps all they have told me has reference to a single existence, the confusion of identities being merely apparent" (*TU* 43). This positing of "a single existence" moves Beckett's "working principle" beyond that of the "absence of rapport" between the human and nonhuman and toward a hybrid subject. We further discover that "[t]he subject doesn't matter, there is none. Worm being in the singular as it turned out" (*TU* 76). Here, the obsessive-compulsive concern with the act of categorizing the subject and, indeed, with grammatical and therefore linguistic placement, appears to have dissipated. But this pause in the obsessive-compulsive quest is temporary.

Certainly, Beckett does not leave us with a simple avowal of the existence of some form of hybrid agency that might transcend the human/nonhuman binary. The glimmer of affirmation that the "principle of change" (*TU* 55) might be embodied, and therefore also categorized, in the form of a clear-cut subject, Worm, soon gives way to further subjective displacement. Even "[p]oor Worm, who thought he was different, . . . is in the madhouse for life" (*TU* 63). Worm too, then, joins the narrator's previous "avatar[s]" (*TU* 27) on their journey into madness. Indeed, it appears that the very act of naming leads to madness in the world of the text as categorization and delineation again become a compulsive pursuit. In the case of Worm, naming occurred because the narrator decided to "give this solitary a name, nothing doing without proper names" (*TU* 51). The latter half of this quotation points to the necessity of the act of naming for the narrator as "nothing do[es] without" such ascription. Moreover, we learn of the narrator's subsequent dislike of the name they have chosen: "I don't like it, but I haven't much choice" (*TU* 51). The act of naming then, whilst necessary for the narrator, does not result in satisfaction, but seems, instead, to be unavoidable habit rather than a signal of a shift to a subject that can finally be named. In its very naming, therefore, Worm's potential as the manifestation of the integrated subject located beyond the human/nonhuman dichotomy is lost.

Nevertheless, we can still register the presence of an agency beyond this divide, even if it is also beyond the reference point of Worm. However, the very possibility of this third agency defining itself through a voice is presented as untenable as the narrator asks, "May one speak of a voice, in these conditions? . . . The fact is all this business about voices requires to be revised, corrected and then abandoned." (*TU* 49) We are thus confronted with the contingency that language itself is inadequate for pinpointing the hybrid subject. This third agency displays an obsessive-compulsive desire to return to a state without language as the narrator refers to themselves as "that unthinkable ancestor of whom nothing can be said" and also speaks "of the impenetrable age when I was he" (*TU* 67). Here, "unthinkable" and "impenetrable" suggest an impasse that bars any qualitative definition of a subject beyond the constraints of the human/nonhuman divide. In relation to this, the narrator states that they will only be able to "speak of him" when "they fall silent" (*TU* 67), which points to both the inadequacy of human language to summon this elusive subject and which also suggests that, in the absence of language, some other form of expression might be possible as, only in this wordless state, might we be able to "speak of him" (*TU* 67).

There are numerous other references to silence throughout the novel, in which it is depicted as an escape from the compulsive need to attain subjective categorization. For instance, the narrator speaks of "taking a step towards silence and the end of madness" (*TU* 36) and also fantasizes that "[they] shall be able to go silent, and make an end" (*TU* 12). In these examples silence offers some form of solace from the cyclical attempts to define subjective identity through language. Ironically, though, the narrator soon also becomes obsessed with attaining this silence as they compulsively state: "I want it to go silent, it wants to go silent, it can't, it does for a second, then it starts again, that's not the real silence, it says that's not the real silence, what can be said of the real silence" (*TU* 128). The repetition of the word "silence" and the obsessive need to pin down a perfect version of "the real silence" re-establishes the futility and impossibility of isolating a qualitative subjective agency beyond the human/nonhuman divide.

What is particularly interesting about the silence figured in the text, however, is that it *is* qualitative. Silence, in *The Unnamable*, cannot be reduced to merely the absence of sound, but, is instead paradoxically described by the narrator as "a dream silence, full of murmurs" (*TU* 134). Just before this, the narrator also suggests that the silence has the potential to span all forms of qualitative subjective definition. Of "the story of the silence," the narrator states "then it will be he, it will be I, it will be the place" (*TU* 133). Here, the silence itself accrues the ability to "be" or encompass "he," "I," and "the place," suggesting that, through it, human and nonhuman identities might be melded. Toward the end of the novel the narrator also identifies with the hybrid agency, stating: "I'm the tympanum, on the one hand the mind, on the other the world, I don't belong to either . . . I don't know how . . . I don't know how" (*TU* 100). However, the problem of cashing this out in any qualitative way beyond the notion of hybridity remains: significantly, the narrator realizes that any qualitative definition of their subjectivity spans both "the mind" (aligned with human agency) and "the world" (aligned with nonhuman agency). But, they "don't know how," and therefore conceptualization of this is, ultimately, denied.

"UN-NAMING" THE ANTHROPOCENE

In the final analysis, we might regard the narrator's unnameable subjectivity in the novel not merely in terms of that which cannot be named, but also as a subject that has the potential to be un-named. As the narrator's attempts at identification with either human or nonhuman agency are unravelled, the textual world also highlights the futility of such rigid categories—categories that, no matter how rigorously adhered to, do not lead to an integrated understanding of the subject. Heeding the novel's portrayal of the inefficacy of simple categorization brings us directly back to the act of naming "the

Anthropocene." While the text alerts us to the difficulty of conceptualizing a qualitative subject beyond the human/nonhuman binary that could be configured in human concepts and language, it does not therefore shut down the need to continue aiming for such a conceptualization. Indeed, we might draw parallels between the narrator's quest and Beckett's own aims for his writing. In his oft-quoted letter to Axel Kaun in 1937, Beckett writes:

> [M]ore and more my language appears to me like a veil which one has to tear apart in order to get to those things (or the nothingness) lying behind it. . . . To drill one hole after another into it until that which lurks behind, be it something or nothing, starts seeping through—I cannot imagine a higher goal for today's writer. (Beckett 2009, 518)

This desire to move beyond language can be aligned with the desire to access that notion of subjectivity that lies beyond the human/nonhuman divide. Beckett's acknowledgment that "those things" beyond language might also be "the nothingness" warns us of the potential inaccessibility of a subject that lies beyond the reach of language, but, nevertheless, still confers on such a quest the status of the "highe[st] goal for today's writer." Beckett's recognition of the conceptual difficulty of conceiving a qualitative entity beyond language does not, therefore, preclude the attempt to "go on" (*TU* 134) with such a quest. Rather, the challenge that Beckett's novel might set for critics of the anthropocentric implications of naming the Anthropocene is how to move beyond this without the spectre of the human framing the definition, or, in the words of *The Unnamable*'s narrator, in a way that is not "clumsily done," where one does not "see the ventriloquist" (*TU* 63).

NOTES

1. For a discussion of these markers, see Walters et al. (2016).

2. This departure from binaries is also evident in recent literary criticism, such as in Joseph Anderton's (2016) survey of the liminal state of "the creaturely" in Beckett's work, and in the collection *Beckett and Animals* (Bryden 2013), which contains essays that explore Beckett's disavowal of the hierarchical superiority of humans.

3. Throughout, I use the words "their" and "they" to refer to the narrator to avoid any over-determination of the narrator as human, nonhuman, or neither of these categories.

4. All further references will be cited as *TU*.

5. I take the term 'agency' to mean the embodiment of an "[a]bility or capacity to act." See the *OED* entry in the reference list.

WORKS CITED

Ackerley, Chris. 2010. "Beckett and Science." In *A Companion to Samuel Beckett*, edited by S. E. Gontarski, 143–63. Oxford: Wiley-Blackwell.

Anderton, Joseph. 2016. *Beckett's Creatures: Art of Failure after the Holocaust.* London: Bloomsbury.

Beckett, Samuel. 2009. "Letter to Axel Kaun, 9 July, 1937." In *The Letters of Samuel Beckett*, edited by Martha Dow Fehsenfeld and Lois More Overbeck. Cambridge: Cambridge University Press.

———. (1953) 2010. *The Unnamable*. London: Bloomsbury.

Boer, Inge E. 2006. *Uncertain Territories*. Amsterdam: Rodopi.

Bryden, Mary, ed. 2013. *Beckett and Animals*. Cambridge: Cambridge University Press.

Chakrabarty, Dipesh. 2009. "The Climate of History: Four Theses." *Critical Inquiry* 35: 197–222.

Cohn, Ruby. 2001. *A Beckett Canon*. Michigan: University of Michigan Press.

Cowie, Fiona. 2008. "Innateness and Language." *The Stanford Encyclopedia of Philosophy.* Stanford: The Metaphysics Research Lab.

Gontarski, S. E. 2014. "Introduction." In *The Edinburgh Companion to Samuel Beckett and the Arts*, edited by S. E. Gontarski, 1–13. Edinburgh: Edinburgh University Press.

Hutchings, William. 1981. "The Unintelligible Terms of an Incomprehensible Damnation": Samuel Beckett's *The Unnamable*, Sheol, and St. Erkenwald," *Twentieth Century Literature* 27 (2): 97–112.

Kerridge, Richard. 2006. "Environmentalism and Ecocriticism." In *Literary Theory and Criticism*, edited by Patricia Waugh, 530–43. Oxford: Oxford University Press.

LeCain, Timothy James. 2015. "Against the Anthropocene. A Neo-Materialist Perspective." *International Journal for History, Culture and Modernity* 3: 1–28.

Malm, Andreas, and Alf Hornborg. 2014. "The geology of mankind? A critique of the Anthropocene Narrative." *The Anthropocene Review* 1 (1): 62–96.

Maslin, Mark A., and Simon L. Lewis. 2015. "Anthropocene: Earth System, geological, philosophical and political paradigm shifts." *The Anthropocene Review* 2 (1): 1–9.

Oxford English Dictionary Online. "Agency." Accessed August 13, 2017. http://www.oed.com/view/Entry/3851?redirectedFrom=agency.

———. "Anthropocene." Accessed August 13, 2017. http://www.oed.com/view/Entry/398463?redirectedFrom=anthropocene.

Raine, Anne. 2014. "Ecocriticism and Modernism." In *The Oxford Handbook of Ecocriticism*, edited by Greg Garrard, 98–117. Oxford: Oxford University.

Saunders, Paul. 2011. "Samuel Beckett's *Trilogy* and the Ecology of Negation." *Journal of Beckett Studies* 20: 54–77.

Van Hulle, Dirk, and Shane Weller. 2014. *The Making of Samuel Beckett's L'Innommable/The Unnamable*. London: Bloomsbury.

Walters, Colin, et al. 2016. "The Anthropocene is functionally and stratigraphically distinct from the Holocene," *Science* 351: 137–47.

Wheeler, Wendy and Hugh Dunkerley. 2008. *Earthographies: ecocriticism and culture.* London: Lawrence and Wishart, 2008.

Part II

PLANETARY TIME AND SPACE

Chapter Five

The Modernist Cosmos

Olaf Stapledon, Pierre Teilhard de Chardin, and the Crisis of Species

Timothy Wientzen

In his 2009 essay, "The Climate of History," Dipesh Chakrabarty argues that because anthropogenic climate change represents a crisis of our species, the Anthropocene demands a collective response that transcends social and political affiliations. The problem, he writes, is one of affect: "We humans never experience ourselves as a species. We can only intellectually comprehend or infer the existence of the human species but never experience it as such. There could be no phenomenology of us as a species" (Chakrabarty 2009, 220). In order to overcome this phenomenological limit, Chakrabarty calls for modes of writing that might allow us to feel the collapse of human and geological timescales that defines the Anthropocene; in lieu of histories in which human actors and institutions neatly bind the historical imagination (limiting us to, at most, thousands of years), he envisions writing that registers the impacts of human activity within the much longer timescales of geology. Such histories, he argues, would be valuable because they would help "produce affect and knowledge about collective human pasts and futures that work at the limits of historical understanding" (Chakrabarty 2009, 221). Without the ability to square these seemingly irreconcilable temporal scales, "knowledge that defies historical understanding," there is "no making sense of the current crisis that affects us all" (Chakrabarty 2009, 221).

While the near-term specter of species collapse was in certain ways foreign to the early twentieth century, Chakrabarty's desire for discourse that collapses human and geological timescales, troubling "the limits of historical understanding," was already central to some iterations of modernism. For modernist writers, advances in fields like geology, paleontology, and physics, as well as the global extension of industrial and political systems, catalyzed a heightened awareness of the long history of the species and its role within even longer temporalities of the planet. These historical circumstances proved beneficial for writers across the disciplinary spectrum, who sought to weigh the long-term pitfalls and potentialities of a world-shaping, dynamic species, and to generate the very kinds of affect that Chakrabarty describes.

This chapter examines Olaf Stapledon's 1937 novel *Star Marker*. Though seldom classed among the pillars of literary modernism, Stapledon's science-fiction classic represents the pinnacle of scalar thinking in the modernist period. Scalar thinking is a way of understanding local or immediate concerns within spatial or temporal perspectives that dramatically change the values we attribute to them.[1] The ability to think across incommensurate spatial and temporal scales is a particularly important aspect of the Anthropocene, which not only collapses the scales of human history and geology, but which demands understanding local and planetary concerns across scales that often set them at odds. In *Star Maker*, Stapledon frames industrial modernity as a planetary and evolutionary dilemma, and suggests the utility of scalar thinking in responding to this crisis of the species. For Stapledon, as I will show, it is in the ability to toggle between the human and the geological, the planetary and the cosmic, the macroscopic and the microscopic, that might allow us to achieve a common purpose as a species and surmount the crises of modernity. By setting the human scale against a cosmic scale, *Star Maker* suggests the inconsequence of the species in the long history of the universe while simultaneously valorizing what Stapledon calls the "self-critical self-consciousness of the human species" (Stapledon 1937, 4). In this sense, Stapledon's modernism offers a particularly apt way of modeling the scalar dilemma that Chakrabarty sees as constitutive of the Anthropocene.

In order to contextualize Stapledon's approach to the question of scale, this chapter reads *Star Maker* in conversation with the work of French Jesuit priest and paleontologist Pierre Teilhard de Chardin. Teilhard's notion of the "noosphere," elaborated in the 1920s, stands as perhaps the most important early twentieth-century attempt to understand the species as a force on a geological scale. Teilhard's interest in the political and spiritual ramifications of scalar thinking neatly mirrored Stapledon's longstanding effort to write a novel that would narrate the long, future history of life in the cosmos. Teilhard's and Stapledon's concerns with world governance, the evolutionary power of culture, and science display a remarkable degree of convergence. These points of contact were not lost on contemporary reviewers. Writing in the *New Republic* in 1959, the British scientist and sinologist Joseph Needham argued that Teilhard's magnum opus, *The Phenomenon of Man*, offered "courageous speculations about the future," which were "sometimes almost reminiscent of Olaf Stapledon, a writer whom Teilhard de Chardin would surely have found sympathetic" (Needham 1999, 87). While Teilhard and Stapledon were ignorant of each other's work, their shared concern with scalar thinking reflects a broader, modernist orientation toward planetary politics and the fate of the species within the longest of *longue durées*. For both Stapledon and Teilhard, the contemplation of scale resides at the center of a salubrious relationship toward industrial modernity as a planetary phenomenon—a perspective that is now badly needed.

In putting the work of these two thinkers in dialogue, I hope to suggest that modernist-era investigations of cosmic scale intersected with inquiry about geological time to produce a body of work on the precarity of the species, cosmopolitan politics, and the aesthetic modes appropriate to both. It is my contention that returning to modernism's modes of scalar thinking now may offer us valuable frameworks for producing the effect of species that Chakrabarty argues is necessary if we are to avoid the most disastrous aspects of the Anthropocene.

MODERNISM AND THE NOOSPHERE

Olaf Stapledon has not traditionally been read among his modernist contemporaries. This is something of a surprise given his longstanding dialogue with H. G. Wells and Naomi Mitchison, and the overwhelmingly positive response his work received from the likes of Bertrand Russell and Virginia Woolf. While Stapledon was often weary of what he called the "cliquish jargon" and "pregnant cross-word puzzles" of modernism, he shared aesthetic and political terrain with many of his contemporaries (Stapledon 1942, 114). For example, upon reading *Star Maker* in July of 1937, Woolf was unrestrained in praising his accomplishment. She wrote to Stapledon,

> I don't suppose that I have understood more than a small part [of *Star Maker*]—all the same I have understood enough to be greatly interested, & excited too, since sometimes it seems to me that you are grasping ideas that I have tried to express, much more fumblingly, in fiction. But you have gone much further, & I can't help envying you—as one does those who reach what one has aimed at. (qtd. in Crossley 1994, 248–49)

Stapledon's interest in the temporal and spatial scales of the cosmos rhymed with Woolf's own efforts to write *The Years* (1937) as a novel that would encapsulate what, in her diaries, she called "cosmic immensities" (qtd. in Henry 2003, 111). Informed by contemporary findings in astronomy, both were attuned to forms of scalar thinking that revealed the fragility of the planet, and both understood the likely event of a second world war as a crisis of evolutionary proportions.[2] In designating Stapledon's work as something other than "fiction," Woolf was not paying him a back-handed compliment.

Rather, like her own work, Stapledon's major fictions exist at the edges of formal convention: his desire to write expansive, defamiliarizing works of literature demanded breaking with generic conventions of plot and character such that he was never wholly convinced that his books were novels at all.[3] As he wrote in the book's preface, *Star Marker* is either "remarkably bad" if "[j]udged by the standards of the Novel," or "it is no novel at all" (Stapledon 1937, 5).

What makes *Star Maker* decidedly un-novelistic is its unparalleled effort to narrate not a life or even an age (as Woolf's would attempt in *The Years*), but rather the entire history of the cosmos—a period stretching to some five trillion years in his account. The narrative begins when an unnamed narrator, having "tasted bitterness" after a fight with his wife, goes for a walk in the hills near his home (Stapledon 1937, 7). Looking back at his house from underneath a sky full of stars, the narrator experiences a defamiliarized perspective on his life. His marriage—this prized "atom of community"—is, he fears, inconsequential and even ridiculous when viewed in its cosmic smallness. The struggle to calibrate the significance of human institutions with the immensity of the cosmos above causes the narrator to experience "a new, strange mode of perception" in which he sees the Earth in its cosmic place and embarks on an interplanetary voyage to discover the unruly diversity of life in the universe at large (Stapledon 1937, 12). Visiting, first, essentially human-like civilizations elsewhere in the Milky Way, the narrator is soon joined by others in a quest to document the many physical, social, and spiritual variations within the galaxy. Much of the narrative concerns these infinite variations, including civilizations of symbiotic beings, swarm-like creatures, life that is both animal and vegetable—a list so long it would take "a world of libraries" (Stapledon 1937, 76) to name them all. In time, the narrator explores not just the millions of civilizations within the galaxy, but the billions of galaxies in the cosmos. Grappling first with one scale of analysis (a planet) and progressing to ever-larger scales (a planetary system, a galaxy, and the entire universe), the narrator glimpses the entire sweep of cosmic history and the "Star Maker" that created it all, before being returned to the hills around his house in the final pages of the novel to contemplate the place of human civilization within the largest of all spatial and temporal scales.

Star Maker's concern with entropy and the endless cycles of life and death at work throughout the physical universe can appear a needlessly philosophical meditation given the pressing political circumstances of Europe in the 1930s. Looking at the events of planet Earth from the perspective of the cosmos as a whole, the novel can seem to render the entirety of modern life (including fascism) inconsequential—a mere millisecond of cosmic time. As Robert Crossley explains, "In 1935, with the danger to human civilization from the fascist powers rising, a philosophical myth composed of arabesque speculations about the nature and purpose of the universe seemed hard to justify" (Crossley 1994, 231). Yet for Stapledon, an avowed pacifist and anti-fascist, the crisis of the day was no trivial thing; as he explained in the preface of *Star Maker*, the rise of fascism represented a planetary crisis that demanded not naked propaganda, but rather literature that would "lead to an increased lucidity" for the human species (Stapledon 1937, 5).[4] The cosmic scale of the novel, Stapledon averred, would prove valuable in furthering the evolutionary life of the species precisely because it would underscore just how rare and precarious life is. He explains that the ability to see "our turbulent world against a background of stars may, after all, increase, not lessen, the significance of the present human crisis" (Stapledon 1937, 4). The wager of *Star Maker*, in short, is that the ability to toggle between incommensurate scales—such as a human lifetime and an eon—might offer the species a sense of direction and value amid one of its most urgent evolutionary crises.

Star Maker's effort to reconcile radically different spatial and temporal scales is a remarkably robust instance of modernist experimentation with scale, but the novel forms part of a much wider concern with scale in the modernist era. In the wake of nineteenth-century discoveries that placed the history of the species at some hundreds of thousands of years, and the age of the Earth at some million years, new inquiry in paleontology, physics, and especially astronomy animated a widespread cultural interest in scale. By the 1920s and 1930s, as physicists were looking at cosmic scales that could only be measured in terms of both space *and* time, astronomers like Edwin Hubble were radically reshaping our sense of how large the cosmos is. In 1925 Hubble overthrew the long-standing notion that the Milky Way comprised the totality of the cosmos by documenting a host of other galaxies existing some millions of light years apart—and in an expanding universe, no less. Stapledon felt it necessary to append a "Note on Magnitude" to *Star Maker* in order to make clear to readers the relative size and distance between celestial bodies in the Milky Way and seven surrounding galaxies. This note drew on W. J. Luyten's *The Pageant of the Stars* (1929), which was part of a much larger body of popular writing by scientists like J. B. S. Haldane and James Jeans, who helped lay readers conceptualize the immense temporal and spatial scales involved in these new models of the universe.[5] The work of these astronomers would inform an emerging popular consciousness about outer space and buttress efforts to synthesize nineteenth-century theories of evolution with fields like paleontology that were beginning to see human culture within geological and planetary contexts.

Perhaps the most important of these latter efforts was the work of Pierre Teilhard de Chardin. Building on his interest in vitalist philosophy, his extensive fieldwork as a paleontologist in China, and his training as a Jesuit priest, Teilhard worked to reconcile the historical scales of evolutionary and geological time discovered by nineteenth-century thinkers like Darwin, with human scales of action. In so doing, Teilhard became one of the major philosophers of scale in the early twentieth century. In books and essays authored between the 1920s and 1950s (but largely suppressed by the Church until after his death in 1955), Teilhard unpacked the spiritual, evolutionary, and ecological significance of scale, and elaborated a theory that represented the species as a remarkable evolutionary feat, but one that was only beginning its developmental ascent. In *The Phenomenon of Man* (finished 1938, published 1955), Teilhard would outline "the future natural history of the world" (Teilhard 1955, 222), diagnose the new ability of humans to act as agents at geological scales, and envision the evolutionary future of a dynamic, though immature, species.

Central to this theory was a term that attempted to articulate the role of human culture within the geological scales of the planet. Teilhard argued that the biosphere—named in 1875 by geologist Eduard Suess—was in fact bisected by another telluric layer of the Earth, the "noosphere." The noosphere constituted not just the layer of living matter on the planet, but a specific kind of living matter—*thinking* matter. With the advent of industrial modernity, Teilhard argued, culture took on a geological and evolutionary significance; whereas transmission of morphological features fueled the early days of the species, within the noosphere, culture plays "an appreciable part, or even a principal part, of the [human] phenomenon" (Teilhard 1955, 176). The term "noosphere" thus suggests both the world-changing power of human culture as well as its role within a geological (as opposed to narrowly historical) timescale: "This sudden deluge of cerebralisation, this biological invasion of a new animal type which gradually eliminates or subjects all forms of life that are not human, this irresistible tide of fields and factories, this immense and growing edifice of matter and ideas"—these are for Teilhard the signs "that there has been a change on the earth and a change of planetary magnitude" (Teilhard 1955, 183). Though the language of the noosphere was never fully adopted by geologists or ecologists, it proved an important predecessor to later theorizations of the Anthropocene, and stands as one of the modernist era's most significant contributions to inquiry about the relationship between human production and the fate of species.

For both Teilhard and Stapledon, the idea that industrial modernity was a singular, but ultimately brief, moment in the much longer history of the planet offered an intellectual framework for examining the moral and evolutionary value of human culture. This mode of scalar thinking is in many ways the engine of both writers' works; it grounds their shared interest in defamiliarizing our sense of time and space in favor of the most evolutionarily-beneficial forms of planetary life. As Teilhard explained in the preface to *The Phenomenon of Man*, he hoped his work would allow readers to see their world from the perspective of planetary time. Until humans develop a sense of the temporal and spatial immensities of life on Earth, he writes, "man will remain indefinitely for us . . . an erratic object in a disjointed world" (Teilhard 1955, 34). What's more, without a sense of scale, the human phenomenon will remain a danger to itself and its planet: "*To see or to perish* is the very condition laid upon everything that makes up the universe . . ." (Teilhard 1955, 31; emphasis added). For both Teilhard and Stapledon, scalar thinking stands as one of the most evolutionarily important capacities of the human species since it offers a framework for addressing difficult philosophical questions about theology, mortality, and the role of humans in directing their own evolution. But considerations of scale also potently raised the specter of evolutionary collapse amid the totalizing, planetary powers of industrial modernity.

In *Star Maker*, Stapledon explored both the positive and negative aspects of industrial modernity as an evolutionary phenomenon. Throughout the novel, Stapledon's narrator encounters species attempting to grapple with the power to shape and destroy their planets. Stapledon's narrator initially journeys to those civilizations that are in the throes of "the same spiritual crisis as that which underlies the plight of *Homo Sapiens* today" (Stapledon 1937, 71). On each planet, the narrator and his co-voyagers encounter a moment in which the fate of the most highly evolved species stands at a decisive fork between evolutionary achievement and cataclysm brought about by technological power. Having achieved a high level of technological sophistication, these beings are able to adapt their planets and themselves to new purposes. But without "the guidance of any well-established tradition," their technological powers are inevitably turned toward near-sighted concerns, "enslaved to individualistic industry," and threaten to undermine the species (Stapledon 1937, 84). For example, on one planet, the narrator encounters a fairly typical example of this noospheric crisis in the "symbiotic" races of the Ichthyoids and Arachnoids. Here, a high state of civilizational achievement has been reached only to be taken over by tribalism and individualism, leading to mass warfare and the poisoning of the planet. Their modernity and "[t]he delicate tissue of knowledge" upon which it depends "began to disintegrate" and endanger the viability of this civilization altogether (Stapledon 1937, 108). Endowed with technical knowledge, these species are without wisdom, and as a result, soon deteriorate. In the course of time, the Ichthyoids and Arachnoids overcome this crisis, but in other species, this planetary drama is not so amicably resolved and many planets meet untimely ends.

Whatever dangers industrial modernity represents, both Stapledon and Teilhard understood it as part of the very fabric of human evolution—an important stage on the journey toward a higher, more evolved and enlightened species. In his 1948 essay, "The Directions and Conditions of the Future," Teilhard argues that "[u]nification, technification, [and the] growing rationalisation of the human Earth" present an increasingly urgent set of conditions of the noosphere (Teilhard 1964, 228). Yet, in spite of the many political and ecological dangers that it presents, Teilhard saw modernization as an essential and necessary force within the longer history of the species: "We must not suppose, even at this early and half-passive stage of our hominisation, that the partly enforced flowering of thought imposed on us by planetary pressure represents a force of enslavement of which we are the victims" (Teilhard 1964, 231). For Teilhard, the noosphere, even in its most dangerous forms, stands as a potential "force of liberation" (Teilhard 1964, 231) since it portends the emergence of a single, unified human culture. In *Star Maker*, Stapledon likewise treats modernization and the emergence of a unified, planetary culture as an evolutionary problem; the "spiritual" crisis that comes of the noosphere is an inescapable part of "the great adventure of biological evolution toward the human plane" (Stapledon 1937, 115). While in many cases, such evolutionary crises end in catastrophe, some of the cultures Stapledon's narrator encounters see the spiritual crisis resolved in favor of a more cosmopolitan, pacifistic, and self-aware species. In the "waking worlds" visited by the narrator, for example, old ideas of evolution as morphological change become secondary to the power of culture; in these civilizations, a "new social environment produce[s] a world population which might well have seemed to belong to a new species" (Stapledon 1937, 138–39). The emphasis in Stapledon's novel is on *society* as an evolutionary phenomenon, and evolution as a spiritual or cognitive change, rather than a purely material one. The question is not whether species *should* attain the power to manipulate their planets, but rather what is to be done with the power once a species passes through this stage of evolution.

In Stapledon's novel, resolution of the spiritual crisis goes hand in glove with a new sense of temporal and spatial scales. Notably, the most highly evolved species in *Star Maker* have no difficulty thinking in terms of immense temporal scale; they are able to lay their "plans to cover periods of many million years" (Stapledon 1937, 150). But this enlightened sense of scale is relatively rare, and for both Stapledon and Teilhard, the new cosmic scales discovered by twentieth-century astronomers threatened to catalyze a genuine crisis of faith—not a faith in God, but a faith in the longevity of the species itself. In Teilhard's telling, the noosphere is marked by an "anguish" that "strikes in the depths of all our hearts and is the undertone of all our conversations" (Teilhard 1955, 227)—what he calls "the modern disquiet."

This modern sensibility entails "a feeling of futility, of being crushed by the enormities of the cosmos" (Teilhard 1955, 227). In *The Phenomenon of Man*, he writes:

> The enormity of space is the most tangible and thus the most frightening aspect [of this anguish]. Which of us has ever in his life really had the courage to look squarely at and try to 'live' in a universe formed of galaxies whose distance apart runs into hundreds of thousands of light years? Which of us, having tried, has not emerged from the ordeal shaken in one or other of his beliefs? And who, even when trying to shut his eyes as best he can to what the astronomers implacably put before us, has not had a confused sensation of a gigantic shadow passing over the serenity of his joy? (Teilhard 1955, 227)

The "[e]normity of [cosmic] duration" suggests a kind of meaninglessness at the heart of the universe, a "[m]alady of multitude and immensity" (Teilhard 1955, 227, 228). This malady is a consequence of scale in all its forms, including evolutionary scale, which in Darwin's analysis offered no discernible telos for human development.[6]

The "spiritual crisis" that Stapledon's narrator encounters in the cosmos is not exactly the same as Teilhard's "modern disquiet." Yet, as his narrator traverses first the Milky Way, then other galaxies, and finally the cosmos as a whole, reckoning with the immensity of space causes him to glimpse the utter precarity of life in the universe. This sense of precarity appears even before he leaves planet Earth. In the novel's first scene, the narrator imagines the curvature of the Earth and perceives "all the swarms of men, generation by generation, [that] had lived in labour and blindness, with intermittent joy and intermittent lucidity of spirit. And all their history, with its folk-wanderings, its empire, its philosophies, its proud sciences, its social revolutions, its increasing hunger for community, was but a flicker in one day of the lives of stars" (Stapledon 1937, 11). The history of the human race is, in this context, not only brief, but, like all life in the cosmos, a fragile flame. As the narrator explores ever-widening vistas of life in the universe, what emerges is a vision of a universe that is riddled with the death of species after species. What meaning can there be in a universe of such "physical immensity and complexity?" he asks (Stapledon 1937, 66). "By itself, plainly, it constituted nothing but sheer futility and desolation" (Stapledon 1937, 66). For every spark of life the narrator encounters in the cosmos, there is an apocalypse to match. Some civilizations die by bacteria or climatic change, some through meteors or cosmic accidents, and others still by the trivial quirks of their biology. Even the most well-adapted and enlightened species are doomed by the universal quiescence of an entropic cosmos. At this galactic scale, Homo sapiens are "burnt up like a moth in a flame by irresistible catastrophe" (Stapledon 1937,

184). From the vantage of cosmic scale, "what had before appeared as a war of titans, in which great worlds manoeuvred in space with inconceivable speed, and destroyed one another's populations in holocausts, was now seen as the jerky motion of a few microscopic sparks, a few luminous animalcules, surrounded by the indifferent stellar hosts" (Stapledon 1937, 185).

For the most enlightened beings in *Star Maker*, scalar thinking involves the contemplation of mortality, but also a sense of sublime awe in the face of its mystery. But Stapledon's narrator is not one of these enlightened beings; he is a representative of a promising but immature species in the throes of an evolutionary crisis that is still ours today. Even when the narrator glimpses the fleeting beauty of a "Star Maker" that orchestrates the endless creation and suffocation of life in the universe, he is troubled by the same dilemmas of scale that Teilhard describes. Returning to Earth in the final pages of the novel, the narrator is disoriented by the experience of scale. Plunged from a perspective on the edges of space-time into a country on the brink of a cataclysmic war, he struggles to make sense of it all. What can the survival of the species possibly mean to a vast and indifferent universe? What can it matter if the human race lives or dies? "How to face such an age?" (Stapledon 1937, 262), he asks.

COLLAPSING SCALE

If the discovery of cosmic scale by Hubble and his contemporaries offered a troubling vision of the precarious place of life in the universe, for writers like Teilhard and Stapledon, scalar thinking was not therefore to be avoided. While situating the human species in the framework of the cosmos inevitably involved, as Teilhard wrote, "the heavy problem of death, not of the individual but on the planetary scale" (Teilhard 1964, 121), the ability to look such precarity in the eye also offered clarity to a species in its technological adolescence. "[A]ccess of consciousness to a *scale of new dimensions*," Teilhard writes, leads not to utter paralysis, but to "the birth of an entirely renewed universe" (Teilhard 1955, 219). This renewed universe is one that offers an illuminated perspective on the role of the human species within a history that is far longer than its modernity, however broadly interpreted.

For Stapledon, scalar thinking involved negotiating these contrary registers. On the one hand, the cosmic scale explored by his narrator in *Star Maker* highlights the necessarily limited, even fleeting, reign of the human species within a much larger history of the universe. In this schema, the life of planet Earth is but one tiny fraction of the age of life in the cosmos, which is itself but one stage of a much longer history of the physical universe. At the same time, however, Stapledon's emphasis on scales of cosmic time is not intended to mortify readers, or heap existential dismay upon them. Like Teilhard, Stapledon believed that scalar thinking was necessary to ensuring the longevity of human civilization and its planetary home. Viewed from the conceptual distance of space-time, the evolutionary plight of the species mandated certain very pragmatic solutions in Stapledon's analysis—solutions without which human civilization would soon find itself extinguished.

Chief among these in *Star Maker* is the ability of the species to coalesce as a unitary collective in a world system. As scholars have broadly noted, *Star Maker* is a deeply utopian novel, one which was inflected by Stapledon's cosmopolitan, pacifist commitments. This interest in planetary collectives takes many forms in the novel, including the narrative voice itself. As the nameless narrator is joined by other interstellar travelers, they become a single narrative voice: "Each [of us] was still at most times conscious of the other and of himself as separate beings; but the pooling or integration of our memories and of our temperaments had now gone so far that our distinctness was often forgotten" (Stapledon 1937, 67). This cosmopolitan ideal of a "contrapuntal harmony" is the political model of *Star Maker*. In the "waking worlds" the narrator encounters, it is just such an ideal that has emerged to solve the most pressing evolutionary problems. Endowed with a new sense of their own temporal scales, these worlds find that all the foibles of the noosphere are swept away: in these communities, "Tribal prestige, individual dominance, military glory, industrial triumphs lost their obsessive glamour, and instead the happy creatures delighted in civilized social intercourse, in cultural activities, and in the common enterprise of world-building" (Stapledon 1937, 139). These world systems are the product of evolutionary necessity; once endowed with the power to destroy themselves and their planets, these civilizations develop compensatory mechanisms for addressing problems that affect the species as a whole. Like Teilhard, who was "deeply concerned with establishing a global unification of human awareness as a necessary prerequisite for any real future progress of mankind" (Huxley 2008, 15), Stapledon regarded a collective planetary culture as necessary to managing the most deleterious aspects of the noosphere.

But even this description of the cosmopolitanism that animated Stapledon and Teilhard's work partly misses the importance of scalar thinking for each of them. In articulating the need for a planetary culture, Teilhard and Stapledon individually returned "cosmopolitanism" to its etymological roots in "cosmos," from the Greek for "order, good order, orderly arrangement." Both imagined a world mind that emerges through an understanding of scale and sustains itself through what Teilhard calls "an overall and completely coherent perspective of the universe" (Teilhard 2008, 248). For both, the ability to navigate the near-term crises of the species depended on our ability to toggle between the discordant scales of cosmic and human matter—to see both the macroscopic and the microscopic as proportionate instantiations of each other. *Star Maker* is structured to show the reader increasingly larger perspectives of cosmic scale, but the narrative is bookended by the experience of a single human and the defamiliarization he experiences upon leaving and later returning to the scale of human endeavors. In the opening and closing scenes of the novel, scale endows human civilization with intrinsic value precisely because it mirrors cosmic structures. The collapsing of scale here shows macroscopic and microscopic concerns to be proportionate and symmetrical. This sense of scalar symmetry is made through the novel's recourse to the language of atomic structures. As he looks down at his house from the hills in the novel's opening scene, Stapledon's narrator questions the meaning of his marriage, what he often refers to as "our prized atom of community" (Stapledon 1937, 9). Bathed in the light of the stars, he wonders whether this bond has any value at all; compared to celestial bodies, it is "so slight a thing" (Stapledon 1937, 9). Yet he remains convinced of its value: "Even the cold stars, even the whole cosmos with all its inane immensities could not convince me that this our prized atom of community, imperfect as it was, short-lived as it must be, was not significant" (Stapledon 1937, 9). In the opening scene of *Star Maker*, the language of the atom anticipates the perspective the narrator will soon acquire as he looks back on the earth from the perspective of the cosmos; here, immense cosmic bodies attain an atomic smallness, like so many grains of sand on a beach or snowflakes in a blizzard. Yet the language of the atom suggests that such relationships, however insignificant they may seem, offer microscopic models for universal structures. What we see at the smallest scale of matter is reproduced at the largest scale; passing from the atomic to the human, and from the planets to the galaxies, Stapledon presents ever-larger scales of a basic, universal symmetry that is precarious and mortal. The metaphor of the marriage as an atomic system employs a scalar imagination in order to suggest the insignificance of human relationships *and* their necessity within the larger systems of the physical universe. Relationships of this sort are, like atoms, the building blocks of the universe.

Over the course of his journey, however, the narrator's faith in the intrinsic value of this "atomic" structure will be shaken. Having glimpsed the entire sweep of cosmic time, he and his fellow travelers contemplate the possibility that the "Star Maker" is not a god of love, but a cruel demiurge who destroys civilization after civilization without pity. This vision of sublime terror suggests that death is the inevitable and shared trajectory of all life in the universe. Yet, the conclusion of the novel is very careful to push against the impulse to accept the death of the human species as meaningless. Returning from the largest of all possible scales to Europe in the late 1930s, the narrator surveys the planet and each continent in turn. In this vision of the entire planet, he glimpses the noosphere in its many forms—industrialism, music and architecture, railways and colonialism, communism and capitalism spreading across every corner of a planet rushing headlong into crisis. What can human achievement mean in a cold, entropic, and quite possibly indifferent cosmos?

Toggling from the "cold light of the stars" to "our little glowing atom of community," the narrator feels not dread but a renewed commitment to the species (Stapledon 1937, 263):

> Strange that in this light, in which even the dearest love is frostily assessed, and even the possible defeat of our half-waking world is contemplated without remission of praise, the human crisis does not lose but *gains* significance. Strange, that is seems *more*, not less, urgent to play some part in this struggle, this brief effort of animalcules striving to win for their race some increase of lucidity before the ultimate darkness. (Stapledon 1937, 263; emphasis added)

The experience of smallness paradoxically catalyzes for the narrator an experience of grandeur and mystery; rather than finding disquiet in the experience of scale, the narrator experiences a new sense of purpose in helping the species gain the "lucidity" of consciousness that might enable it to overcome the coming crisis. Even as the experience of scale underscores the mortality of the individual, the species, the planet, and the physical cosmos itself, it has a strangely humanizing force. The individual and the species are revealed to be part of a much larger, universal movement through which "the cosmos was seeking to know itself, and even see beyond itself" (Stapledon 1937, 72). In this context, the experience of scale endows individual relationships and the collective enterprise of industrial modernity with a supreme importance, a sensibility without which the cataclysm of the species is virtually assured.

FEELING LIKE A SPECIES

When Stapledon's narrator looks at the globe in the final pages of the novel and worries about the "coming storm," it is clear that Stapledon had the Second World War in mind (Stapledon 1937, 262). While the prospect of global warfare stands as a typically twentieth-century source of anxiety, the conclusion of the novel nevertheless offers a useful commentary on the power of scalar thinking to the historical moment of the Anthropocene—a moment that presents an even more dire (and decidedly more planetary) threat to the species than the war Stapledon feared. According to Chakrabarty, the pragmatic challenges of the Anthropocene depend to a large degree on a collective experience of species that lies outside of our immediate perceptual capacities. "Even if we were to emotionally identify with a word like *mankind*, we would not know what being a species is," he writes, because "one never experiences being a concept" (Chakrabarty 2009, 220). For Chakrabarty, the need for the affect of species is urgent and demands a recalibration not just of disciplines like history, but of the very foundations and assumptions upon which such disciplines have been built. In the case of history, the Anthropocene throws into "contradiction and confusion" our "usual historical practices for visualizing times, past and future, times inaccessible to us personally" (Chakrabarty 2009, 198) and demands "affect and knowledge about collective human pasts and futures that work at the limits of historical understanding" (Chakrabarty 2009, 221).

Chakrabarty's call for writing that engages the affect of the species is a project that was well understood by Stapledon and Teilhard. The scalar imagination of modernism was, to be sure, a product of the immense transformations of industrialization and the findings of the sciences; but it was also a moment of profound utopianism, which (in spite of two world wars) saw the foundation of global political institutions. The spirit that made these institutions possible depended on an understanding of culture as part of our evolutionary story. (It is not for nothing that the first head of UNESCO was the evolutionary biologist, Julian Huxley.) Stapledon and Teilhard in their different ways looked upon these institutions as necessary to the future of the species, but also as institutions that would crumble without a shared consciousness of species. In book four of *The Phenomenon of Man*, entitled "Survival," Teilhard looked toward the emergence of a single planetary culture and noted that such an event depended as much on the material conditions of interconnection as on a coalescence of consciousness. "The outcome of the world, the gates of the future, the entry into the super-human," he writes, "these are not thrown open to a few of the privileged nor to one chosen people to the exclusion of all others. They will open only to an advance of *all together*, in a direction in which *all together* can join and find completion in a spiritual renovation of the earth" (Teilhard 2008, 245). Without a spiritual renovation in which humans came to feel themselves bound by a shared fate, the path to our evolutionary ascent would be blocked. Teilhard quite consciously oriented his philosophy toward spreading a spirituality appropriate to the "noosphere"—a philosophy that would allow people to feel themselves wedded to the collective enterprise of the species and part of a historical trajectory that stretched well beyond our limited modernity.

Star Maker participates in this effort very deliberately. Stapledon embraced modes of formal experimentation common to modernism but without fetishizing form for its own sake. He understood literature as part of culture's increasingly important role across evolutionary time. As such, it had an important role to play in helping the species surmount its deepest challenges. As he explained in his1934 essay, all education should be geared toward engendering in students a "loyalty to the enterprise of the human species" and invigorating the "struggle toward ever more awakened mentality" (Stapledon 1934, 155). *Star Maker* makes this loyalty its very goal. The scalar experiment of *Star Maker*, which leaves behind traditional literary conventions of character and plot, appeared to Stapledon as the most appropriate way of representing modernity as a forking evolutionary path. Working at the edges of historical understanding, *Star Maker* suggests that many aspects of our collective life are evolutionarily myopic—noospheric shortcuts toward planetary collapse. But *Star Maker* is not just a tale of the cosmos. It is a deeply human novel that places scalar thinking at the center of our collective deliverance. Inviting readers to think across incommensurate scales of time and space, *Star Maker* takes an activist stance in the contest between contrary forces within industrial modernity—both those which would hasten the demise of the species, and those which would work to preserve it by acknowledging the importance of difference and collectivity to our planetary future. In this sense, Stapledon's novel attempts to generate an affect of species in which we can *feel ourselves* as a planetary collective—bound, whether we like it or not, to thrive together or die together.

The Anthropocene challenges our understanding of historicity because it forces us to confront the power of humans to impact systems that would seem eternal and impervious to us—systems legible at geological temporal scales. Yet the realization that human culture is intervening in planetary processes is not without its promises. For in confronting the incommensurate scales of human history and geological time, we are also able to tap into the resources of scalar thinking themselves. Toggling between cosmic scales and human ones, as Teilhard and Stapledon suggested, we gain the ability to see political crises as evolutionary ones, and thereby link ourselves to a planetary collective. To see ourselves in this new context is to open up cognitive space that might allow us to keep our fragile modernity measured always against the backdrop of the stars.

NOTES

1. Timothy Clark explains, "[W]hat is self-evident or rational at one scale may well be destructive or unjust at another." For example, "progressive social and

economic policies designed to disseminate Western levels of prosperity" may appear
inherently good at one scale of analysis while appearing like "an insane plan to destroy the biosphere" at another. For more on scalar thinking, see Clark 2012.

2. See Henry 2003, which grounds Woolf's and Stapledon's pacifism in popular
astrological discourse of the 1930s.

3. Patrick A. McCarthy notes that Stapledon was often uncomfortable with the
term "novel," and that his books *Last Men in London* (1932) and *Death into Life*
(1946) both rehearse an anxiety with the term. See McCarthy 1989.

4. Teilhard made much the same argument about WWII as an evolutionary crisis.
In his 1945 lecture, "Life and the Planets: What is Happening at this Moment on
Earth?," Teilhard argued that the events of the war "are unquestionably bound up
with the general evolution of terrestrial life; they are of *planetary dimensions*. It is
therefore on the planetary scale that they must be assessed" (Teilhard 1945, 97).

5. Stapledon himself was deeply affected by Jeans's 1926 article in *Nature*, "Recent
Developments in Cosmical Physics." Some of these ideas would be rehearsed by Jeans
for lay audiences in books in the 1920s and 1930s. According to Crossley, "Jeans's
account of the philosophical implications of the inhuman distances between us and
the stars, the vast disproportion between human and cosmic interests, excited Olaf's
imagination" (Crossley 1994, 177). Teilhard likewise cited Jeans approvingly in his
1945 essay, "Life and the Planets: What is Happening at this Moment on Earth?"

6. As opposed to Darwin, Teilhard believed that evolutionary scales revealed a
clear developmental telos in humans. *Phenomenon of Man* presents a vision of the
noosphere as a necessary (if vexed) evolutionary stage in the unceasing organization of matter into ever-more diversified and resplendent patterns of being. Here
Stapledon's fiction stands at its greatest distance from Teilhard's philosophy. Where
Teilhard foresaw an inevitable "Omega point" in the future of the species, Stapledon
imagined the rise and fall of civilizations in the cosmos as a sure sign that evolution
lead nowhere in particular. Stapledon's "Star Maker" is the god of an agnostic, not
the God of a Jesuit priest. For more on the cosmic pessimism of *Star Maker*, see
Canavan 2016.

WORKS CITED

Canavan, Gerry. 2016. "'A Dread Mystery, Compelling Adoration': Olaf Stapledon's
    Star Maker and Totality." *Science Fiction Studies* 42 (2): 310–30.
Chakrabarty, Dipesh. 2009. "The Climate of History." *Critical Inquiry* 35 (2):
    197–222.
Clark, Timothy. 2012. "Scale: Derangements of Scale." Telemorphosis: *Theory in
    the Era of Climate Change*, Vol. 1. Edited by Tom Cohen. Michigan Publishing:
    University of Michigan Library.
Crossley, Robert. 1994. *Olaf Stapledon: Speaking for the Future*. Syracuse: Syracuse
    University Press.
Henry, Holly. 2003. *Virginia Woolf and the Discourse of Science: The Aesthetics of
    Astronomy*. Cambridge: Cambridge University Press.

Huxley, Julian. 2008. Introduction to *The Phenomenon of Man*, by Teilhard (1955). Translated by Bernad Wall. New York: HarperCollins.

Jeans, James. 1926. "Recent Developments of Cosmical Physics." *Nature* 4: 29–40.

Luyten, Willem J. 1929. *The Pageant of the Stars.* London: Stanley Paul & Co.

McCarthy, Patrick A. 1989. "Stapledon and Literary Modernism." In *The Legacy of Olaf Stapledon: Critical Essays and an Unpublished Manuscript*, edited by Patrick A. McCarthy, Charles Elkins, and Martin Harry Greenberg. Westport, CT: Greenwood Press.

Needham, Joseph. 1999. "Cosmologist of the future." *New Statesman*. November 7, 1959. In *The Biosphere and Noosphere Reader: Global Environment, Society and Change*, edited by Paul R. Samson and David Pitt. New York: Routledge, 85–87.

Stapledon, Olaf. 1934. "Education and World Citizenship." In *Manifesto: Being the Book of the Federation of Progressive Societies and Individuals*, edited by C. E. M. Joad. London: Allen and Unwin, 142–63.

———. (1937) 2004 *Star Maker*. Edited by Patrick A. McCarthy. Middletown, CT: Wesleyan University Press.

———. 1942. "Literature and the Unity of Man." In *Writers in Freedom: A Symposium*, edited by Hermon Ould. London: Hutchinson & Co, 113–19.

Teilhard de Chardin, Pierre. (1945) 1964. "Life and the Planets: What is Happening at this Moment on Earth?" *The Future of Man*, 97–123. Translated by Norman Denny. New York: Harper & Row, 1964.

———. (1955) 2008. *The Phenomenon of Man*. Translated by Bernad Wall. New York: HarperCollins.

———. 1964. "The Directions and Conditions of the Future." (Originally published in *Psyché*, October 1948. In *The Future of Man*. Trans. Norman Denny. New York: Harper & Row, 227–37.

Chapter Six

Modernist Planets and Planetary Modernism

Joshua Schuster

The Anthropocene is the name for a new phase of the planet's geology, but it also is a new name for the Earth itself. Humans have inscribed themselves in the geological work of the planet, changing what is meant by the planet Earth and what a planet can do. The Anthropocene is also another name for modernity, marking the moment when human modernization has taken on planetary scale and power. We live on a planet that has been altered in our own image, and our task at the very least is to come to know just what kind of planet we have made.

The fact that the Earth has been redefined so thoroughly by modernity raises the question of how theoretical discussions of modernity and works of modernism might offer a uniquely powerful resource for understanding this new phase of the planet. However, the convergence between a modernized planet and modernist studies goes further. The urgent need to rethink the status of the planet today intersects with a recent emphasis in modernist studies to push the bounds of its own disciplinarity by considering how modernism has become a global cultural phenomenon. Indeed, in order to grasp how modernism has spread across the globe in various locations and in different cultural forms, Susan Stanford Friedman asserts that modernist studies needs to take a "planetary turn" (Friedman 2015, ix). In Friedman's view, modernism needs a planetary frame to break from narrow habits of restrictively periodizing the time and space of modernist culture. In taking up the scale of the planetary in modernist studies, there is a recognition that modernity "is understood as multiple, polycentric, and recurrent instances of transformational rupture and rapid change across the full spectrum of political, economic, cultural, technological, demographic, and military arenas of interlocking societies and civilizations" (Friedman 2015, ix). Multiplying perspectives on modernism across the planet also leads to a multiplying of perspectives on the planet itself. Friedman points to how "Planetary also gestures at a world beyond the human, even beyond the Earth, by invoking the systems and networks of inner and outer space that are both patterned and random. Planetary suggests the Earth as a place of matter and climate, life and the passage of time, and an array of species of which the human is only one" (Friedman 2015, 8). In a similar vein, Ursula Heise has called for an "eco-cosmopolitan" perspective that brings environmentalism and globalist thinking together (Heise 2008, 60), while Christian Moraru has declared now a "planetary turn" for the humanities (Moraru 2015, 5).

How, then, can one use the planet to know modernism, and modernism to know the planet? How can this planetary thinking of modernism inform us about the modernization of the planet we have made in the Anthropocene? To begin to respond to these questions, the modernist reader must cultivate a method to make sense of the planet as both form and content. Planetary modernism registers the Anthropocene not just by thematizing all the global ecological shocks that have ensued due to modernization, but also by considering the frames of knowing and the cultural modes that have accumulated and made planetarity thinkable and sensible.

One place to begin in thinking the conjunction of planet and modernism in the Anthropocene is to welcome how all the conversation around naming a new geological age has forced us to scramble over how one defines a planet. The origin of the word "planet" comes from the ancient Greek, "to wander," a descriptive term to account for how the planets moved in the sky in a way unlike the stars. Yet wandering as metaphor seems particularly apt. Planets wander in the sky but also wander from themselves, as their geological, atmospheric, and chemical properties change over time. Planets wander, but to explore a planet, one must become a wanderer too. Only by wandering the Earth can one come to know it and to imagine its globality. The same applies to planets in the skies. To think planetarity, one must wander across one's planet and think beyond one's planet. The need to look up and look down at the same time to understand Earth has been an ancient practice that takes on renewed urgency in the Anthropocene. Carl Sagan eloquently speaks of how we will fail to know Earth if we think of it only from Earth as if it were an only planet:

> If we're stuck on one world, we're limited to a single case; we don't know what else is possible. Then . . . our perspective is foreshortened, our insights narrow, our predictive abilities circumscribed. By contrast, when we explore other worlds, what once seemed the only way a planet could be turns out to be somewhere in the middle range of a vast spectrum of possibilities. When we look at those other worlds, we begin to understand what happens when we have too much of one thing or too little of another. We learn how a planet can

go wrong. We gain a new understanding . . . called comparative planetology. (Sagan 1994, 175)

Earth then can only make sense if we find a way to leave it and reflect on it at the same time in the company of other planetary bodies. Yet I want to still push the metaphor of wandering further. The English word "wander" has etymological ties to the word "wonder." Wondering and wandering are related activities that co-implicate curiosity and knowledge, being lost and being found. One must wander physically and mentally, wandering through the mind and on land, to come to know the Earth as one kind of ground among others. Yet in the concept of wonder, there is also the possibility that knowledge may not arrive, as there is no guarantee that one's course of inquiry will yield answers. Wondering and wandering may bring upon oneself a sense of confusion, a loss of orientation, becoming a wanderer with no clear sense of where one is or where one is going. This uncertainty connects to epistemological and ontological problems of knowing an object that wanders by definition. Planets can wander from our ways of knowing; they can remain inaccessible by scientific instruments or become unknowable in other ways as they challenge human ways of cognizing. A planet populated by living organisms will always change its inhabitants and be changed by them; in this sense, only knowledge that is itself wondering and wandering will be adequate to cognize the people and planet.

Thinking planets and the Anthropocene in the face of the ideas just introduced could quickly spiral out and lead well beyond the purview of this chapter. Here my task will be to point to how some modernist texts and methods in modernist studies can offer a compelling window into some of the epistemological and ontological questions raised in trying to understand the modernized Earth as one kind of planet in the midst of other ways of being a planet. In particular I will examine how two science fiction authors, Olaf Stapledon and Stanislaw Lem, made comparative planetary thinking the basis for pushing the limits of the scientific romance genre. Both authors also developed planetary fictions that raised powerful questions about the role of modernism and modernity as frames for cosmological thinking. However, before I turn to these literary examples of the conjunction of modernist planets and planetary modernism, I want to examine briefly an early argument for rethinking the Earth as a problem of comparative planetary study in the work of Vladimir Vernadsky. We see in Vernadksy's modernist sense of the planet an insistence that theorizing the Earth must take in to account the special role of life's impact on earth.

In the early 1920s, Vernadsky, a Russian geologist, elaborated a theory of the Earth's physical systems around the concept of the biosphere. Effectively, Vernadsky claimed that one could not understand earth without life, and life

without earth. "Living matter gives the biosphere an extraordinary character, unique in the universe" (Vernadsky 1998, 53). The earth was not just a
strictly geochemical system with preset laws but a composite of interactive
forces including biological life that had pronounced effects on the earth's
crust and atmosphere. "Life is, thus, potently and continuously disturbing the
chemical inertia on the surface of our planet. It creates the colors and forms
of nature, the associations of animals and plants, and the creative labor of
civilized humanity, and also becomes a part of the diverse chemical processes
of the Earth's crust" (Vernadsky 1998, 57–58). Vernadsky's theories shifted
geosciences away from passive models of the Earth that treated geology as
a churning set of independent mechanical processes, and proposed instead a
planet whose geological history was inseparable from its biological history.
The diversity of life made a direct impact on the diversification of geological eras and landscape formations. Furthermore, Vernadsky fostered an early
form of comparative planetology by arguing for a comparison of Earth's
biogeochemistry to planets without any apparent biological history. To understand Earth, one had to look back at the Earth from outside, comparing
Earth to other planets, and compare the current state of Earth with previous
states, thus comparing Earth to Earth. Not surprisingly, this methodology led
Vernadsky also to make prescient claims for the emergence of a new geological age made in the image of humans.

In an essay published just after his death in 1945, Vernadsky evoked the
notion of an "anthropogenic era in which we now live" (Vernadsky 1945, 8).
Vernadsky describes how "man, under our very eyes, is becoming a mighty
and ever-growing geological force" (Vernadsky 1945, 8). The term Vernadsky offers to define this new geological moment is *nöosphere*. The coinage,
from the ancient Greek *nous* (mind), is usually first credited to Pierre Teilard
de Chardin, although de Chardin in turn was influenced by Vernadsky. Citing the colonization by humans of almost all inhabitable zones on the planet,
and the rise of industrialization that has created an abundance of "artificial
minerals" (Vernadsky 1945, 9) such as aluminum, Vernadsky asserts that,
"The *nöosphere* is a new geological phenomenon on our planet. In it for the
first time man becomes a large-scale geological force" (Vernadsky 1945, 9).
Vernadsky does not shade into as much mysticism as de Chardin, who ultimately extended the *nöosphere* into the cosmos and saw it as the propensity
of a universal mind and a theological presence. Vernadsky rather is more
interested in describing the effects on Earth of how humans are changing the
biological and geochemical properties of the biosphere: "Chemically, the face
of our planet, the biosphere, is being sharply changed by man, consciously,
and even more so, unconsciously" (Vernadsky 1945, 9). The notion that the
biosphere has been shaped by human psychological states can mean two

things here: humans have consciously and unconsciously produced a new biosphere as they remake the planet for their own benefit, and humans are both consciously and unconsciously aware of the impact they have had in re-defining the conditions of the planet Earth. As Vernadsky seems to imply, the split between human consciousness and unconsciousness is now embedded in the Earth's systems. Perhaps then even the concept of the *nöosphere* is ridden with psychic conflicts and splitting, a situation that will become crucial to the modernist literature of planets that I will examine here.

STAR MAKER AND PLANETARY-SIZED UTOPIAS

In the Anthropocene, the question "what can a planet do?" converges with the task of trying to understand what humans have done to the planet Earth. To think the planet in its changing form, one must find a way to represent the planet as it is changed by natural and industrial means and respond to the way the planet itself changes the means and modes of representation. In other words, one must represent the planet as well as account for how the planet contributes to making and remaking modes of representation. What I want to focus on here is how two works of science fiction, Stapledon's *Star Maker* (1937) and Lem's *Solaris* (1961), depict versions of comparative planetology at work as they attempt to stretch the bounds of the literary. These two works can be said to enact a literary planetology, which involves narrating planets as agential characters as well as background setting for human self-exploration. In both these novels, the aim of the narrator is to try to come to terms with the extreme otherness of planets unlike Earth. Yet the means available to each narrator comes from the conceptual toolbox of modernity built on Earth. Both novels then end up posing questions about how to narrate contact with another planet without narrating that planet as a lesser or greater version of Earth. Thus each novel suggests that to cognize a planet one also needs to record how that planet changes cognition.

Stapledon positions *Star Maker* with a preface where he sets the novel at the precipice of planetary-scale war. On the eve of the outbreak of World War II, Stapledon writes that "year by year, month by month, the plight of our fragmentary civilization becomes more serious" (Stapledon 2008, 3). Stapledon does not address directly Earth's own impending war in the novel, but instead crafts a plot that seemingly allows for a look at every other planet in the universe to see how everyone else has dealt with planetary-scale crises. The novel begins with a solitary male figure taking a stroll outdoors after experiencing some personal, domestic troubles. The narrator, who is never named, soon starts to reflect on the smallness of his worries in the context of millions of others on the planet with their own problems. Upon gazing at the skies, the narrator finds himself quickly shifting to wider perspectival scales as he starts to contemplate the meaning of "us" (Vernadsky 1945, 10) at human species-wide levels. Yet this initial scale jump is just the beginning. To cognize at this bigger scale, the narrator imagines himself taking an elevated, aerial viewpoint by visualizing himself moving farther and farther away from Earth, like a hot air balloon floating away. This journey is entirely mental, and it keeps going. Suddenly, somehow, the narrator seems to have found a way to travel in time and space just with his mind. Upon leaving Earth mentally, at first other planets beckon, then other galaxies, then the outer reaches of the universe. The mind becomes the sole means for wandering among the cosmos. The whole novel is predicated on a plot device of the utmost fictionality, yet the novel also winks at the notion that all fiction is a kind of mind travel in space and time. Stapledon's novel offers the formula that fictional space is as comparatively vast in imagination as the universe is vast in distance. The optimism toward the expansiveness of literary form as well as for nearly limitless psychological wandering is palpable. Stapledon ties a modernist sense of planetarity to a kind of cosmological constructivism that is run through at such speed that one can get a sense of the entire universe in less than two hundred pages. This brief sweep through the cosmic, as Fredric Jameson remarks, makes *Star Maker* "so idiosyncratic that it seems to have no genre, not even those of SF or Utopian literature, and that it is a somehow unique and unclassifiable work" (Jameson 2005, 124).

Once this tremendous narrative conceit of mental interstellar travel is installed, the novel whisks us away to planet after planet, some teeming with life similar to humans, while others swarm with organisms that are anatomically unlike anything on Earth. The narrator spends extended time exploring the first humanoid planet he finds, which he dubs "the Other Earth," and examines their social and political features. Here Stapledon sees versions of capitalism, communism, and fascism battling it out on another planet. At first, there is a sense that Stapledon lacks some imagination as he blatantly projects existing social relations on Earth into the context of other planets. But there is a different argument to be made here that grapples with the perennial problem of mass political organization, namely, that planets that are humanoid will invariably construct some social system around versions of these socio-political principles because each planet would face the same problem of environmental constraints, expanding population needs and interest diversifications, and the use of advanced technology for discovery and civilizational expansion. Each human-like planet would have to deal then with its own version of civilizational crisis as the constraints of biology, ecology, technology, and ideology would be similar from planet to planet. The novel then points to how a problem like the Anthropocene, created when one species dominates a planet to the detriment of its other inhabitants, could be understood as a recurrent planetary problem and not just specific to Earth.

Stapledon's account of other humanoids is just one stop in a series of differently populated planets. The narrator makes brief visits to a planet inhabited by flying "bird-men," one full of echinoderm-like beings, another teeming with nautiloid-shaped beings, and one planet replete with a kind of swarm intelligence of avian creatures flying together to form group minds. With the platform of limitless space travel that Stapledon has set up, he could conjure any kind of world, yet the novel spends much of the time considering how civilizational crises appear in humanoid and non-humanoid contexts. Stapledon wants to use the vehicle of the novel to foresee different kinds of planetary crises and envision how post-crisis worlds might be formed. Ultimately, Stapledon envisions a universe where planets either figure out how to get out of their own version of the Anthropocene problem and arrive at a planetary utopia, or run themselves into self-destruction.

The narrator joins up telepathically with a humanoid from the Other Earth and together they explore these biologically and culturally disparate lands, paying special attention to the alternative forms of psyche and thought elsewhere in the universe: "In this state of heightened lucidity we, or rather the new I, began deliberately to explore the psychological possibilities of other types of beings and intelligent worlds" (Stapledon 2008, 51). At first, they encounter a number of planets seemingly going through their own version of an Anthropocene moment: "[I]n this novitiate stage of our work we invariably came upon these worlds when they were passing through the same spiritual crisis as that which underlies the plight of *Homo Sapiens* today" (Stapledon 2008, 53). The reference to "spiritual crisis" stands in for any planetary-scale problem that puts a civilization at a precipice, and would include the condition of the Anthropocene even though Stapledon had not intuited this problem specifically. The term "spirit" also alludes to a loosely Hegelian motif of interplanetary spiritual becoming that guides Stapledon's novel. For Hegel, the becoming of spirit involves the realization of reason in and through self-consciousness. The Hegelian self-conscious reasoning spirit must reconcile in actuality the laws of nature and the laws of right in order to build an ethical world-state.

Stapledon writes of "the spirit's struggle to become capable of true community on a world-wide scale" (Stapledon 2008, 55), indicating that "spirit" stands for a communal and enduring form of civilization that, as Hegel argued, combines law, morality, and religion. This community of spirit needs to be able to get along with its own planet and with other planets in "the age-long task of achieving the right, the finally appropriate, the spiritual attitude toward the universe" (Stapledon 2008, 55). Is there, however, an appropriate and right spiritual attitude that can extend to planetary and interplanetary scales? Is Stapledon projecting a somewhat anthropomorphic sense of communal and collaborative spirit as the only reasonable frame for universal history? A Hegelian would say that one should reverse the question and assert that "spirit" has its own agency and works as the immanent cause of historical reason coming to know itself as such. However, the "spirit" that Stapledon describes is one that is focused on how any form of civilization in the universe might avoid self-destruction and instead find a way to flourish and achieve some sense of knowledge and peace in a well-populated cosmos. Stapledon proposes that a properly spiritual attitude to one's planet and other planets would involve seeking a shared enlightened consciousness and collaborative connection rather than a controlling, acquisitive, or individualist triumph over neighboring worlds. The "right" spirit then is the project for a planetary-scale accomplishment of a form of utopia. To put it in the terms of this chapter, enlightened "spirit" allows for a planet to overcome the version of its own Anthropocene so that a more sophisticated and globally aware society can emerge and be shared with other planets.

But even when a planet approaches this utopian spirit in Stapledon's narrative, problems remain. The narrator comes across case after case of planets that achieve a higher state of self-consciousness but then find out that relating to neighboring planets brings about its own social and psychological conflicts. Even a planet that achieves "spirit" at home can become a problem: "When such worlds mastered interstellar travel, they might conceive a fanatical desire to impose their own culture throughout the galaxy" (Stapledon 2008, 107). The narrator ends up realizing that interplanetary civilizations are caught in a version of Freudian psychic conflicts and progressive maturations. The Anthropocene bottleneck, the period of global crisis that occurs before a planetary culture either manages to achieve the proper cosmological perspective or ends up in self-destruction, appears first on a planetary scale, then on an interplanetary scale. The narrator remarks, "We were inclined to think of the psychological crisis of the waking worlds as being the difficult passage from adolescence to maturity" (Stapledon 2008, 101). Traveling across the universe, the narrator finds that "many galaxies were in many stages of mental, as of physical, development" (Stapledon 2008, 136). Indeed, the psychological well-being of a planetary-scale civilization is of such paramount importance in the novel that it seems to be the determining factor in the fate of each planet. Stapledon's novel spends just as much time assessing the psychological profiles of planetary cultures as it does in developing the classical science fiction work of describing an alien life-form. A number of times, the travelers encounter the scene of whole planetary cultures turning insane. These "mad worlds" (Stapledon 2008, 110) can lose their marbles by falling into world-wide "social neurosis and civil strife" (Stapledon 2008, 111), often stemming from a motive of religious imperialism that comes to define the planet's identity. Planetary cultures can also go mad by seeking out another planet and trying to manipulate or impose upon that other planet to force it to become civilized or "spiritual" according to the terms of the dominant planet. A mad planet can spread its madness across a galaxy, often provoking other planets to turn to war or enact a kind of suicide. "We could not long endure the spectacle of scores of worlds falling into psychological ruin" (Stapledon 2008, 124), the narrator bemoans. Every commentary on other worlds is meant as self-commentary, so Stapledon wants readers to ask: would an alien visitor to Earth describe it as a mad planet? Upon seeing a world at war, or generating enough weapons to wipe itself out, or even ultimately destroying itself through its own prosperity by redefining everything on the planet as beholden to the improvement of one species—would one not call the Anthropocene Earth a mad world falling into psychological ruin?

Stapledon depicts how psychological conditions are played out at planetary and galactic levels, in effect proposing that a version of psychoanalysis should expand to cosmic scales. Stapledon's novel suggests one must develop a psychoanalysis of being in space and being interplanetary, with the added complication that this psychoanalysis seems to have to pass largely through the epistemological gate of science fiction, since aside from a few probes interplanetary contact today has to be creatively imagined. Freud himself once thought that certain geological and historical periods of the Earth's history brought about specific psychological profiles that contributed to the phylogenetic development of the modern human mind. In his unpublished essay "A Phylogenetic Fantasy," Freud suggested that the harsh coldness of the late Pleistocene ice age pushed humans out of their animal comforts and brought forth a sense of anxiety about hunger and sex that remains embedded in the mind today.[1] Freud also invoked a number of geological and geographical metaphors throughout the course of his work, from his references to "oceanic feeling" behind religion to describing the mind as layered in sediment like an archeological site. Stapledon does not delve into Freud's geological and planetary metaphors, but he does promote the notion that the psychological condition of a species is one of the prime determinants for the fate of a planet. What Stapledon adapts from Freud then is less Freud's own occasional geological thinking than his tendencies toward theorizing species-wide psychic constitutions and the psychic discontent inextricable with civilization.[2] Stapledon imagines the same attractions and repulsions that compose personal and collective dramas reappearing at interplanetary relations: "Between the minded planetary systems occurred infinite variations of personal intercourse. As between human individuals, there were loves and hates, temperamental sympathies and antipathies, joyful and distressful intimacies, cooperations and thwartings in personal ventures and in the great common venture of building the galactic utopia" (Stapledon 2008, 127). Stapledon's novel perhaps could be subtitled "Interplanetary Civilizations and Their Discontents."

At the end of the novel, as the narrator tries to get yet another cosmic perspective on all these planetary encounters, he has a brief encounter with the figure of the Star Maker, the original builder of the universe. This encounter attempts to reconcile theological and scientific theories of the universe, but what I want to focus on here is the evocation of a panpsychist power that the Star Maker represents. The Star Maker is described as a "cosmic mind" (Stapledon 2008, 160), and there are suggestions of a nöosphere-like presence in the universe. The Star Maker shows the narrator what will be the fate of this current universe, but also offers brief glimpses of other universes, some that run on different scientific laws. What is most relevant here is that the Star Maker offers another layer of cosmic psychology and a further motif for the realization of universal spirit. Ultimately, Stapledon's novel provides at least three distinct versions of interplanetary psychology—Freudian conflicts, telepathic communion, and panpsychism. The reason I have spent so much time examining the psychological motifs here is that Stapledon suggests that planetary thinking, and the resolution of planetary-scale problems, has to include a well-developed psychological knowledge that can scale to planetary and cosmic levels. This brings us back to the Anthropocene on Earth, which viewed from outside might suggest a planet gone "mad" and incapable of achieving collective enlightenment about how to deal with its own problems. Stapledon's novel proposes that any way of dealing with the Anthropocene has to deal with psychological conflicts and spiritual conflicts along with ecological conflicts in order to build toward a kind of planetary communion. Comparative planetology needs to work with comparative psychological theories to be able to model how worlds fall into crises and either pull themselves out or fail. For Stapledon, the modernist science fiction novel, which can use narratological tools to expand to any scale to access inner or outer space, provides the vehicle by which to tell the story of how the fate of a planet is tied to the vicissitudes of consciousness of the species on planet.

SOLARIS AND THE MELANCHOLY OF PLANETS

What does a planet want? Setting aside the question of whether or not planets can have wants or desires, in Stapledon's novel, the least we can say is that a planet does not want to be wasted, undone, or stunted by its inhabitants. Planets, it would seem, do not want to be stuck in versions of an Anthropocene bottleneck. Finally, in Stapledon's view, planets want to be known, and to recognize and be recognized by other planets. Writing less than three decades later, Stanislaw Lem takes up Stapledon's challenge to know other worlds and to formulate a planetary psychology. However, in complete opposition to Stapledon, Lem writes of planets that refuse contact and cognition. Lem tells the story of a planet that has powerful psychic effects on its visitors but cannot be assimilated to any psychological models that pertain to Earth. There is no universal cosmic mind in Lem, only an account of the desires and traumas experienced by humans who try to study the minds of other worlds but end up just revisiting their own psychic conflicts and hang-ups in the process.

In Lem's eyes, Stapledon's *Star Maker* was an ultimately failed work because of its initial premises. In a short essay on Stapledon, Lem questions the assumption of the existence of a "Star Maker" figure and adds that Stapledon never explains how and why planets should end up in conflict or self-destruct if they are all somehow expressions of this maker. According to Lem,

> Stapledon thus raises the typical dilemmas and antinomies of every religion to a cosmic scale, elevating them from an earthly plane and earthly scale of magnitude to the dimensions of the fictive universe. . . . [A]lthough *Star Maker* is an artistic and intellectual failure, at least the author was defeated in a titanic battle. . . . Stapledon's book is a completely solitary creation. No other work in fantastic literature has begun from similar premises. For this reason, it defines the boundaries of the SF imagination. (Lem 1987a, 7)

Solaris, in stark contrast to *Star Maker*'s universal reach, takes a minimalist approach by focusing only on contact with a single planet. Instead of raising personal problems to a cosmic scale, the novel lingers on the struggles of a few planetary scientists to understand just one particular planet that is completely covered by an ocean. Although Lem radically reduces the scale of the planetary novel to focus on just one story of contact, he shows that the gathering of comparative planetary knowledge is not necessarily more secured. If Stapledon fails in his narrative by assuming an overly optimistic view of the novel's cognitive access to thinking exoplanets, Lem writes of the failure of each of the characters in his novel to fully cognize the planet Solaris. Ultimately the narrative of *Solaris* could be said to conclude with the adage: nothing alien is human to me.

Solaris is told from the point of view of the crew member Chris Kelvin as he visits the planet for the first time. Kelvin's expertise is in psychology, an unusual background for planetary science but one that has made his doctoral research on the planet Solaris stand out. The planet Solaris is covered by some kind of living and conscious ocean that continually produces elaborate topological shapes and can respond to stimuli. The planet has already been studied and theorized about for over a century by the time Kelvin arrives at the space station orbiting the planet, and little is expected from his visit. Immediately upon arrival, Kelvin finds the station's two occupants, Snow and Sartorius, each to be haunted by some kind of presence that takes the form of a person who is the manifestation of a desire harbored within the mind of each crew member. Kelvin himself soon is confronted with what appears to be the living and breathing reincarnation of his deceased wife, Rheya. The novel weaves through a double plot of the astronauts who try to come to terms with the nature of these visitors and the nature of the oceanic planet.

Already prior to Kelvin's arrival, a continual stream of planetary thinkers and scientists had offered so many different theories of Solaris that whole journals and libraries are filled with explanations trying to account for this living planet. The novel divulges these theories in chunks, letting the reader feel the weight of theory after theory. Among the hypotheses for Solaris: it is a brilliant "ocean-brain"; it is a child-like organism that has little knowledge of itself; it is a planet that is capable of manipulating its own space/time properties; it is a planet that is intelligent but has no consciousness or perhaps even has gone insane; it is a kind of planetary genius, a "cosmic yogi." The piling up of so many "Solaristics" points to a theoretical fatigue. Even Kelvin comes to feel that "the ocean of Solaris was submerging under an ocean of printed paper" (Lem 1970, 176).

All the scientists seem to agree that the ocean is one giant organism that has managed to achieve a symbiosis with the planet. The organism "had reached in a single bound the stage of 'homeostatic ocean,' without passing through all the stages of terrestrial evolution, by-passing the unicellular and multicellular phases, the vegetable and the animal, the development of a nervous and cerebral system. In other words, unlike terrestrial organisms, it had not taken hundreds of millions of years to adapt itself to its environment—culminating in the first representatives of a species endowed with reason—but dominated its environment immediately" (Lem 1970, 19). Any time a single species dominates its environs, there is the suggestion of a problem comparable to the Anthropocene. Yet in the case of *Solaris*, the ocean has in effect evolved in a way that makes biodiversity irrelevant. There is only one form of life on the planet, even though the ocean takes many shapes. The ocean is not in conflict with its environment and there is not the case that one form of life threatens other life on Solaris. There is no possibility for an Anthropocene-like crisis on Solaris because the ocean has already taken over and "dominated its environment." Solaris, presumably, will forever be in one geological phase, an ocean-cene. How should one understand and evaluate this planet in which there is only one life form without any apparent selection pressure or need to evolve? Some Solaris theorists argue that the ocean-planet has achieved an exponentially more sophisticated form of intelligence compared to humans because it has found a way for life and planet to be inseparable, an apparent harmony of organism-environment. Should one then say that the smarter option for a planet is to achieve a life-and-planet synthesis, or is the Anthropocene problem due to the very attempt of humans to dominate their environs and achieve a synthesis with the planet that would largely just satisfy human interests? The notion that planet is life and life is planet on Solaris points to an extreme case of symbiosis and coordination. The wholeness and totality that defines the ocean planet is completely unlike the biodiversity and plurality that is spread across the Earth.

The ontological composition of the ocean remains a question throughout the novel; at the same time, the ocean questions the ontological status of its visitors. The planet has somehow made appear as if alive the fantasies buried in the unconscious of each crew member's mind. The crew members interact in deeply emotional ways with these manifestations even as they try to perform experiments on them to discover their material composition, which they conclude is made from some kind of subatomic particle. Kelvin's invitation to apply psychological methods to the planet already indicated that the study of exoplanets, and Solaris in particular, needed a psychological component, what might be called exopsychology or astropsychology. Yet at the same time as the crew studies the geology and psychology of the planet, the crew realizes they too are being studied psychologically. Visiting Solaris effectuates a kind of scene of psychoanalysis. The crew members do not know if this infiltration of their unconscious is an aggression or a form of friendly and inquisitive contact. They are only left with the thought that a whole planet "has performed a series of . . . experiments on us. Psychic vivisection" (Lem 1970, 201). Solaris stimulates a psychic rush in its visitors that can be described as Freudian in its destabilizing of the psyche, leading to the shattering of the crew's composure.

Lem's novel expands the scale of psychological inquiry to planetary size, but he does not go further like Stapledon to hypothesize a cosmic mind. Instead, the encounter between crew and Solaris is fraught with individual fears, desires, and misunderstandings that blend scientific study and emotional response. The crew members feel certain that Solaris is teaching them a lesson about contact with other planets. They debate vigorously whether this lesson of contact is enriching or diminishing of the status of the human. Snow, one of the crew members, offers a darker view that would dissociate interplanetary contact from any notion of progress:

We take off into the cosmos, ready for anything: for solitude, for hardship, for exhaustion, death. Modesty forbids us to say so, but there are times when we think pretty well of ourselves. And yet, if we examine it more closely, our enthusiasm turns out to be all sham. We don't want to conquer the cosmos, we simply want to extend the boundaries of Earth to the frontiers of the cosmos. For us, such and such a planet is as arid as the Sahara, another as frozen as the North Pole, yet another as lush as the Amazon basin. We are humanitarian and chivalrous; we don't want to enslave other races, we simply want to bequeath them our values and take over their heritage in exchange. We think of ourselves as the Knights of the Holy Contact. This is another lie. We are only seeking Man. We have no need of other worlds. We need mirrors. We don't know what to do with other worlds. A single world, our own, suffices us; but we can't accept it for what it is. (Lem 1970, 75)

In response to this lecture, Kelvin interjects, "But what on earth are you talking about?" (Lem 1970, 75)—an interesting question since Snow is exactly talking about the repetition compulsion that humans show in trying to find another Earth elsewhere in the universe. Snow's response: "I'm talking about what we all wanted: contact with another civilization. Now we've got it! And we can observe, through a microscope, as it were, our own monstrous ugliness, our folly, our shame!" (Lem 1970, 76). Contact with other planets has brought out the shameful realization that contact with Earth is still not well valued or much understood.[3] Snow says that all this travel and exploration really could be avoided by looking in a mirror and looking at "Man," but he should also have added that they need to look at how the human psyche is embedded in a desire for Earth. And yet, the imagination of other planets, particularly ocean-like ones, is a stimulus to reimagine the terraqueous Earth. Sometimes one has to travel extremely far to get a glimpse of a mirror that is planetary in size.

Solaris does not exactly refuse contact, but it refuses to be known and to be reduced to a theory. The planet also refuses to be colonized—it offers neither resources nor exploitable knowledge to its human visitors. This refusal to be identified and theorized also thoroughly unsettles the crew, who must question the stability of their psyches as well as the meaningfulness of their scientific and conceptual models of planets. After admitting such frustrations, Snow claims that humans should focus on exploring their own psyches before trying to meddle with other planets. The implication is also that humans have yet to really examine their psychic bond to Earth, and the way the Earth has formed and informed human unconscious and conscious desires. For Kelvin, the encounter with Solaris leads him to a depressive state where he recognizes that he has had his unconscious exposed, making him realize that he longs for a form of human intimacy he can never have since he can never return to a world that would include his lost wife. Among the crew, Kelvin seems the most capable of coming to terms with the appearance of his unconscious made real in the form of his deceased wife, Rheya. Kelvin ultimately comes to an understanding with the ersatz Rheya that while he cannot know what she is made of and why she appeared, he values the time he has with her and resists the urge to banish her. Rheya comes to understand that Kelvin truly does love her even in this uncanny artificial form she has taken. Rheya then realizes that the most honest way to respond to this love shown by Kelvin is to destroy herself. Her dissolution frees Kelvin to put his unconscious desires to work elsewhere, although Kelvin is left burdened with a kind of planetary melancholy where he feels he no longer belongs to Earth or Solaris.

At the end of the novel, Kelvin is resigned to return to Earth, but he is disenchanted with that prospect and feels a distinct loss of psychic energy. "What did that word mean to me? Earth?" (Lem 1970, 205). Solaris has undone Kelvin's sense of authority over his own psyche and over his own planet. Imagining how his return to Earth will proceed, Kelvin ruminates: "For a while, I shall have to make a conscious effort to smile, nod, stand and perform the thousands of little gestures which constitute life on Earth, and then those gestures will become reflexes again. I shall find new interests and occupations; and I shall not give myself completely to them, as I shall never again give myself completely to anything or anybody" (Lem 1970, 205). The sadder and wiser Kelvin is burdened by the knowledge that he came closest to gaining an understanding of Solaris and appreciating the appearance of Rheya when he stopped trying to come up with definitive classifications and let the planet and Rheya be in their otherness. The novel closes with Kelvin taking his first voyage to the surface of Solaris. He comes as close as he can to the undulating ocean, not aiming to gather knowledge about the planet but just to be with it. As Kelvin prepares to return to Earth, he tells himself, "I hoped for nothing. And yet I lived in expectation" (Lem 1970, 214). To have no hope but to live in expectation suggests an openness to the unknown without assurances. To be without hope is not to rely on any system of belief or knowledge that the universe will be favorable to one's desires, while to live in expectation means to be ready to meet whatever happens in the universe without pre-set theories. This is the lesson that Solaris offers for Kelvin, and the suggestion is that this attitude may be a more honest way to connect with planetary otherness, including the otherness of the Earth.

The arc of this chapter has been to examine how the Anthropocene has prompted a rethinking of the Earth and the conceptualization of the planetary. The modernization of Earth became a topic for representation in modernist literature that also began to imagine the Earth's problems in the context of other ways of thinking and encountering planets. Stapledon's *Star Maker* puts the massively expansive space of the novel in service of imagining encounters with the plurality of planets across the universe. Stapledon's account is largely positive and optimistic that planetary problems can be overcome just as psychic conflicts are overcome at an individual level. Lem's story of the liquid opaqueness of Solaris and its refusal of colonization stands as a rebuttal to the notion that the human psyche and planetary otherness can be wilfully reconciled. Lem's story of failed contact serves as a warning that the problems of Earth, and its Anthropocene, may not be resolved by looking to other planets. Furthermore, it seems as if Solaris somehow knew that the human visitors might shift from contact to colonization, even if unintentionally, and thus made contact become a barrier. In Lem's novel *Fiasco*, a crew of interstellar surveyors ultimately admit that "exploration of a world without causing harm is impossible" (Lem 1987b, 107). With Solaris, the crew must admit that perhaps the most honest lesson is to realize that the troubles of Earth must not be spread to other planets. If the Anthropocene represents the sum of these troubles on a planetary scale, then, at the very least, one needs to keep the Anthropocene on just one planet. There is a kind of geology of morals involved in every exoplanet landing such that it is incumbent upon the visitor not to irremediably change the planet for self-serving reasons or project one's troubles onto the planet. Humans have already changed Earth, and if our planet can be said to have a psyche, it is largely shaped after ours. The Earth has our morals embedded in its geology. Thinking and acting in the Anthropocene certainly requires planetary thinking and thinking like a planet. But as Earth changes, so do our representations and understandings of what a planet can do, as well as our responsibilities toward that changing ground.

NOTES

1. See Freud 1987.

2. The term "geopsychoanalysis" might be apt to describe Stapledon's approach. The notion of a geopsychoanalysis was briefly suggested by Jacques Derrida but ultimately left underdeveloped in his work. Derrida's essay on geopsychoanalysis states at the outset, "I'm sure it will come as no surprise to you that my speaking of 'geopsychoanalysis'—just as one speaks of geography or geopolitics—does not mean that I am going to propose a psychoanalysis of the earth of the sort that was put forward a few decades ago, when Bachelard evoked 'The Earth and the Reveries of Rest' and 'The Earth and the Reveries of the Will.' But as inclined as I may be today to distance myself from such a psychoanalysis of the earth . . . it is nevertheless upon the earth that I wish to advance—upon what the psychoanalysis of today considers to be the earth" (Derrida 1998, 66).

3. Stefan Helmreich makes a brief comparison with the treatment of the ocean on Solaris and the oceans on Earth. Helmreich remarks that both oceans are seen as alien

yet also as "a realm that scientists, managers, and policy makers seek to domesticate, to tame" (Helmreich 2009, 276).

WORKS CITED

Derrida, Jacques. 1998. "Geospychoanalysis: '. . . and the rest of the world.'" In *The Psychoanalysis of Race*, edited by Christopher Lane, 65–90. New York: Columbia University Press.

Freud, Sigmund. 1987. *A Phylogenetic Fantasy: Overview of the Transference Neuroses*. Edited by Ilse Grubrich-Simitis. Translated by Axel Hoffer. Cambridge, MA: Harvard University Press.

Friedman, Susan Stanford. 2015. *Planetary Modernisms: Provocations on Modernity across Time*. New York: Columbia University Press.

Heise, Ursula. 2008. *Sense of Place and Sense of Planet: The Environmental Imagination of the Global*. Oxford: Oxford University Press.

Helmreich, Stefan. 2009. *Alien Ocean: Anthropological Voyages in Alien Seas*. Berkeley: University of California Press.

Jameson, Fredric. 2005. *Archaeologies of the Future: The Desire Called Utopia and Other Science Fictions*. London: Verso.

Lem, Stanislaw. 1970. *Solaris*. Translated by Joanna Kilmartin and Steve Cox. London: Faber.

———. 1987a. "On Stapledon's 'Star Maker.'" Translated by Istvan Csicsery-Ronay Jr. *Science Fiction Studies*, 14 (1): 1–8.

———. 1987b. *Fiasco*. Translated by Michael Kandel. New York: Harcourt, Brace, Jovanovich.

Moraru, Christian. 2015. *Reading for the Planet: Towards a Geomethodology*. Ann Arbor: University of Michigan Press.

Sagan, Carl. 1994. *Pale Blue Dot: A Vision of the Human Future in Space*. New York: Random House.

Stapledon, Olaf. 2008. *Star Maker*. Mineola: Dover.

Vernadsky, Vladimir. 1945. "The Biosphere and the Nöosphere." *American Scientist* 33 (1): 1–12.

———. 1998. *The Biosphere*. Translated by David B. Langmuir. New York: Copernicus.

Chapter Seven

Early Ecology and Climate Change in the Future Histories of H. G. Wells and Olaf Stapledon

Ted Howell

Virginia Woolf's *Between the Acts* is bookended by geological time, which intrudes via Lucy Swithin's favorite reading: "an outline of history" (Woolf 1941, 8). Two references to H. G. Wells's *The Outline of History* thus frame the novel's multilayered narrative and exemplify how the natural world, the history of England, and the lives of its characters overlap within Woolf's book. The presence of Wells's bestselling tome in *Between the Acts* introduces a handful of themes that remain largely buried: recognition of the brevity of human history on a geological scale, the story of the species as separate from the story of civilization, and slow climate change across millennia. One thread running through *Between the Acts*, and Woolf's broader oeuvre, is the recognition of humanity as interwoven with nature; for this reason, Woolf's novels have consistently provided go-to examples for critics who wish to make connections between ecocriticism and modernism.[1] So the fleeting presence of geological time and climate change in *Between the Acts* offers one possible point of entry into a conversation about modernism and the Anthropocene, and Woolf was, especially late in her life, keen to incorporate long, even geological timelines into her fiction. Perhaps this is why, when she wrote a letter to the philosopher and science fiction writer Olaf Stapledon after reading his 1937 book *Star Maker*, Woolf replied that "sometimes it seems to me that you are grasping ideas that I have tried to express, much more fumblingly, in fiction. But you have gone much further and I can't help envying you—as one does those who reach what one has aimed at" (qtd. in Crossley 1994, 248–49).[2] What, exactly, did Woolf envy about Stapledon's *Star Maker*, a genre-defying work of fiction that follows its narrator across galaxies over billions of years? To say that Stapledon had "gone much further" is a colossal understatement, for both *Star Maker* and his earlier *Last and First Men* (1930) outpace even geological timelines. Stapledon and

115

Wells both certainly go "much further" than Woolf, presenting speculative histories of the future shaped by an emerging sense of humanity as one species among many, the influence of early forms of environmental thinking, and the effort to develop and nurture a truly planetary response to the increasingly globalized political, economic, and environmental issues of their day. Casting a glance long into the future, the fiction of Wells and Stapledon demonstrates the influence of the burgeoning discipline of ecology on fiction, exhibits a remarkable prescience that anticipates key elements of the Anthropocene, and offers a vibrant glimpse into a form of interwar writing radically different from the more familiar modernist fiction of Virginia Woolf.

Situating the foundational science fiction of Wells and Stapledon within the context of early ecology fosters a connection between its moment and current narratives of the Anthropocene. At its most broad, the concept of the Anthropocene describes the environmental impact of anthropogenic climate change resulting from human technology, but more exactly it sees human beings as a species evolved into a planetary force, points to the disintegration of any clear boundary between what is "natural" and what is "social" or "cultural," and, often, carries with it undertones of ecological apocalypse.[3] Each of these narratives finds an early echo in Wells and Stapledon. Further, the writing of Wells, to a great extent, and Stapledon, to a lesser extent, bears an uncanny and possibly disquieting resemblance to the philosophy of contemporary "ecomodernists" who call for a "good Anthropocene" where humankind manages its environment more purposefully. Ecology in its early form, as it solidified as a discipline in the 1920s and 1930s, was taken up by popularizers like Wells as a shining example of the possibilities of scientific management, as a way of grasping and managing complex wholes like ecosystems. Ecology quickly began to bring human beings into its purview, recognizing humankind's intricate connections to nature while elevating scientists above their object of study. Wells's late-career nonfiction, most explicitly the 1929 book *The Science of Life* he co-authored with Julian Huxley and his son G. P. Wells, eagerly adopted ecology as one of its guiding principles. Wells's awareness of ecology's theories and findings influenced his fiction from the 1920s onward, culminating with the publication of *The Shape of Things to Come* (1933), a novel that was in turn influenced by Stapledon's *Last and First Men*. Stapledon's fiction too intersects with ecology, and its grand theory of planetary change and the capacity of the human species to evolve (and devolve) portrays terraforming, fossil-fuel dependence and depletion, and bioengineering. The future histories of Wells and Stapledon depict a human species that has learned to live sustainably not by adjusting to the natural environment, but by mastering it.

By looking back at Wells's and Stapledon's predictions for the future we encounter not a "literature of cognitive estrangement"—Darko Suvin's famous definition of science fiction—but rather a literature of cognitive resemblance: not the shock of the strange, which enables us to see the old as new again by coming to it aslant, but rather the shock of the familiar, the realization that the concerns, conversations, and arguments that dominate current conversations about the Anthropocene date back nearly a century. Finding Anthropocene antecedents in the writing of Wells and Stapledon can enrich and further historicize studies of the contemporary literature on climate change, like Adam Trexler's recent book *Anthropocene Fictions*, which establishes and then analyzes a canon of contemporary climate change literature, claiming that "climate change and all its *things* have changed the capacities of recent literature" (Trexler 2015, 13). I wholeheartedly agree, and add that the anticipation of climate change and all of the things that accompany it, as it appears in the fiction of Wells and Stapledon, changed the capacity of literature in their own moment. Even more interesting is the way their writing from the 1920s and 1930s more closely resembles that of our own time than it does their immediate successors. By midcentury, plenty of science fiction was concerned with environmental issues, and science fiction has long acted as an essential site for imagining a radically different future.[4] But Wells and Stapledon are more than early exemplars of ecological science fiction. They anticipate the Anthropocene, a concept that thrives on its own radical newness, forcing us to evaluate critically any narrative of the Anthropocene that views its reflexivity, scientific or technological discovery, or species-decentering moves as game-changing.

WELLS, EARLY ECOLOGY, AND ECOMODERNISM

The Science of Life continued H. G. Wells's efforts to write what his biographer David C. Smith calls "textbooks for the world" (Smith 1986, 245), forming the second part of a trilogy that began with *The Outline of History* and concluded with *The Work, Wealth, and Happiness of Mankind* (1931). Wells and Huxley decided to base the style of the book on the writing of "Dickens, Meredith, T. H. Huxley, Darwin" and consistently break from the form of information-conveying science writing to reflect on both the implications of these findings and the reaction of the authors to them.[5] In a typical move, the authors boldly declare the aim of their book on the first page by suggesting that it is a sequel to *The Outline of History* in that the first book ended with an account of human history where "at last man was revealed, becoming creative, becoming conscious of the possibility of controlling his destiny" (Wells

1936, 1). Thus, *The Science of Life* offers to its readers the knowledge needed to consciously control their future. The book became possible, and was perceived by Wells to be so urgently necessary, because of the radical changes in the life sciences in the early twentieth century. The history of ecology, as the textbook's authors and subsequent historians of the term explain, traces back to Ernst Haeckel's coinage of the term as *Ökologie* in 1866 to describe the relationship between individual organisms and their environment.[6] Ecology launched as a subfield of botany, but eventually began to cast itself as a meta-discipline capable of synthesizing all the life sciences. Wells and Julian Huxley both played a significant role in ecology's expansion and popularization in the 1920s.

Apart from its explicit treatment of ecology, two particular strands running through the book are pertinent to Wells's and Stapledon's future histories. The first is a storytelling device that more than any other aspect demands to be read as Wells's individual contribution: the daily life of a "Mr. Everyman," which from his introduction on the first page of Book One grounds detailed scientific descriptions and explanations within recognizable scenarios, thereby insisting on discussing humans as products of their biological make-up and as powerfully molded by their environment. Mr. Everyman's hunger for breakfast is "his machinery demanding fuel" (Wells 1936, 25) and his house in the suburbs is a habitat in which "the whole assemblage of lives is biologically entwined" and "forms an interlocking whole" (Wells 1936, 823). But the book is equally willing to invite the reader into current debates in the life-sciences and their significance, as the second strand I wish to pull out reveals: its counterpoint to the philosophy of vitalism and Bergsonian élan vital. Early ecology was profoundly shaped by debates between vitalist and mechanical accounts of evolution that accounted for the connections between organisms and the whole.[7] *The Science of Life* stands on the side of mechanism, dismissing Bergson's account of a purposeful, creative "Life Force" (and its popularization by G. B. Shaw) as "not a scientific explanation" (Wells 1936, 639). But even though the authors are contemptuous of the notion of a purposeful Life Force with its own agency, they continually rely on language that imagines the environment in terms of energy flows and argue that evolution "has at least the possibility of becoming purposeful, because man is the first product of Evolution who has the capacity for long-range purpose, the first to be capable of controlling evolutionary destiny" (Wells 1936, 642). With these words that sound very much like a theory of creative evolution, the authors double-down on their argument that humanity can and must take charge of its future by arresting control of the forces that flow through nature.

The Science of Life's means of engaging then-cutting-edge research demonstrates how deeply ecological science was embedded within social norms and expectations, and how ecology in turn is used to reinforce two of Wells's favorite arguments: against overpopulation and toward utopia. The textbook borrows heavily from and copiously cites the work of the ecologist Charles Elton, a colleague of Huxley's who reviewed the ecology chapter and had recently published *Animal Ecology* (1927). Elton's book is responsible for the famous image of lemmings crowding one another over a cliff, a piece of folktale that Elton absorbed without question, never observing it for himself, likely because it appealed to his own scientific interest in population control (Anker 2009, 97). Its section on "Storms of Breeding and Death" closes with one of the least palatable sentences in *The Science of Life*: "Unrestrained breeding, for man and animals alike, whether they are mice, lemmings, locusts, Italians, Hindoos, or Chinamen, is biologically a thoroughly evil thing" (Wells 1936, 1011). Wells, of course, consistently exhibits deep anxieties about overpopulation, which often results in one of the most Wellsian of themes, what John Carey memorably calls "H. G. Wells Getting Rid of People" (Carey 1992, 118–34). A counterpoint to the fear of overpopulation is the idea of the "climax community," a pervasive concept in early ecology, in *The Science of Life* as elsewhere figured as an end-goal of ecological succession in which ecological communities become more and more efficient. Applying the concept to the human community, the authors wonder if man "will make a mess of things and fail, or will succeed and hold on from climax to climax. If he fails the forest will return" (Wells 1936, 989). With this one line at the end of a section, the authors briefly reveal their fears about the future while reaffirming their belief, dominant throughout the book, that humanity will indeed be able to not only hang on but push their environment towards an increasingly climactic state.

With this context in mind, the implications of "The Ecological Outlook" come into focus. Wells and his coauthors, having spent more than sixty pages educating readers about ecology, are ready to make some suggestions about its application. The key to the section is its focus on what the authors call "man's general problem" and how ecology can solve it:

> [T]o make the vital circulation of matter and energy as swift, efficient, and wasteless as it can be made; and, since we are first and foremost a continuing race, to see that we are not achieving an immediate efficiency at the expense of later generations. . . . At last [man's] difficulties are driving him back to first principles. In the last couple of centuries he has accelerated the circulation of matter—from raw materials to food and tools and luxuries and back to raw matter again—to an unprecedented speed. But he has done it by drawing on reserves

of capital. He is using up the bottled sunshine of coal thousands of times more quickly than Nature succeeds in storing it. (Wells 1936, 1029)

With some edits for style, this passage could easily pass as being written by an American environmentalist. Voicing a key concern raised by the Anthropocene—development via fossil fuels without regard for the effect on future populations—*The Science of Life* looks toward a future of energy scarcity. The authors' call to action is equally familiar when they argue that humanity's "chief need to-day is to look ahead . . . as one community, one a world-wide basis; and as a species, on a continuing basis," thereby quilting together Anthropocene discourse's focus on global scale and on humanity as species (Wells 1936, 1030). And if the book's emphasis on future generations, its cosmopolitan politics, and its bullishness on alternative energy strike contemporary readers as familiar and even satisfying, its extension of the point—humanity "must plan his food and energy circulation as carefully as a board of directors plans a business" (Wells 1936, 1030)—will be more divisive, for it strikes at the heart of current reactions to the concept of the Anthropocene: will it be a catastrophe or an opportunity?

Wells's and his coauthors' idea about humanity's need to gain increasing mastery over nature run counter to the ways environmentalists have adopted the concept of the Anthropocene as a way of explaining the consequences of industrial modernity, fossil-fuel burning, and philosophies that instrumentalize nature. For this reason, it's easy to dismiss *The Science of Life* as outdated; while there certainly is a tension in the textbook between efforts to embed humanity within its environment and calls for humanity to master it, the authors ultimately see the outcome of ecological knowledge as means to mastery. By contrast, environmentalists have consistently called for restraint rather than control of the environment, and "ecology" in the common parlance is often used to deliver a blow to human hubris—against industrial modernity in favor of harmony with nature. But this is not at all what "ecology" meant in 1929, and in recent years a strain of arguments about the Anthropocene and the future of environmentalism has emerged that makes hopeful calls for humanity to take charge of its growth. When the textbook's authors insist that "the whole process must be conscious" (Wells 1936, 1028), they voice the core concept of today's "ecomodernists," who write, as their manifesto explains, "with the conviction that knowledge and technology, applied with wisdom, might allow for a good, or even great, Anthropocene" ("Ecomodernist" 2015, 6).[8] As it often does, the meaning of "modernist" here announces a break from the past and adopts the manifesto form to announce its ideals, which include a call to use "natural ecosystem flows and services more efficiently" and to own up to humanity's force and responsibility as a developing species ("Ecomodernist" 2015, 17). Again, the authors of *The Science of Life* know these arguments and the tension between them, and the textbook's description of the human species as a "collective human organism" profoundly influencing its environment and other species anticipates the Anthropocene's reliance on a narrative of humanity as a species. At its close, *The Science of Life* reiterates the Wellsian theme of "collective purpose of continuation and growth" with these words: "At the end of our vista of the progressive mental development of mankind stands the promise of Man, consciously controlling his own destinies and the destinies of all life upon this planet" (Wells 1936, 1475). The conclusion and closing view of *The Science of Life* starkly resembles the opening salvo of the ecomodernist Mark Lynas's book *The God Species*, a title that aptly names the Wellsian view of humanity. Lynas: "we must recognize that we are now in charge—whether for good or ill—we need to make conscious and collective decisions about how far we interfere with the planet's natural cycles and how we manage our global scale impacts" (Lynas 2011, 8). Lynas's next move is to describe how earth systems analysis can give humanity the necessary knowledge to take control. From its origin moment, when Paul Crutzen and Eugene Stoermer closed their short piece on the Anthropocene saying that an "exciting, but also difficult and daunting task lies ahead of the global research and engineering community to guide mankind towards global, sustainable, environmental management" (Crutzen and Stoermer 2000, 18), a significant chunk of the scientific research around the Anthropocene has focused on identifying the "planetary boundaries" that will shape development in the future (Steffen et al. 2015, 736). As a result, its language of mastery has taken on a new tone: rather than being chastened by the recognition of humanity's impact on the earth, thinkers are using this knowledge to bolster arguments for a more conscious, more sustainable form of control that will lead to a brighter future—another argument, as his future history shows, that Wells mounted.

HUMAN ECOLOGY AND *THE SHAPE OF THINGS TO COME*

By the time Wells began writing *The Shape of Things to Come* in 1932, his knowledge of ecology had expanded dramatically, and its influence is vividly registered in the novel. Wells envisioned *The Shape of Things to Come* as another, this time fictional, "textbook for the world," but rather than writing an outline of history he thought of writing "An Outline of the Future" or a "History of the Future" (Wells 1933, xxxiii). Wells had been producing detailed forward-glancing works since 1901's *Anticipations*, but *The Shape of Things to Come* is his most extensive future history, one that strives to match his textbooks in scope despite being (largely) fictional. After one book of recent nonfictional history, Wells's novel, continuing its framing device as the "dream book" of Wells's fictional contemporary, Dr. Phillip Raven, tells the story of humanity's struggle through World War, an "Age of Frustration" (1930s–1960s) accompanied by a plague that halves the world's population, the slow rise of the global "Modern State" beginning in the 1970s, and the increasing development and "modernization" of this utopian society up to the year 2106. Ecological details from *The Science of Life* enter the book at the critical juncture where it moves from past to future history; the introduction of the term "human ecology" offers an explanation for efforts to control the world economy and global society. "Human ecology" was a brand-new term in 1933, so new that a footnote in the 2005 Penguin edition of *The Shape of Things to Come* mistakenly claims, based on evidence from the *OED*, that Wells coined it in the novel. But the term appears in the ecology chapter of *The Science of Life*, where economics is described as "merely Human Ecology . . . the narrow and special study of the ecology of the very extraordinary community in which we live" (Wells 1933, 962).[9] Wells had made the concept of human ecology fundamental to his work of political economy *The Work, Wealth and Happiness of Mankind*, and as it appears in *The Shape of Things to Come*, Human Ecology is called upon to describe how humanity managed to purposefully guide the progress of society and achieve a utopian world state. The roadblocks to utopia, as Wells presents them, lie in a dearth of knowledge about the workings of human society and a lack of willpower needed to overcome centuries of mental stagnation and resistance to change. Human ecology, by offering a material explanation for the workings of society, provides the necessary know-how, system of ideas, and willpower to revolutionize the world and institute a Modern State.

The most significant aspect of Wells's future history is its account of how the Modern State manages the Earth on a planetary scale and envisions it as a changing and changeable whole—ideas that predate Anthropocene concerns with earth systems analysis, reforestation, climate change, and geoengineering.[10] One of the Modern State's most impressive accomplishments is its effort "to become the landlord of the planet" (Wells 1933, 309). Wells links this accomplishment to what he sees a restoration of human vitality, which had ebbed (worldwide) in the days before the Modern State and helps to account for its rise when it returns in decaying towns and the abandoned countryside. Here Wells is in line with the increased attention to the country and the return to the rural that accompanied it in the 1930s; but what makes Wells's account unique is how insistent he is to think of the Earth as a single, global unit through which vitality flows, rather than remaining limited to nostalgic pastoralism. The Modern State, building upon a recently completed "general survey of the natural resources of the planet," makes a case for itself in a manifesto form that relies on a managerial rhetoric steeped in ecology, arguing that the Earth's resources have been improperly used, that the new "Council for World Affairs" has authority over the entire Earth, and that it is calling for "the preservation of order and security throughout our one home and garden, our pleasure ground and the source of all our riches—the earth, our Mother Earth, our earth and yours" (Wells 1933, 337). The "riches" found in the earth take on a more than metaphorical meaning, for the Modern State is founded on an "energy unit" of money, a concept that makes literal Wells's application of ecology to the world of economics and applies the ideas of energy flows from *The Science of Life*. What separates Wells's human ecology from contemporary forms of "ecological economics" is that in Wells's Modern State, in a move away from Malthusian conceptions of the earth's finite carrying capacity, while there are theoretically limits to growth and overpopulation is a recognized problem, the predominant concern is with finding new resources to exploit more efficiently.

The fifth and final book of *The Shape of Things to Come*, "The Modern State In Control of Life," tells the story of a twenty-first century utopia controlling the earth on a massive scale, thereby completing the project of ecological management laid out in *The Science of Life* (its final chapter: "Life Under Control"). Two chapters in *The Shape of Things to Come*, "Keying Up the Planet" and "Geogonic Planning," provide a compelling constellation of Wells's anticipations of the Anthropocene. The Modern State essentially acts like Clive Hamilton's *Earthmasters*, starting massive geoengineering projects made possible by an increase in applied biological knowledge in an effort to adapt to a changing climate.[11] Wells sets up his Modern State's planetary management in terms of anthropogenic climate change, along the way previewing one of most commonly cited sentences in Anthropocene studies, Dipesh Chakrabarty's argument that "anthropogenic explanations of climate change spell the collapse of the age-old humanist distinction between natural history and human history" (Chakrabarty 2009, 201). Wells's "Human Ecology" already begins to disintegrate this distinction by mashing together the two words. In *The Shape of Things to Come*, "From the point of view of the ecologist the establishment of the Modern State marks an epoch in biological history. It has been an adaptation, none too soon, of our species to changing conditions that must otherwise have destroyed it" (Wells 1933, 441). The social and political aspects of Wells's future history are at the same time landmarks in biological history. Among the ways the Modern State "keys up" the planet to improve life upon it are a comprehensive system of reforestation, the creation of a "world garden" spotted with nature reserves and newly designed species of plant and animal life, the extraction of minerals from deep in the earth's crust, the "greening" of industry, and even attempts to alter the composition of the atmosphere and the surface of the earth to create more desirable habitats. Each of these ideas finds a correlative in contemporary ecological concerns: recent innovations in fracking shale oil, carbon capture and sequestration, the "rewilding" of ecomodernism (Marris 2013), the "half earth" proposal of Edward O. Wilson (Wilson 2016), "de-extinction" science (Shapiro 2015), and a wide array of geoengineering schemes (Hamilton 2013). What unites these ecological visions, past and present, is a narrative of the human species adapting to radically changing conditions of its own making through scientific, specifically ecological, management of its environment.

STAPLEDON'S STAR-SPANNING SPECIES

If Wells's novel offers an overview of humanity's adjustments to change and planetary management, the future histories of Olaf Stapledon—*Last and First Men* and *Star Maker*—are grander, vaster, and more detailed. While *Last and First Men* begins with a history of its "First Men" that resembles Wells's *The Shape of Things to Come* in scope and style, it soon picks up speed before eventually ending two million years into the future. *Star Maker* extends this by billions of years. The theoretical and imaginative richness of Stapledon's writing, combined with its overall lack of memorable characters, general indifference to plot and pacing, and often comically vast timescales make it easier to mine for ideas, images, and inventions than to analyze formally or thematically.[12] But even as the *Last and First Men* moves through eighteen new "types" of human species, and as its efforts to convey scale through the repetition of large numbers becomes wearisome, its emphasis on the continuity of humanity across eons remains capable of surprise, particularly in its preview of Anthropocene concepts.

Stapledon's future history of the First Men and their "Americanized planet" antedates Wells's lengthier account, and it's within this section of the book that Stapledon most clearly influenced Wells. But even within this tamer portion of *Last and First Men*, Stapledon's insights far outstrip those of Wells. Like Wells's utopian Modern State, Stapledon's First Men attain mastery over nature; they too urbanize their world while setting aside some areas for wild nature, and their efforts at geoengineering are successful: the Sahara is now a lake, the Arctic Circle is warmed by redirected ocean currents, and the vast material wealth below Antarctica has been made accessible by thawing. But all is not well. In exaggerated terms, Stapledon's account of the rise and fall of the First Men narrates a possible future for humanity in the Anthropocene. Their civilization is powered by "the buried remains of prehistoric vegetation," but because the earth's reserves of oil and coal are depleted after three centuries of heavy use the First Men must seek alternative sources of fuel—a timeline (1800–2100?) that chillingly resembles our own (Stapledon 1968, 63). The loss of their primary source of power has a momentous impact. In a startling paragraph, Stapledon writes:

> The cessation of oil had taught men a much needed lesson, had made them feel the reality of the power problem. At the same time the cosmopolitan spirit, which was learning to regard the whole race as compatriots, was also beginning to take a broader view temporally, and to see things with the eyes of remote generations. (Stapledon 1968, 63)

Having learned to abide by the precautionary principle and put aside national and racial differences, the First Men seek to reduce their use of fossil fuels and run their civilization on "more permanent sources of power" (wind, water, geothermal) (Stapledon 1968, 63). But even though they cover their hills with windmills and tap volcanoes, the First Men are unable to maintain their carbon-dependent culture, with its worship of movement and its cult of flying, while living sustainably; when their supply of coal finally fails, the civilization collapses into a dark age, and the population dwindles as people throw themselves into the sea like lemmings leaving a tiny "remnant of a population" able to "scrape a living from the soil" (Stapledon 1968, 72) "Elsewhere, utter desolation," Stapledon's eco-catastrophist narrative of the First Men concludes. "With easy strides the jungle came back into its own" (Stapledon 1968, 73).

As does his extended account of the First Men, Stapledon's chronicle of the rise-and-fall movement of his multiple species depends on a theory of planetary climate change, sometimes anthropogenic (as in the case of the First Men) and sometimes natural. But the dominant narrative of *Last and First Men* is one of human and human-like species adapting to changing material circumstances. Humanity shapes its environment, and is in turn shaped by it. Throughout, Stapledon relies on vast geological timescales—the Second Men, for example, only emerge after a period of millions of years restores the Earth and makes it possible for a new civilization to emerge. Patrick Parrinder traces this theme across *Last and First Men* and *Star Maker*, pointing out that Stapledon relies on a plot in which civilizations proceed through a period akin to industrial revolution before they either use up their world's resources or achieve a utopian world state. In this sense, every civilization in Stapledon's future histories passes through something like its version of the Anthropocene, with some coming out well on the other side and others collapsing. In *Star Maker*, Stapledon figures this process as one in which a species either changes itself in response to planetary pressures or allows its environment to remake it; the civilizations who emerge, newly awakened, are then capable of building a new, more sustainable, world. That Stapledon's societies complete the process over thousands or millions of years marks an important divergence from its otherwise noteworthy alignment with the Anthropocene. But even though Stapledon's timescales are vast, they are in many ways artificial: no matter how often he repeats some variation of the phrase "millions of years"—Jameson calls this Stapledon's "empty temporality," his "childish reiteration of large numbers" (Jameson 2005, 126)—the fact remains that the majority of the predictions Stapledon made about the future were either already on their way to being realized, realized within a matter of decades, or purely fictional. As Stanislaw Lem points out in a seminal essay, "decades have already completed Stapledon's Billion Year Plan" (Lem 1986, 288). But the speed with which Stapledon moves through millennia itself challenges the impact of his timelines, which remain unreal and pale in comparison to the richness of his vision of the future, which stands out (as Lem notes) more for his capacity to imagine the cultural and environmental impacts of the technologies he invents, rather than the inventions themselves, and for his willingness to subsume the rise and fall of cultures into a story about climate and geology. For Stapledon, the human civilizations and the history of planets they inhabit are two halves of the same story.

The most strikingly ecological aspect of Stapledon's future histories is how his account of the evolution of human species freely draws upon both vitalist and scientific language.[13] While Wells and his coauthors dismissed vitalism as unscientific, but consistently spoke of ecology as the study of vital flows, Stapledon at critical moments uses the language of vitalism to present concepts and themes that in Wells take the form of the language of ecological management. Stapledon's Third Men exemplify this thread that runs throughout his work, in that they worship "Life," yet believe it is their responsibility to assume godlike powers of bio-engineering to guide the evolution of their species (Stapledon 1968, 146). The most conspicuous feature of the Third Men is that "their worship of Life, as agent or subject, was complemented by worship of environment, as object to life's subjectivity" (Stapledon 1968, 146). The Third Men develop a "vital art," in which they make the whole of their environment, on a planetary scale, into a shared, civilization-wide, masterpiece through a "whole vital economy of the planet" (Stapledon 1968, 152). Here, in the Third Men's "vital economy," is Stapledon's version of Wells's "Human Ecology." The difference is that Stapledon's Third Men are organicists, largely uninterested in industry, striving to create a planetary garden and assimilate their society into a collaborating world-organism. The organicist Third Men represent Stapledon's arcadia, a moment of ecological balance stemming from a means of management rooted in a philosophy of care and artistic achievement—but even in this Eden are seeds of its downfall, in the form of a eugenic philosophy that strives to perfect humanity and instead creates a new species of "Great Brains," super-minds doomed to be the last humans on earth; when the moon's orbit shrinks, these Fifth Men have to search the solar system for a new home, eventually colonizing Venus, adjusting to its conditions as they change across geological time, absorbing apocalypses and managing to continue. Once Stapledon's account leaves the earth behind, its ecological focus weakens, but his insistence on the coevolution of species and climate is sustained.

H. G. Wells, for his part, only amplified his concentration on ecology, and his final books exhibit an even greater degree of insight into the climatic changes he was beginning to notice. *The Fate of Homo Sapiens* (1939) rounds out Wells's career as an ace anticipator. Emphasizing the possibility that the human species is by no means guaranteed to survive—a note he had been sounding since *The Time Machine*—Wells posits that biology has invaded history, history has become ecology, and humanity is out of balance with its environment. Wells writes:

> there can be no question that to-day we are, from the geological point of view, living in a phase of exceptional climatic instability, in a series of glacial and interglacial ages, and witnessing another destruction of animal and plant species on an almost unprecedented scale. . . . And this time the biologist notes a swifter and stranger agent of change than any phase of the fossil past can show—*man*, who will leave nothing undisturbed from the ocean bottom to the stratosphere, and who bids fair to extinguish himself in the process. (Wells 1939, 29–30; emphasis in original)

On the strength of this passage, together with his knowledge of ecology and his futurism, Wells has to be considered alongside other figures from the past who have been lauded as forerunners of the Anthropocene: Antonio Stoppani, George Perkins Marsh, and Vladimir Vernadsky.[14] What differentiates Wells from these scientific figures is that his forecast emerged not from an array of scientific evidence but from a lifetime of future forecasting, often in fictional form. Wells's solution to the problem, that humanity is changing its environment faster than it can possibly adapt, is that only a "mental readjustment" will suffice (Wells 1939, 48). And from point through the remainder of the book, Wells expounds upon his belief in the collective power of humanity and the importance of universal education to social progress. Four compelling chapters on the survival of the species and the promise of human ecology are followed by twenty-two chapters on world government, religion, and contemporary politics. A strong pivot, certainly, but if the concept of the Anthropocene has taught us anything, it's that the social and the natural can no longer be separated, that humanity and geology are intertwined. Wells knew in 1939 that "many readers will be quite unaccustomed to seeing human social life in the light of ecological science" (Wells 1939, 33), a limited outlook he and Stapledon both worked hard to overcome, and one we must continue to set straight.

NOTES

1. For examples of ecocritical work on Woolf, see Alt 2010, Bryson 2007, Scott 2012, and Westling 1999. Most recently, Kelly Sultzbach reads Woolf alongside Merleau-Ponty to show how Woolf's diaries, reviews, and fiction stress embodied relationships with the nonhuman world more broadly, especially animals, resulting in an "an ecophenomenological representation of an embodied existence intertwined with a more-than-human sensory world" (Sultzbach 2016, 84).

2. In an earlier letter, Woolf told Stapledon that she admired his earlier books; she would have most likely read *Last and First Men*, Stapledon's best-known work (Crossley 1994, 433). Interpreting Woolf's remarks to Stapledon, Kim Stanley Robinson argues that Woolf's writing changed after she read Stapledon, as it turned toward longer histories and departed from her trademark stream of consciousness style. "Woolf's last pages," Robinson claims, "were a kind of science fiction" (Robinson 2009, 47).

3. My breakdown of the Anthropocene is indebted to Christophe Bonneuil's, who identifies "four grand narratives of the Anthropocene: (1) the naturalist narrative, currently the mainstream one; (2) the post-nature narrative; (3) the eco-catastrophist narrative; and (4) the eco-Marxist narrative" (Bonneuil 2015, 18). All four are relevant to the writing of Wells and Stapledon; even if I use alternative means of describing them, connections to each narrative emerge below.

4. A fact comprehensively demonstrated by the collection *Green Planets: Ecology and Science Fiction* edited by Gerry Canavan and Kim Stanley Robinson. See especially Canavan's supplement, "Of Further Interest" (Canavan and Robinson 2014, 261–79).

5. Julian Huxley reports on this decision in his book *Memories* (Huxley 1970, 65). The textbook was composed primarily by Huxley, with Wells acting as taskmaster, editor, and reviser, responsible for its shape and thrust. Huxley's composition of the book is intricately entwined with modernist literary history; he wrote much of it during the winter of 1927, in a chalet in the Swiss Alps that he shared with his brother Aldous and their wives Juliette and Maria. D. H. Lawrence and his wife Frieda were living nearby, and while Juliette typed Julian's script, Maria was typing out *Lady Chatterley's Lover* for D. H. Lawrence (Huxley 1970, 160).

6. While the histories of ecology found in Worster, Bramwell, Anker, and Phillips inform my reading of *The Science of Life*, I largely limit my account of ecology to the textbook's detailed explanations.

7. For more on these debates, see Bramwell 1989 and Anker 2009.

8. Among the most visible ecomodernists are Erle Ellis, Mark Lynas, Ted Nordhaus, and Michael Shellenberger, the latter two as founders of the Breakthrough Institute, authors of "The Death of Environmentalism" (2004), and co-editors of *Love Your Monsters: Postenvironmentalism and the Anthropocene* (2014). Crucially, the ecomodernist account relies on the "early Anthropocene" hypothesis, which argues that the Anthropocene should not be tied to industrialization but rather to the onset of agriculture.

9. The earliest use of "human ecology" was by a group of American sociologists interested in urban planning; Huxley and Wells almost certainly adopted it from Charles Elton's *Animal Ecology*, which takes up the phrase on its final page to argue that human communities and animal communities can and should be studied along similar lines (Anker 2009, 102; Elton 1927, 190).

10. When *The Shape of Things to Come* receives attention from critics, its account of the near future gets top billing, particularly Wells's prediction that a world war would result in early 1940 from a conflict between Germany and Poland. And in many ways the most noteworthy thing about the book is that it inspired the landmark 1936 film *Things to Come*.

11. Hamilton himself makes this comparison in his first chapter. After briefly summarizing some popular geoengineering proposals, he quips that some of them "seem properly to belong in an H. G. Wells novel" (Hamilton 2013, 4).

12. As a counterpoint, John Huntington has demonstrated how *Last and First Men* can be read in terms of its symphonic form, and the rewards of this approach are how it accounts for the continual shock of freshness that comes with reading Stapledon.

13. It's important to note that Stapledon does not ascribe to a fully vitalist concept of Life, in which a separate, non-physical life force is posited, even if at times the language he uses comes close to this meaning. Stapledon was intimately familiar with vitalism, but more in line with Alfred North Whitehead's philosophy of organism. See Stapledon's 1928 lecture, "Thoughts on the Modern Spirit."

14. For two competing views on the degree to which the Anthropocene was anticipated by scientists, see Steffen, Grinevald, Crutzen, and McNeil 2011 for a historical summary and Hamilton and Grinevald 2015 for a response that argues in favor of the Anthropocene's novelty.

WORKS CITED

Alt, Christina. 2010. *Virginia Woolf and the Study of Nature*. New York: Cambridge University Press.

"An Ecomodernist Manifesto." 2015. Accessed March 16, 2021. http://www.ecomodernism.org.

Anker, Peder. 2009. *Imperial Ecology: Environmental Order in the British Empire, 1895–1945*. Cambridge: Harvard University Press.

Bonneuil, Christophe. 2015. "The Geological Turn: Narratives of the Anthropocene." In *The Anthropocene and the Global Environmental Crisis: Rethinking Modernity in a New Epoch*, edited by Clive Hamilton, Christophe Bonneuil, and François Gemenne, 17–31. New York: Routledge.

Bramwell, Anna. 1989. *Ecology in the 20th Century: A History*. New Haven, CT: Yale University Press.

Bryson, J. Scott. 2007. "Modernism and Ecological Criticism." In *Modernism*, edited by Astradur Eysteinsson and Vivian Liska, 591–604. Amsterdam: John Benjamins Publishing.

Canavan, Gerry, and Kim Stanley Robinson, eds. 2014. *Green Planets: Ecology and Science Fiction*. Middletown, CT: Wesleyan University Press.

Carey, John. 1992. *The Intellectuals and the Masses: Pride and Prejudice among the Literary Intelligentsia 1880–1939*. London: Faber.

Chakrabarty, Dipesh. 2009. "The Climate of History: Four Theses." *Critical Inquiry* 35 (2): 197–222.

Crossley, Robert. 1994. *Olaf Stapledon: Speaking for the Future*. Liverpool: Liverpool University Press.

Crutzen, Paul J., and Eugene F. Stoermer. 2000. "The 'Anthropocene.'" *Global Change Magazine* 41: 17–18.

Elton, Charles. 1927. *Animal Ecology*. New York: Macmillan.

Hamilton, Clive. 2013. *Earthmasters: The Dawn of the Age of Climate Engineering*. New Haven, CT: Yale University Press.

Hamilton, Clive, and Jacques Grinevald. 2015. "Was the Anthropocene Anticipated?" *The Anthropocene Review* 2 (1): 59–72.

Huntington, John. "Olaf Stapledon and the Novel about the Future." 1981. *Contemporary Literature* 22 (3): 349–65.

Huxley, Julian. 1970. *Memories*. New York, Harper & Row.

Jameson, Fredric. 2005. *Archaeologies of the Future: The Desire Called Utopia and Other Science Fictions*. New York: Verso.

Lem, Stanislaw. 1986. "On Stapledon's 'Last and First Men' ('Les Derniers et Les Premiers' de Stapledon)." Translated by Istvan Csicsery-Ronay, Jr. *Science Fiction Studies* 13 (3): 272–91.

Lynas, Mark. 2011. *The God Species: Saving the Planet in the Age of Humans*. Washington, DC: National Geographic.

Marris, Emma. 2013. *The Rambunctious Garden: Saving Nature in a Post-Wild World*. New York: Bloomsbury USA.

Parrinder, Patrick. 2015. *Utopian Literature and Science: From the Scientific Revolution to Brave New World and Beyond*. Basingstoke: Palgrave Macmillan.

Phillips, Dana. 2003. *The Truth of Ecology: Nature, Culture, and Literature in America: Nature, Culture, and Literature in America*. New York: Oxford University Press, 2003.

Robinson, Kim Stanley. 2009. "Why Isn't Science Fiction Winning Any Literary Awards?" *New Scientist* 203 (2726): 46–49.

Russell, W. M. S. 1990. "H. G. Wells and Ecology." In *H. G. Wells Under Revision: Proceedings of the International H.G. Wells Symposium, London, July 1986*, edited by Patrick Parrinder and Christopher Rolfe, 145–52. Selinsgrove, PA: Susquehanna University Press.

Scott, Bonnie Kime. 2012. *In the Hollow of the Wave: Virginia Woolf and Modernist Uses of Nature*. Charlottesville: University of Virginia Press.

Shapiro, Beth. 2015. *How to Clone a Mammoth: The Science of De-Extinction*. Princeton, NJ: Princeton University Press.

Shellenberger, Michael, and Ted Nordhaus, eds. 2011. *Love Your Monsters: Postenvironmentalism and the Anthropocene*. Oakland, CA: Breakthrough Institute.

———. 2004. "The Death of Environmentalism: Global Warming Politics in a Postenvironmental World." https://s3.us-east-2.amazonaws.com/uploads.the breakthrough.org/legacy/images/Death_of_Environmentalism.pdf. Accessed January 15, 2016.

Smith, David C. 1986. *H. G. Wells: Desperately Mortal*. New Haven: Yale University Press.

Stapledon, Olaf. 1968. *Last and First Men and Star Maker*. New York: Dover.

———. 1997. "Thoughts on the Modern Spirit," in *An Olaf Stapledon Reader*, 148–63. Syracuse, NY: Syracuse University Press.

Steffen, Will, Jacques Grinevald, Paul Crutzen, and John McNeil. 2011. "The Anthropocene: Conceptual and Historical Perspectives." *Philosophical Transactions of the Royal Society A* 369 (1938): 842–67.

Steffen, Will et al. 2015. "Planetary Boundaries: Guiding Human Development on a Changing Planet." *Science* 347 (6223): 736.

Sultzbach, Kelly. 2016. *Ecocriticism in the Modernist Imagination: Forster, Woolf, and Auden*. New York: Cambridge University Press.

Suvin, Darko. 1979. *Metamorphoses of Science Fiction: On the Poetics and History of a Literary Genre*. New Haven, CT: Yale University Press.

Trexler, Adam. 2015. *Anthropocene Fictions: The Novel in a Time of Climate Change*. Charlottesville: University of Virginia Press.

Wells, H. G. 1939. *The Fate of Homo Sapiens*. London: Secker and Warburg.

———. 1936. *The Science of Life*. Garden City: Doubleday.

———. (1933) 2005. *The Shape of Things to Come: The Ultimate Revolution*. Edited by Patrick Parrinder. London: Penguin.

———. 1931. *The Work, Wealth and Happiness of Mankind*. London: William Heinemann.

Westling, Louise. 1999. "Virginia Woolf and the Flesh of the World." *New Literary History* 30 (4): 855–75.

Wilson, Edward O. 2016. *Half-Earth: Our Planet's Fight for Life*. New York: Liveright.

Woolf, Virginia. 1941. *Between the Acts*. San Diego, CA: Harcourt.

Worster, Donald. 1994. *Nature's Economy: A History of Ecological Ideas*. 2nd ed. New York: Cambridge University Press.

Chapter Eight

Second Modernism and the Aesthetics of Temporal Scale

Charles M. Tung

The question of how to register and anticipate massive change over time has become one of the most pressing aesthetic and political problems in what we might call the post-Holocene moment. In the absence of the "eye-catching and page-turning power" of "falling bodies, burning towers, exploding heads, . . . and tsunamis," how is it possible, asks Rob Nixon, to "convert into image and narrative the disasters that are slow moving and long in the making, disasters that are anonymous and that star nobody" (Nixon 2011, 3)? The bad fit between "our flickering attention spans" and the un-spectacular, uneventful nature of "slow violence," the incompatibility of the satisfactions of narrative form with the enormous temporal scale necessary to conceive of anthropogenic dangers, and the uneven distribution of harm across rich and poor regions of the planet have for a long time rendered hazards such as global climate change invisible to perception and politics. To counter this invisibility, Columbia University's Center for Research on Environmental Decisions (CRED) doubles down on the downscaled forms of the human: "in order for climate science information to be fully absorbed by audiences, it must be actively communicated with appropriate language, metaphor, and analogy; combined with narrative storytelling; made vivid through visual imagery and experiential scenarios" (Shome and Marx 2009, 2).

Metaphor, storytelling, and vivid scenarios are undoubtedly good ways of motivating immediate decision-making, which is the principal goal of CRED's mission. But it is also true that the twentieth century witnessed a great acceleration of geological consciousness, stratigraphically inscribed in many cultural objects that sought to test and expand narrative capacities in unprecedented ways, often pushing "appropriate language" deliberately to its breaking point. Even without the specific element of temporal scale, this period's cultural production is to a large extent defined by its experimental movement beyond absorbing language and absorbable narratives. Moreover, early attempts to think the explosive speed-up in industrialization, population growth, and other high-impact conditions of modernity that are now legible in sediments and ice often aimed explicitly to critique human downscaling and short-term thinking—as a way of not only engaging our epistemological and aesthetic limitations, but also examining these accelerated conditions as primary hazards in their own right, causal factors turning up in stratigraphic readings of the ongoing aftereffects of modernity.

We have often interpreted the time obsession of modernism to have focused on either short-term temporalities or backward-facing, primitivist returns. But there was a speculative strain of modernism that scoped out to the temporal scales of the Anthropocene and tacked from the imperative to "make it new" to the worries of what has been called a second modernism. To alter the line from Pound, this second, Anthropocenic modernism might be said to have tracked and reflected on the news of the twentieth century that will have STAYED NEWS for unimaginable lengths.[1] This chapter will explore modernism's scalar zoom as a response to the anthropogenic hazards of second modernity unfolding on imperceptible timescales. The quintessentially modernist interest in differently-scaled clocks contributes to our current understandings of this new epoch and its distension of periodization, exemplified by the project of the Clock of the Long Now (CLN) to elongate human thinking about the future, but it also reminds us to resist the temptation to collapse all temporal scales down to one fundamental timescape. By investing in the value of thinking and feeling disjunctiveness, modernist clocks underscore the need for a multiplicity of scales rather than for aesthetic downscaling and conversion. The appearance of these clocks is the result of the period's interest in time travel as a mode of tracking massive change over time. The specific technique of time lapse arises as a way to make change visible, but it also becomes a way of implicating multiple rates of change in relation to one another.

There are two main reasons why this volume is timely for modernist studies. The first and very obvious reason that twentieth-century scholars are or should be deeply invested in this particular question of geological periodization has to do with the increasingly clear provenance of massive planetary changes: the specific historical moment that scientists have begun to read in the lithosphere, a clear stratigraphic signal that beacons and tracks impending/ongoing environmental catastrophe, is the moment of "accelerated technological development, rapid growth of the human population, and increased consumption of resources" (Waters et al. 2016, 2). Crutzen and Stoermer initially backdated the start of the Anthropocene to the rise of high-powered steam engines, but later collaborations with the Dahlem Conference working group discovered, in the famous set of twelve graphs, major increases around 1950 in "atmospheric composition, stratospheric ozone, the climate system, the water and nitrogen cycles, marine ecosystems, land systems, tropical forests, and terrestrial biosphere degradation" (Crutzen and Stoermer 2000, 17–18). Many scientists now agree that these dramatic changes, known as "the Great Acceleration," make the twentieth century a better starting point for the new epoch than the eighteenth century (Steffen et al. 2015, 83). Indeed, in the vote of the ICS Working Group on the Anthropocene, announced on August 29, 2016, at the International Geological Congress in Cape Town, South Africa, the majority of scientists agreed that the Anthropocene, whose stratigraphic reality they almost unanimously confirmed, began in the middle of the twentieth century. When the International Commission on Stratigraphy (ICS) eventually formalizes the Anthropocene as a chronostratigraphic series and a geochronological epoch, it will be because our evidence of our long, post-Holocene moment will have been underwritten millions of years from now by conditions broadly known as modernity, whose signal was broadcast in toxic chemicals, nuclear fallout, heavy metals, ancient plastics, and other technofossils and anthropogenic deposits (Waters et al. 2016, 2).

The second reason modernist studies should be interested in the Anthropocene is less obvious and has to do with an underexplored aspect of modernist cultural production itself—its similar interest in extreme temporal forms, in this case the forward distension of deep time. In geochronology, an epoch is a unit of time that normally functions to identify an enormous swathe of the *past* on a scale of *millions (and tens of millions) of years*. However, scientists have been reading stratigraphic signatures in the outermost layer of the earth that will have indicated in the *future* a major shift that our current epoch of the Holocene, a mere twelve thousand years, and our dominant aesthetic temporalities do not satisfactorily encompass. The temporal scenario of the Anthropocene reads so far forward that the present becomes a trace of an enormously distant past from the perspective of a far future: it features the absence of all familiar protagonists or antagonists, save for that force which radically distends and dissipates the dramatic. To quote climate scientist Tim Lenton, "The alien geologist arriving in the future would see a change in the sedimentation rates, novel metals, pollutants, microplastics. They might find something more dramatic, the remains of an ancient civilisation flooded out by rising sea levels or something, but they'd definitely find the changes in the sediment" (qtd. in Chivers 2014, n.p.). Maybe some human remains to suggest an aestheticizable situation (to the alien geologist?), but certainly changes in sediment—this scene that issues from the inhuman, forward-facing, geological periodization of the Anthropocene suggests a type of drastic

expansion for the study of new modernisms, recalculating the waning of historicity in a "long now" as the multiply historical risks of the "long new," and
refocusing not just on futurity but on the scale of futurity as a consequence of
the present and the scale of the present.

Modernism is not usually associated with the far future and massive,
forward-facing timescales. Instead, it is most often understood to be a set of
short-term responses to a culture of brevity and transitoriness—a gathering of
family resemblances bearing the mark of a world compressed by speed and
coordinated by different kinds of synchronization. Indeed, beyond a mere
reflection of that accelerated world, modernism could be said to be a part of
its synchronizing machinery. As Peter Galison writes, if one were to pull on
a late nineteenth-century wire, you'd discover an "opalescent" mesh connecting that transatlantic cable to academic and technical fields, government institutions, and the technology of clocks and their regulation (Galison 2003, 40).
This meshwork forms a major part of the infrastructure responsible for organizing and coordinating faster and more efficient movement, communication,
and production. Modern time in its most familiar form—synchronized, precise, and increasingly brief—emerges from this set of connections and itself
becomes load-bearing. As Adrian Mackenzie points out, "clocktime may well
be the most ubiquitous of modern technical infrastructures," since "clocks are
deeply embedded in diverse scientific, cultural, institutional, economic, and
military realities" (Mackenzie 2002, 88). Modernism's cultural circuits were
directly patched in to this network, and its fascination with the moment can be
considered a significant aesthetic trait of industrial culture, because this small
unit of time was both the instrument and byproduct of modern infrastructure
(the railway, the telegraph, the factory system), and because so many late
nineteenth- and early twentieth-century writers attempted to reappropriate the
moment as a perceptual and aesthetic vertex/vortex that might free us from
this regulatory matrix.

However, there was a strand of modernism that turned away from the
moment and the familiar aesthetics of transitoriness, a strand that seemed
to recognize that the forms, media, and crumbling remains of the short-term
infrastructure would inscribe themselves in the geological record and become
the message, so we now worry, that we could not think larger timescales. This
aspect of modernism instead pursues instead a range of enormous durations
that lies beyond the scope of modern networks and serves to critique them,
and seems to relate precociously to a different stage or mode of modernity.
That is, against the pervasive fetish for the accelerated and the fleeting, there
emerged an interest in the temporal scale on which modernity's hazards
slowly unfold, an interest, distinct from the paleomodernist nostalgia for
mythic permanences, in what Ulrich Beck theorized as "reflexive" or "sec-

ond" modernity. In second modernity, the myopic focus on the circulation and distribution of goods is replaced by the wide-angle concern for the management of long-term bads, the dangers produced by industrial modernity that lie far beyond the circuits of the present. As Beck writes, "In the struggle over risks of modernization, the subject of controversy as to its degree of reality is [not the sensible but] instead what everyday consciousness does *not* see, and cannot perceive: radioactivity, pollutants, and threats in the future" (Beck 1992, 73). Thus, the risk society, as he goes on to say, "marks the dawning of a *speculative* age in everyday perception and thought" (Beck 1992, 73).

This long-range modernist aesthetic—a reflexive, "second modernism"— was already thinking about the long half-life of the modern and about the reconceptualization of the present, even of time itself, that would be necessary for such speculation. That is, as Aaron Jaffe has pointed out in *The Way Things Go: An Essay on the Matter of Second Modernism*, a "second modernism . . . was implicit from the start," since its obsession with temporal scale extended forward the "future effects of the deep time of modernity" and projected "an unknowable future determinate of the present" (Jaffe 2014, 18–19). Jaffe's focus on the object matter of modernist imaginaries—the stuff and things that persist as junk littering the waste lands of twentieth-century texts—prompts a reconsideration of things that appear as presentist detritus or pastist artifacts. Such things become, rather, the pieces of a gigantic, temporal Rube Goldberg machine performing and figuring a kind of side-effectuality. To the accounts of modernism as an ephemerality fetish, or as a critique of modernity's microtime by means of a retreat into a deep and singular past (ironically the very one that anchored the progressivist history producing ever shorter moments and marking up parts of the globe as irremediably regressive and anterior), we must add a chapter on the temporal scales necessary to track the long-term dangers of the instant itself, the risks of a unified, world-standard time, and the hazards of small-scale forms. Second modernism critically imagines the itineraries of ecstatic intervals, "primitive" pasts, and customary aesthetic shapes—epiphanies, Magdalenian cave paintings, downscaled form—as strange sites of varying timescales and as timelines to planetary futures that vindictively, in Lily Briscoe's words, "outlast by a million years . . . the gazer" (Woolf 1981b, 20).

There is not enough space in this chapter to detail fully the ways in which modernism's interest in differently-sized clocks not only sought to disrupt modern infrastructure and reveal its failures, but also imagined participating in a counter-infrastructure, one that produces desynchronized states for the purpose of undergirding longer and different nows in different timelines.[2] And I will return to modernism's aesthetics of temporal sale later in order to emphasize the multiplicity that I think is the crucial contribution of a specifically modernist Anthropocene. For now, I point to a brief example of second modernism's scaled-up prolepsis in Virginia Woolf, whose fascination with multiple clocks includes her exploration of timescales drawn out not only by "the age of the tusk and mammoth," at one end, but also by the heat-death of the sun and the closure of "the pageant of the universe" at the other, a way of tracking the impact of the moment that shares a great deal with rise of aesthetic and critical time machines to travel in and among enormous timelines.

Woolf is often seen as a connoisseur of the short *durée* peppered with intermittent deep-past meditations, but her telescopic treatment of distant views also fares forward in a way that resembles the futural historicizing that Fredric Jameson identifies in science fiction—as the imagination of a future in which the now is transformed into "the determinate past of something yet to come" (Jameson 2005, 211). Consider the shift in Woolf's *Mrs. Dalloway* (1925), for example, from the famous motor car scene to the "ruins of time." There, in the middle of the week, in the middle of year 1923, in the heart of London's posh shopping on Bond Street, a motor car appears as a part of the novel's thematic exploration of the "changed temporal context" or post-war "timescape" symbolized by Big Ben, which like the clock (and the skywriting aeroplane) draws the attention of citizens from all walks of life "to one centre" (Woolf 1981a, 15). As Barbara Adam points out, the domination of clock time began with the synchronization of the globe to Greenwich at the International Meridian Conference in 1884, and the worldwide, wireless transmission of standardized time, first broadcast from the Eiffel Tower in 1913. This "rationalized time" drew the world and its previously disparate and distant time horizons together "at near the speed of light, displaced variable local times, and imposed one uniform, hegemonic world time for all" (Adam 1998, 107). The motor car, which is conjectured as housing the "Queen, Prince, or Prime Minister" (Woolf 1981a, 16) and sparks a common "thought of the dead; of the flag; of Empire" (Woolf 1981a, 18), is often read as adding the consideration of state power and imperial coordination to the novel's treatment of the hegemonic imposition of world time.

However, this passage also shoots forward from the "enduring symbol of the state" on Bond Street and its violently backfiring technology to a time far in the future. In this proleptically imagined scene, "London is a grass-grown path and all those hurrying along the pavement this Wednesday morning are but bones with a few wedding rings mixed up in their dust and the gold stoppings of innumerable decayed teeth" (Woolf 1981a, 16). If not quite alien geologists, Woolf's "curious antiquaries, sifting the ruins of time" are figures of modernist speculation—not just about the inevitable nothingness of death on existential and historical scales, but also about the distended timescales necessary for thinking the future effects of the present, effects of imperialist nationalism, yes, but also of what it takes to fuel and propel that level of global hegemony. What Holly Henry calls Woolf's "narrative scoping strategies," which frequently zoom out temporally to a world "when you're not there" (Woolf 1981b, 23), remind us that modernism's scalar meditations should not be confined to the paleomodernist aesthetic alone—in which Piccadilly rewinds beyond its medieval history to the site of "rhododendron forests" and the prehistoric traffic of "elephant-bodied, seal-necked, heaving, surging, slowly writhing . . . monsters; the iguanodon, the mammoth, and the mastodon; from whom . . . we descend" (Woolf 2008, 7). Rather, Woolf's temporal hyperopia also shoots forward in a way that raises clear questions the relationship between the myriad rhythms of social life, synchronized in this novel by clocks, cars, and biopolitical discourses, and the inhuman timescales on which planetary and cosmic consequences play out. That is, the various tempos of modern life, so skillfully and conspicuously treated in Woolf's work, are not brought to a halt by her various characters' reflections on the ends of things; rather, activated by the distant view, they provocatively gesture at a variety of possible timelines that "outlast by a million years . . . the gazer," as Woolf writes in *To the Lighthouse* (Woolf 1981b, 20), because they are in fact put in motion by a modernity that, much like the implications of interstellar gaps in *Night and Day*, will have turned "to cinders the whole of our short human history" (Woolf 2005, 172).

This ability to fast-forward to many different kinds of death and closure is a way of exploring the multiplicity of temporal scales and rates, and the more extreme versions of this prolepsis, which have obvious connections to science fiction, have yet to be counted among modernism's toolbox of formal interrogations, especially in their subversion of the aesthetic as a technology of the short term. Such experiments probe in explicit ways art's default periodicity—centered on moments, days, decades, generations, centuries, and of course, most radically, the career of the human itself. While moving across these scales toward the end of the human and beyond tends to lead one out of modernist studies into science fiction (SF), second modernist scope encompasses SF's alternative futurity as a modernist gesture; together they form a large part of a cultural meshwork wired to defamiliarize time itself. But going big, in both, is often not simply about the dissolution of smaller-scale temporalities into the largest, most fundamental timescale but about the relations among them.

As the scientist J. B. S. Haldane's "The Last Judgement" ([1927] 2002) showed, the thought experiment of imagining time itself from a distance, that is, estrangement not simply of commonsense measures but of earthly units based on planetary rotation, owes as much to modernist thinking as it does to

H. G. Wells's *Time Machine* (1894), from which it explicitly drew inspiration. In Haldane's scientific fiction (an essay that contains within it a fantasy that goes ten million years beyond Wells's thirty-million-year trip), a schoolteacher on Venus is instructing our descendants about the demise of the earth, caused by our exploitation of the planet—first for its fossil fuels, and then for its tidal energy. All species slowly go extinct, and the fundamental temporal unit of the day continually changes and lengthens as the Earth's rotation slows until the planet finally grinds to a halt. As the Venusian teacher points out, the biggest hazard for humanity turned out to be its temporal myopia: "it was characteristic of the dwellers on earth that they never looked more than a million years ahead. . . . The continents were remodelled, but human effort was chiefly devoted to the development of personal relationships and to art and music, that is to say, the production of objects, sounds, and patterns of events gratifying to the individual" (Haldane 2002, 295). In this comic over-statement of under-preparation, human beings had foresight that extended for a million years, which was not far enough to curb their self-destructive extraction of energy from the planet. Haldane ends his piece with a return to the expository, as if the fiction cannot fully grasp "the proper time-scale [since] . . . [o]ur private, national, and even international aims are restricted to a time measured in human life-spans" (Haldane 2002, 310–11). For Haldane, as for second modernism, the very act of getting distance on the medium that narrative is meant to organize (time) means departing from the aesthetic, as well as reconfiguring its object (experience) to include, in Beck's words, "general knowledge devoid of personal experience" (Beck 1992, 72).

Second modernism's interest in the issue of scale—the stark contrast between the human and inhuman or nonhuman—brings together its estranging distance from the everyday, the reflexive exploration of making it new in post-Holocene literature and culture, and what critics have been working to identify as the general Anthropocenic forms that have blossomed at the start of the very-long-post-45. In Annie McClanahan's and Hamilton Carroll's special issue on "Fictions of Speculation," the general aesthetic form that is "better equipped to accurately represent a world changing beneath our feet than realism itself" is "genre fiction": because realism's scale is so limited, with its "emphasis on 'psychical' interiority," *speculative* fiction is the better instrument for gauging "inhuman systems, alternative worlds, and the drama of event"—by means of its anti-mimetic interests in "what-wasn't, what-isn't, what-might-be, what-could-have-been-if" (Carroll and McClanahan 2015, 658). Moreover, our contemporary conditions "of crisis capitalism and neoliberal ideology" are best represented by this "genre whose proleptic and anticipatory temporality has long made it appear to the aesthetic correlative of speculative finance capital" (Carroll and McClanahan 2015, 658). Likewise, Andrew Hoberek, who also sees recent economic crises as dominant features of the present, believes that genres such as postapocalyptic fiction are now not only highly literary but also capable of scenarios "paradoxically more real than the ones realism can manage" (Hoberek 2015, n.p.). Genre fiction's domain is now populated by "respectable" authors making deeply political reference to contemporaneity precisely by starting beyond the end or looking far forward. By recasting the present's thrownness in far more extreme terms, such authors work "to unwind narratives of contemporary life" less from below and before than from beyond (Hoberek 2015, n.p.).

But looking forward beyond narrative scenarios often produces failures of setting and scope, a kind of general/generic badness produced by the impossibility of aligning the aesthetic's typical scale of the sensuous and intersubjective with the inhuman scale of second modernity. These provocative scalar misalignments in thinking ahead and imagining forward have come to serve as important signifying gestures, part of the arsenal of "new modes of articulation" required by the Anthropocene's immanent imperative to know and articulate "species-being within a reflexively produced era," as Kate Marshall and Tobias Boes put it (Boes and Marshall 2014, 66). Such negative, symptomatic techniques mark the difference between the everyday and the highly uncertain day after tomorrow. This speculative aesthetic mode is best when it begins to function the worst, exhibiting the disjunctive effects of stretching toward its own limits in its attempt to grapple with the scale of hyperobjects and the distances of various futures. For instance, as Eugene Thacker argues, the contemporary "ecothriller" features the disruptive entrance of the catastrophic in awkward ways as the scale of human life runs up against the intractable and halting presence of speculative exteriority—almost as if "the desire for the nonhuman," "a kind of ecological death drive" were the structuring force of the narratives' absurdities (Thacker 2012, 138–39). Whereas so many conventional human dramas treat disaster as a "narrative way-station" en route to "coping, managing, [and] surviving" (Thacker 2012, 140), eco-thrillers such as Kim Stanley Robinson's *Forty Signs of Rain* allow the tautology of a ruined nature (i.e., *it is what it is*, and can't stand for anything else) to highlight the "disconnect between the level of human drama and the level of nonhuman, planetary shifts, a rift between the world-as-human and an anonymous world-in-itself . . . evacuated of human meaning" (Thacker 2012, 140). Aesthetic form seems to rely on its malfunctions or impending crash as its primary (last) method for representing the big futures built into and built by the Anthropocenic present.

Anthropocenic representational modes call for certain kinds of formal badness, lapses that derive from the scale of the objects engaged by aesthetic structures. Although critics like Jameson have distinguished between SF's estrangement of the present and modernism's defamiliarization of time, we might think of both second modernism's and SF's scalar aesthetics as active modes of rendering the Anthropocenic futures that follow from their long modernist pasts. In this light, Danny Hillis's and Stewart Brand's Clock of the Long Now (CLN) would seem to stand as an example of general Anthropocenic form. It is full of the science-fictional and second modernist badness of going big, especially in its critical contrast with the modernity's short-term bads and small-scale clocks—but crucially it lacks modernism's corresponding interest in the disjunctiveness of scalar relations, the incoherent, unnestable temporal multiplicity revealed by scoping out. This enormous clock, currently being built directly into Mount Washington in Nevada, was conceived to make the immense and the invisible available to politics. It is meant to function as a foresight-and-responsibility machine that they hope will inspire and plug into "abiding charismatic artifacts; extreme longitudinal studies; . . . human life extension; highly durable institutions; [and] . . . widespread personal feeling for the span of history" (Brand 1999, 133).

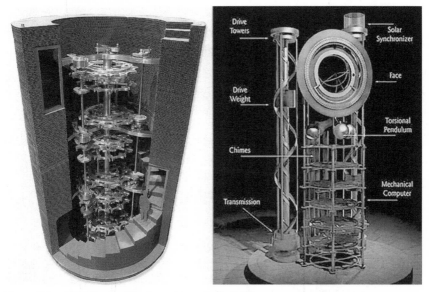

Figure 8.1. The Clock of the Long Now. Kelly 1996.

Brand, who co-founded the Long Now Foundation with Hillis in 1996, says that the clock is meant to function like the whole earth photos he famously used on the covers of his intermittent counterculture zine the *Whole Earth Catalog*. "Just as the Earth photographs gave us a sense of *the big here*," he writes, "we need things that give people a sense of *the long now*" (Brand 1999, 133). Though he prefers "rigorous and objective" future studies to mere futurism, Brand nevertheless cites the mathematician Freeman Dyson on the fact that "economic forecasting makes predictions by extrapolating curves of growth from the past into the future. SF makes a wild guess. . . . For the future beyond 10 years ahead, SF is a more useful guide than forecasting" (Brand 1999, 114). However, compared to both second modernist and SF scales, the clock's imaginative range is unambitious—it is meant to keep time for a mere ten thousand years.

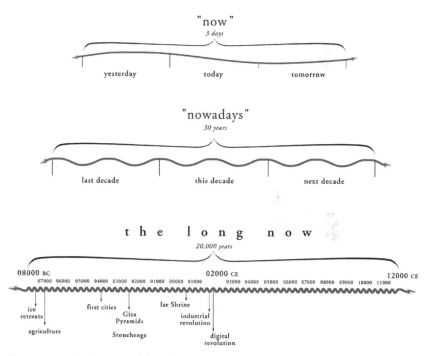

Figure 8.2. The duration of the Clock of the Long Now. Brand 1999.

The experience that the CLN is supposed to inspire is the sublime effect of continuity that we will have survived for another 10,000 years. The best description of the clock and its SF ambition of triumphant survivalism is actually found in Brand's huge quotation from the Long Now Foundation's 501(c)3 IRS form for nonprofit tax exemption (an irony compounded by the fact that the prototype model is being built by Jeff Bezos, founder of Amazon, on his property in Van Horn, Texas). Written by the executive director Alexander Rose, this description of the CLN is said to have cut through

bureaucratic delays in its successful appeal to the generic pronoun "you"—
the IRS reviewer and contemporary visitor, but also, in a narrative twist, the
surviving species millennia from now. To visit the clock, "you" exit a vehicle
"at the base of a mountain somewhere in the high desert of the Southwest"
(qtd. in Brand 1999, 46):

> Looking up, you see a flight of shallow steps, each carved from a layer of rock
> representing approximately 10,000 years of geologic time. After climbing one
> hundred of these steps, or one million years into the future . . . [y]ou arrive at a
> flat knoll where you see a cave ahead. (qtd. in Brand 1999, 46)

After this high-speed pedestrian time-travel, you/the visitor enters the cave
and its progressive decelerations, where you see "a giant pendulum swinging
back and forth": "you realize that you are actually within the clock mechanism itself and you are aware of the pendulum beating out its 10-sec period"
(qtd. in Brand 1999, 46).

It is clear that the aesthetic function to which Brand and Hillis are attracted
is not scalar disjunction but, like CRED, the successful sensuous apprehension in small-scale narrative features of a smooth expansion into something
incrementally bigger and slower. The IRS description continues: after taking
a spiral staircase, the visitor ascends into the "first layer of the clock mechanics," where "you see the fastest of the calculation devices, which ticks once
per day" (qtd. in Brand 1999, 47). "As you go up flight after flight, you see
each progressive mechanism with its relatively slower tick, the last being
the precession of the equinoxes, a 25,784-year cycle" (qtd. in Brand 1999,
47). At the top of the stairs, you enter "a huge room several stories tall," in
which a shaft to the surface directs light at solar noon to a synchronizing
mechanism triggered by the light beam's heat. It is in this final control room
that the IRS form delivers the estranging "novum" of science fiction: on the
great dial "reads the year 11,567" (qtd. in Brand 1999, 47). From this future
point of survival, the government bureaucrat was able to imagine staring at
the "diagram of the current night sky" on the sphere in the center of the dial,
from which "you are able to work backward . . . to your newer and more familiar time scale. But you are struck that the people of this ancient time had
the foresight to think this far into their future and create this place" (qtd. in
Brand 1999, 47).

Perhaps to highlight the contrast between this project of the Long Now
Foundation and Hillis's past work in supercomputing, which he sold to
entities such as AMEX to crunch massive amounts of data, Brand touts the
CLN as the "world's slowest computer" and emphasizes the capacity of its
narrative mechanics and appeal as an attraction to inspire us to take the far
future "personally" (Brand 1999, 49). In Brand's account, the machine is

constructed out of with Bronze Age materials, powered by human winding (and the temperature differential between day and night), and run on a "mechanical digital logic" to calculate different period movements. Its millennial scale of four hundred generations remains unapologetically human (Brand 1999, 49). While the CLN seeks to desynchronize from a present diminished by short market horizons, election cycles, attention spans, it is also meant to prompt the question, "Are we being good ancestors?" (qtd. in Kelly 1996, n.p.). It hopes to generate the conditions for the future self-congratulatory answer, "Yes we were." The 10,000-Year Library attached to it will even have a "Time Mail" service by which we can lob slow-mo messages across the ages to our descendants. Although Brand says that we need to encourage the "ability to live both in the present and in a handful of imagined but uncertain futures [which] is the basic skill of foresight, planning, and responsibility" (Brand 1999, 100), it's worth remembering that this clock adjusts constantly to solar noon. The clock is an attraction of the most resolutely *narrative* nature, smoothing over its most salient, intractable seams—the economic, political, and social timescales that overlap but refuse to nest fully within what Srinivas Aravamudan calls catachronism—the unification of time in which the entirety of the line until now can be "re-characterize[d] . . . in terms of a future proclaimed as determinate" (Aravamudan 2013, 8). The idea for the CLN came to Hillis while he was R&D vice president at Walt Disney Imagineering. When he described his dream of an enormous clock with many different chambers, his colleagues remarked on its resemblance to a Disneyland ride (indeed Disney owns "the right to make a replica of the finished clock") (Bronson 1998, n.p.). According to Brand, Hillis replied that "Time *is* a ride . . . and you are on it" (Brand 1999, 69).

There are elements of this grand ride—the story that ends with the surprise that ten thousand years earlier humans were smart enough to have sufficiently enlarge their temporal scope to have saved the visitor—that of course attest to what Fred Turner identifies as the "New Communalism" in Brand's countercultural activities of the late 1960s. Brand's *Whole Earth Catalog*, founded in 1968, was created for an audience withdrawing from bankrupt bureaucracies and heading "back to the land." Far from retreating to a romantic past, argues Turner, this youthful audience "turned away from political action and toward technology and the transformation of consciousness as the primary sources of social change" (Turner 2006, 4). For Turner, Brand's counterculturalism was responsible for the "digital utopianism" of later cyberculture, because to drop out of mainstream culture and institutions was also to turn on and tune in technologically, to learn to use new tools "ranging from axes and hoes to amplifiers, strobe lights, slide projectors, and LSD—to bring people together and allow them to experience their common humanity" (Turner 2006, 4).

There is no doubt that the CLN is meant to be a tool for surviving and a technical marvel for imagining survival. As Thomas Allen has pointed out, the CLN is, like a number of monumental clocks built in the nineteenth century, an aesthetic and temporal scaling-up that shifted focus from liberal subjectivity in largely domestic spaces to large populations and their collective destinies. As Allen writes, such clocks were crucial to "grand temporal visions inspired by problems of population, by the need for narrative structures to manage the movement of people as populations across historical time" (Allen 2015, par. 4). I would add to Allen's account that the CLN's twin fantasies of managing the human species across geologically-significant durations and of outlasting anthropogenic catastrophe are coupled with a blindness to scalar disjunction and a strong desire, to the extent that taxes are the price of civilization, for a withdrawal from the infrastructure of the very public good necessary for survival.

It is the very ability of narrative and technological structures to generate a pleasing trip to sublimity that makes CLN inadequate as a second-modernist device. What Allen eloquently describes as "the eros of unbecoming" (Allen 2015, par. 36) our desire for the shift in scale from individual lifetimes and agency to a fantasy of "our own dissolution within time" and in massive populations—leads smoothly in Brand's and Hillis's theme-park clock into the pleasures (rather than the defamiliarizing vertigo) of what Dana Luciano calls "affective geology" (qtd. in Rodeau 2015, par. 4) and what David Nye calls the "technological sublime" (Nye 1994, 60). The former refers to the transformation of the "speculative work of geology into a form of aesthetic and sensory experience" (qtd. in Rodeau 2015, par. 4); the latter, to "the awe induced by seeing an immense or dynamic technological object . . . [which becomes] a celebration of the power of human reason . . . [and which] granted special privilege to engineers and inventors" (qtd. in Allen 2015, par. 30). The tracks of this ride—geeky billionaire donations, Disney machinists carving out tunnels in mountains, tax exemption—suggest that the universal problem of the survival of the species can be scoped out to and solved without engaging the other histories that refuse to nest comfortably in it—most glaringly, in this case, that of capitalism.

The remedy for the ills of the Anthropocene's temporal scale might not be the big-history approach in which one simply dissolves smaller histories into the ultimate timescale of the planet, but rather the awareness of more scales and their relations. Without an awareness of the multiplicity of scales that resist being nested in one another, the interest in going big is simply a smooth, seamless extension of what Noah Heringman calls "evolutionary nostalgia," the longing for a "a deep human past so legible that it displaces more transient cultural inscriptions": instead acknowledging the radical discontinuities that mark the rock record of the past, "civilization has presented itself as the culmination or completion of geological and anthropological time . . . encoded in the very name of the Anthropocene" and therefore written too smoothly into a catachronic future record featuring our survival (Heringman 2015, 74–75, 57). What modernism's multiple clocks and timescales reminds us is that the Anthropocene cannot be about unified temporal containment from the top but about the complex interactions among temporal scales that threaten many of the scales, big and small. Articulating the Anthropocene is about registering scalar incompatibility—not in order to remain mired in a single timescape and timeline, but to negotiate productively both practical challenges and possibilities, for instance, in articulating the social to the ecological, but also to track the reverberations and boomerangs within any particular timeframe.

I want to conclude with a brief examination of modernist time lapse in order to suggest that modernism not only looked to the far future in surprising ways, but that the technique of deep prolepsis and time lapse served to reveal the heterochronic multiplicity of scalar zoom. While there are numerous texts in the modernist canon that feature multiple clocks and varying scales—think not only of Woolf's oeuvre but also of Faulkner's jeweller shop and Joyce's Dublin, for instance—I want to focus on H. G. Wells's *The Time Machine* as featuring the first second-modernist time lapse. The time machine is a trope that allows the text to speculate on the social outcomes of economic organization, imperial adventure, and technological developments eight hundred thousand years into the future, and on the yet-more-scaled-up consequences thirty million years from 1894, under an expiring sun. Wells describes his time traveler's speed-up through time as a "melting and flowing"—from one second per second to "over a year a minute," and later, in "great strides of a thousand years or more"—in obviously cinematic terms (Wells 2001, 76, 78, 147). As the machine moves through "the palpitations of night and day," the traveler notes "the slowest snail that ever crawled dashed by too fast for me" (Wells 2001, 77). In George Pal's 1960 film version, the flicker of moving rapidly across time is represented in the chronophotographic cells of the traveler's solarium windows, followed by the time-lapse shots of a snail, the bloom and wilt of flowers, the shift of fashions on a mannequin in a shop window, and of course hands spinning around the dial of one of scientist's many clocks. This mode of making massive change over time visible is central to ecological representations, as for instance in the 2012 documentary *Chasing Ice* James Balog's record of melting arctic glaciers.

Time lapse makes change over time spectacular by slowing down frame capture relative to the number of projected frames per second. While time lapse might seem to rely on the reduction of all processes down to one smoothly scannable timeline, and thereby the reassertion big history as singular, it is in fact, like the trope of time machine itself, a relativity technique in which the relations among various rates is a fundamental condition for perception itself. There are obvious problems with time lapse as a technique and with speculative aesthetics in general. In resizing disasters "slow moving and long in the making" to spectacle, the extreme acceleration and ellipses can seem to leave out everything that matters: if the cuts are too far apart, as Wells's time traveler realizes is the case with his Victorian present and 802,701, then epistemologically there can be "no convenient cicerone in the pattern of the Utopian books" (Wells 2001, 111). As critiques of speculative perspectives point out, the function of scalar thinking might in fact be to unperceive the social. As Robin Mackay, Luke Pendrell, and James Trafford sketch the caricature, speculative aesthetics desires to free art from politics and language, and reaches out to science in order to bypass its culpable situatedness. Speculative realist thinkers evade the correlationist bubble, inspiring flights from interpretation and culture by "stressing the presence of objects speaking for themselves," sometimes in what amounts to "a cosmic reinvigoration of the readymade" (Mackay et al., 2014, 2).

Stephen Sawyer says that the Braudel's longue durée, popular again because of the breakdown of the spatial scale of the nation as an organizing principle, was attractive in its promise to unite the social sciences under history's disciplinary ability to "combine multiple temporalities into one narrative" (Sawyer 2015, par. 15). However, what if the goal is not to generate a unified narrative but a modernist one? While big history usually appears as a tent for a unified time, it also holds the ability to call attention to temporal differences, varying rates of change, and the relation among a plurality of timescales. Perhaps the most useful lesson of speculative aesthetics is not the destruction of relationality and context; rather, as Jane Bennett and Katherine Hayles have suggested separately, it is that various levels of zoom generate a multiplicity of contexts; technologies "from optical microscopes to particle accelerators, radiocarbon dating to seismic detectors," to use Hayles's examples, expand the range of the aesthetic and inquiry (Bennett 2012; Hayles 2014, 176). By thinking reflexively of specific scales and local horizons in relation to other scales and horizons, and of objects' speaking for themselves within them, we generate, as Hayles says, an "understanding of the world as comprised of a multitude of world views, including those of other biological organisms, human-made artefacts, and inanimate objects" (Hayles 2014, 176). These "views" are agents in their own right, as many contemporary thinkers have been arguing; they are also different scales of time necessary for seeing rates of change themselves disjunctively assembled.

NOTES

1. I take this joke from Mark McGurl: "Like literature as conceived by Ezra Pound, the information [marking the storage of nuclear waste] . . . will be 'news that STAYS news'" (McGurl 2010, 330).

2. For more on modernist heterochrony, see Tung 2015.

WORKS CITED

Adam, Barbara. 1998. *Timescapes of Modernity: The Environment and Invisible Hazards*. London: Routledge, 1998.

Allen, Thomas. 2015. "Toward Endless Life: Population, Machinery, and Monumental Time." *Transatlantica: Revue D'études Américaines* 1. Accessed August 12, 2020. https://journals.openedition.org/transatlantica/7379.

Aravamudan, Srinivas. 2013. "The Catachronism of Climate Change." *Diacritics* 41 (3): 6–30.

Beck, Ulrich. 1992. *Risk Society: Towards a New Modernity*. Translated by Mark Ritter. London: Sage.

Bennett, Jane. 2012. "Systems and Things: A Response to Graham Harman and Timothy Morton." *New Literary History* 43 (2): 225–33

Boes, Tobias, and Kate Marshall. 2014. "Writing the Anthropocene: An Introduction." *Minnesota Review* 83 (1): 60–72.

Brand, Stewart. 1996. "About Long Now." Accessed 22 March 2016. http://longnow.org/about.

———. 1999. *The Clock of the Long Now: Time and Responsibility*. New York: Basic Books.

Bronson, Po. 1998. "The Long Now." *Wired*. May 1, 1998. Accessed August 12, 2020. https://www.wired.com/1998/05/hillis-2/.

Carroll, Hamilton, and Annie McClanahan. 2015. "Fictions of Speculation: Introduction." *Journal of American Studies* 49 (4): 655–61.

Chivers, Tom. 2014. "The Anthropocene Age: What World Will Humans Leave Behind?" *The Telegraph*. October 17, 2014. Accessed August 12, 2020. https://www.telegraph.co.uk/news/science/11167165/Scientists-wonder-what-in-the-world-will-we-leave-behind.html.

Crutzen, Paul J., and Eugene F. Stoermer. 2000. "The 'Anthropocene.'" *Global Change Newsletter: The International Geosphere–Biosphere Programme Study of Global Change* 41: 17–18.

Galison, Peter. 2003. *Einstein's Clocks, Poincaré's Maps: Empires of Time*. New York and London: W.W. Norton and Company.

Haldane, J. B. S. (1927) 2002. "The Last Judgment." In *Possible Worlds*. New Brunswick: Transaction Publishers.

Hayles, N. Katherine. 2014. "Speculative Aesthetics and Object-Oriented Inquiry (OOI)." In *Specculations V: Aesthetics in the 21st Century*. Edited by Ridvan Askin et al., 158–79. Brooklyn, NY: Punctum.

Heringman, Noah. 2015. "Deep Time at the Dawn of the Anthropocene." *Representa-tions* 129 (1): 56–85.

Hoberek, Andrew. 2015. "The Post-Apocalyptic Present." *Public Books.* June 15, 2015. Accessed August 10, 2020. https://www.publicbooks.org/the-post-apocalyptic -present/.

Jaffe, Aaron. 2014. *The Way Things Go: An Essay on the Matter of Second Modern-ism.* Minneapolis: University of Minnesota Press.

Jameson, Fredric. 2005. *Archaeologies of the Future: The Desire Called Utopia and Other Science Fictions.* London: Verso.

Kelly, Kevin. 1996. "The 10,000 Year Clock." Accessed August 13, 2020. http://longnow.org/clock.

Mackay, Robin, Luke Pendrell, and James Trafford. 2014. *Speculative Aesthetics.* Falmouth: Urbanomic.

Mackenzie, Adrian. 2002. *Transductions: Bodies and Machines at Speed.* London and New York: Continuum.

McGurl, Mark. 2010. "Ordinary Doom: Literary Studies in the Waste Land of the Present." *New Literary History* 41 (2): 329–49.

Nixon, Rob. 2011. *Slow Violence and the Environmentalism of the Poor.* Cambridge: Harvard University Press.

Nye, David. 1994. *The American Technological Sublime.* Cambridge, MA: MIT Press.

Rodeau, Cècile. 2015. "How the Earth Feels: A Conversation with Dana Luciano." *Transatlantica: Revue D'études Américaines* 1. Accessed August 12, 2020. https://journals.openedition.org/transatlantica/13007.

Sawyer, Stephen W. 2015. "Time After Time: Narratives of the Longue Durée in the Anthropocene." *Transatlantica: Revue D'études Américaines* 1. Accessed August 12, 2020. https://journals.openedition.org/transatlantica/7344.

Shome, Debika, and Sabine Marx. 2009. *The Psychology of Climate Change Com-munication: A Guide for Scientists, Journalists, Educators, Political Aides, and the Interested Public.* New York: Center for Research on Environmental Decisions.

Steffen, Will, et al. 2015. "The Trajectory of the Anthropocene: The Great Accelera-tion." *The Anthropocene Review* 2 (1): 1–18.

Thacker, Eugene. 2012. "Notes on Extinction and Existence." *Configurations* 20 (1): 137–48.

Tung, Charles. M. 2015. "Modernism, Time Machines, and the Defamiliarization of Time." *Configurations* 23 (1): 93–121.

Turner, Fred. 2006. *From Counterculture to Cyberculture: Stewart Brand, the Whole Earth Network, and the Rise of Digital Utopianism.* Chicago: University of Chi-cago Press.

Waters, Colin N., et al. 2016. "The Anthropocene Is Functionally and Stratigraphi-cally Distinct from the Holocene." *Science* 351 (6269): 1–10.

Wells, H. G. 2001. *The Time Machine: An Invention.* Edited by Nicholas Ruddick. Peterborough: Broadview Press.

Woolf, Virginia. 1981a. *Mrs. Dalloway.* New York: Harvest.

———. 1981b. *To the Lighthouse.* New York: Harvest.

———. 2005. *Night and Day.* New York: Barnes and Noble.

———. 2008. *Between the Acts.* New York: Houghton Mifflin.

Part III

WRITING MATERIALS

Chapter Nine

Comics

Worldmaking in the Anthropocene

Glenn Willmott

The idea of the Anthropocene supposes human activity to have irrevocably conditioned the destinies of our planetary environment. The global world, human and nonhuman, while never simply appropriated to our aims and often wayward to them, is nevertheless everywhere anthropotropic, inescapably turned to human history and exposed to human activity. Small wonder, then, that an art of global fabrication or worldmaking—one that openly pursues what Donna Haraway calls "relentless artefactualism" (Haraway 2004, 63)—is to be found in comics.

Comics emerges as a flourishing cultural institution precisely together with the hegemony of modern industrial and consumer society. At its most vibrant and compelling, comics explicitly reflects this birthright as a mode of anthropotropic but post-humanist storytelling founded on thoroughly plastic, stylized, fabricated worlds and their struggling, strangely vulnerable denizens. I will argue that in doing so, comics texts always express an *ecological unconscious*, inevitably mixing ecological fact, fantasy, and fear, and not infrequently, they offer a deliberately environmentalist vision. The following pages will therefore concern themselves with the emergence of comics as a unique worldmaking art of the modernist Anthropocene. I will begin with a theoretical and formal account of worldmaking in comics and its ecological implications. Upon this foundation, I will then explore how the ecological worldmaking of key early comics artists in different genres, Winsor McCay, George Herriman, and Tarpé Mills, reveal provocative, unconventional visions of ecological life.

THE ECOLOGIES OF COMICS: THEORY AND FORM

Worldmaking can refer to at least two different activities. One results from the compositional activity of the artist and refers to form and content belonging to a text, which in keeping with the most common usage I will call *worldbuilding*. The other stems from the cognitive activity of the reader and refers to the inference of an imagined storyworld from the data and forms provided by a text, which I will here call *worldreading*. Worldbuilders need world-readers, so I will reserve the term *worldmaking* to refer to the combined process as it variously plays out for authors, texts, and audiences. Comics have long been associated with worldmaking, the cocreation by artist and reader of holistic worlds larger than their constitutive fragments. This is not only due to the fantasy and science fiction heritage of worldbuilding in comics, but also to the long recognized, formal specificity of its worldreading. There is what we see, what we are given: the sequence of fictional spaces and events represented in actual space graphically, a musical stuttering of visual mimesis and iconology. But that is not enough. To this we add, continuously while reading, a fictional connective tissue that is our own making. We fill the existential gaps between objects, between panels and between pages, and tie these all up on the fly, as best we can.[1] Here we see a heroine kiss her lover, next we see her alone with a blush, so we likely imagine her lover has just stepped aside. But if her lover is a ghost or other fantasy being, we might as readily assume the lover has vanished back into the spirit plane, reverted into a frog, or rearranged its quantum self in some invisible way; or perhaps the first event was a dream or parallel world glimpsed through the reality of the second event. How we cross the gutters and gaps between panels will depend on the particular story and our understanding of the rules of its background storyworld—its imagined ecology of creatures and physical history. Comics generate not only mimetic stories we see, but also inferential worlds we don't. The latter are *unrepresentable*. We must inductively develop from panel to panel and even story to story an understanding of how these fictive worlds work, what is possible in them and what is not, and why. This world logic must involve both natural and historical logics, thus ecology.

  The inference of an imagined storyworld is hardly limited to comics, and it has been studied as a dimension of all storytelling by worldbuilding and narrative theorists. In her foundational 1985 work, *Narratology*, Mieke Bal discusses the dialectic of spatial description and inference in written stories, as well as the framing of represented spaces as unified locations, and their focalization (Bal 1985, 43, 94–99); but in this work she pursues the significance of thematized or symbolic locations rather than of worldbuilding. More recent scholarship has developed a transmedial narrative theory of the *story-*

world, which David Herman defines as the "ecologically" imagined world in which story events take place and make sense—which we will see has specific implications for comics (Herman 2002, 13–14).[2] Such ecologies, in an expanded naturalcultural sense, may involve a great range of worldbuilding elements—as media theorist Mark Wolf catalogues them, all the way from orders of space and time, to those of genealogy and social structure, organic nature and physics, culture, language, mythology, and philosophy (Wolf 2012, 154–55). All narratives imply worldmaking and storyworlds as such, and profoundly affect what we expect and accept as meaningful and possible in a story, including all its shadowy, non-narrated, alternative vectors of development. But worldmaking is usually only noticed, and named by readers as such, when it stands out from the story. This happens, according to Wolf, when texts are designed so that efficient narrative economy, which is the minimal description necessary to advance the plot, is arrested or slowed down by "data, exposition, and digressions that provide information about a world" that is in striking *excess* of narrative (Wolf 2012, 29–30). This notion of worldbuilding as an excessive and even somewhat incommensurate supplement to plot is saliently developed by narratologist Pirjo Lyytikäinen, who shows how literary narrative, in the hands of literary modernists drawn to awarenesses and experiences not captured by conventional employment, abandons storyworlds configured by plot for storyworlds configured by varieties of worldbuilding (Lyytikäinen 2012, 68–69).

The same insistent *exceeding* of plot data by worldbuilding data is manifest in literary modernism's historical sibling, the popular comics, where spatial form and causal plot are normally observable in (but not restricted to) its parallel reading structures of image and word. Pictorial narratives are intrinsically fragmented or abstracted forms of legibility, and enlist an especially demanding gap-filling activity in worldreading (Ranta 2014, 12). In addition to this, in comics the reader follows narration and dialogue anchored in the linear (for example, left to right, up to down) progression of its written text and its iterated character images, thus moving the plot forward, while he or she simultaneously scans all the descriptive and expressive elements in the space of each panel and page. One *cannot not* see ahead or behind any given narrative moment, in the composition of a panel, strip, or page. Comics are designed with this synoptic perception in mind. Scanning the page opens the comics narrative to a wandering eye that may move backward, forward, or linger in moments free of linear plot order. Thus, worldmaking in comics undoes any strong distinction between the reading of plot foreground versus the reading of contextual background, or figure versus ground, in their comprehension.

The pioneer of comics formalism, Scott McCloud, views this spatial form of comics worldreading as a process that is always in tension with our (especially Western) training in linear progression (McCloud 1994, 104–5); and when comics devote themselves to worldbuilding that exceeds story data, he shows how comics use spatial poetics to disrupt this training and produce a "licence to wander" within panels and across the page (McCloud 2006, 165). How do comics do this, precisely? Here, Herman's schema for transmedial narration of storyworlds (Herman 2013, 108–12) offers a general plan adaptable to comics.

The simplest worldreading process in Herman's schema involves an act of narration (N) that uses one semiotic mode (SM) to refer to a particular fictional world (or "reference world," RW) that in turn comprises the text's whole storyworld (SW). This process may be diagrammed:

$$N \rightarrow SM \rightarrow RW = SW$$

In literature, perhaps a novel like *Middlemarch*, best approaches this simplicity of worldmaking process, however masterfully complex in spatial and plot detail. If there are more than one fictional world that a reader must switch between—for example, with a framed narrative such as *Heart of Darkness* or *Wuthering Heights*, or with multiple ontologies as in the historical worlds of *The Time Machine*, the virtual versus material worlds of *Neuromancer*, or the mental versus actual worlds of *Kiss of the Spider Woman*—then there will be more than one reference world comprised by the storyworld. If there is more than one semiotic mode—for example in the theatrical staging and the verbal language of a Shakespeare play—then multiple modes of communication will make up a text that may each refer to more than one reference world (as in *Hamlet*'s play within a play), all contributing to the production of a manifold storyworld. Such a multimodal process may be diagrammed:

$$N \rightarrow SM1, SM2, \ldots \rightarrow RW1, RW2, \ldots \rightarrow SW$$

For comics, it seems there will always be a double track of semiotic modes corresponding to word and image, along with any number of reference worlds making up a storyworld. But this is not precisely right: McCloud reminds us that in comics, words are always also graphic icons (McCloud 1994, 27) with effects in the pictorial semiotic mode. Their visual appearance is always expressive or connotative in some way and may be read, by artistic design, both as pictures and as words. And vice versa: because graphic figures that iterate from panel to panel are icons or signifiers to be decoded into signifieds, what McCloud calls "ideas" of characters and objects, usually enchained to and constituted in part by a sequential grammar of language reading (for example, from left to right and up to down), pictures are, in this sense, conversely read as words.[3]

When we worldread comics, then, we infer a whole storyworld by gradually constructing a text's reference worlds through verbal reading and visual scanning of both words and pictures. These fictional worlds may be realist—directly mimetic of what worldbuilding theorists call the Primary World, the actual historical world of the reader; they may belong to other genres of fiction (ghost stories, science fiction, or funny animals); or they may defy broad generic classification, and play by their own world-logic rules (for example, *Sandman*). Such distinctions are important because the filling in the gaps process of worldreading, of imagining storyworlds from narrative data, depends on defaults and suppositions. Given a narrative or world-logic gap that needs to be closed, a reader will use either Primary World or generic fictional world expectations as default sutures. If Batman drives out of the bat cave and arrives at the docks, we assume he has driven through the streets of Gotham, as a car in our Primary World would do. If a zombie is shot down but later appears to attack our hero, we assume its body is indifferent to bullets, as it normally is in the genre. The logic of worldbuilding genres must also be viewed from the broader perspective of world types categorized by narratologist Brian Richardson, as adhering to types of cosmic order: naturalistic, supernatural, chance/absurdist, or metafictional (Richardson 2012, 107). In constructing imaginary ecologies, a storyworld must rely on the reader's Primary World experience as well as these kinds of generic defaults for ecological conditions and relations. But the reader also fills gaps without defaults, using deductions or suppositions made possible by the specific worldbuilding narrative itself. If Superman jumps out an office window and is then seen tackling a criminal on the street, we assume that he flew using his unique alien powers, not that he fell with gravity. In imagining the storyworld that supports a comics story, we depend on knowledge from our Primary World, from genre experience, and from our training by the particular narrative we are reading, to go beyond what we see.

I wish now to build on this summary of narrative and worldmaking theory to propose ways in which worldmaking is specific to comics and implies ecological representation:

1. Comics synthesizes a linear reading practice and a nonlinear or synoptic viewing practice in the production of its storyworlds. Thus the wandering or arrested comics reader is always caught up in the direct apprehension, distinct from plot, of a storyworld *ecology*—a world-logic comprising

space, time, nature, and genealogy—which makes plot and its alternatives, hence ethical meaning, possible.

2. Comics storyworlds are always marked by *explicit worldmaking*, because their rendering always depends on graphic manifestations or disclosures of space and perceivability that *exceed* narrative economy. You cannot avoid actually seeing that bit of a story's world space that is depicted in a given panel *as one that is manifestly cut off* or fragmented from an implied larger space it cannot show, whether by a framing line or by a more vague but no less abrupt bleeding of unmarked space. In comics, the mimesis of space makes full display of its boundaries, inadequacy, its framing, and its occultations.[4] Far from being frustrating, this imposition on the reader of an uninterrupted, nonlinear, manifest and practical dialectic between explicit fragment and inaccessible totality is seductive, evoking active immersion. This dialectic in comics is also a common feature of modernism in literature and across the arts, and along with innovations in character plasticity, it grounds their experimental affinities.

3. The imposition of worldmaking upon the creator and reader of comics suggests the inescapability of some kind of ecological imagination, and indeed of an *ecological unconscious*, that cannot help but express, whether realistically or fantastically, the desires and fears evoked by the Anthropocene.

4. A storyworld may be a unified or fragmented space, its framing orders intelligible or left uncertain. The tendency of worldmaking to unity and stability I call *global*, for its connotations of wholeness and closure. But worldmaking that tends to heterogeneity and indeterminacy I call *planetary*, a more relational term resistant to holism or closure, with etymological roots in "wandering." In her ecocritical discussion of the poetics of global representation, of scales and complexity beyond ready comprehension, Ursula Heise suggests that *allegory*, or holistic metaphor, is a strategy for representing the global as such; while *collage*, or parataxis, is one of the strategies for representing the planetary welter of autonomous lives, agencies, and dynamics that escape global coherence (Heise 2008, 64). These concepts find correlation in comics poetics.

Set against the backdrop of the above general principles, the poetics of worldbuilding in comics specifically includes:

1. The use of graphic *style* to express continuity or discontinuity among objects and spaces, degrees of play in material mutability, and ontological unity or variety. Style is the most powerful allegory for the global storyworld—as in the clarity, consistency, and unity of a Disney strip.

2. *Perspective* as a structure of relations among objects, senses, and focalization, including relative scale, distance, horizon, and ground (as orientations and limits for focalization). McCloud usefully demonstrates different techniques of perspective, which he defines broadly as "any attempt to represent a 3D world on a 2D surface": conventional illusionistic vanishing point perspective, flattening non-vanishing point perspectives, diagrams or abstract perspectives, biomorphic landscape perspectives, and anamorphic or warped perspectives (McCloud 2006, 171). Storyworlds based on either biomorphic or diagram perspectives, for example, will express ecologies that are respectively more fluid and indeterminate (as in Jim Woodring's Unifactor) or more atomized and discretely organized (as in Chris Ware's worlds). Herman's discussion of figure-ground relationships (Herman 2002, 274–77) converges with McCloud's notion of perspective in comics. Perspective that plays with what counts as foreground and background in composition can be a powerful ecopoetic strategy, as in Alan Moore's *Swamp Thing*, whose art frequently flip flops the reader's attention between characters, their built world, and the vaster natural world in which both are embedded.

3. *Iterability* of signs, in modular forms or multimodal rhymes, to represent continuities and linkages—whether spatial, as with braided motifs of green space or cellular form, or temporal, as with characters from panel to panel (on *braiding* forms in a nonlinear structure across composition, see Groensteen 2007, 146).

4. World *genres* and cosmic types: a didactic ecopoetics might insist upon a naturalistic world of meaningful creature agencies and projects, rather than an absurdist world of chance (which risks nihilism) or a magical world (which risks anthropomorphic romance, as in the villainization of the vegetable in *Invasion of the Body Snatchers*, or in the control of natural elements in Pokémon). But a chance world might usefully expose limits to human knowledge and power, while a magical world might illuminate agencies and power beyond those limits.

5. Rules of object emergence and *transformation*, including genealogy and mortality. Are there limits to what kind of things can exist, how they come to be or disappear, and how they are bound or not to others? In the supernatural world of *Archie*, nobody ages and the work that reproduces Riverdale is ephemeral or nonexistent. Its abundance is ceaselessly renewed, an abundance which is normally naturalistic but ready to generate anything a story might need; a fantasy ecology of life free of any ecological restrictions except to remain in Riverdale (see further Beaty 2015, 29–31).

6. The use of facial conventions, focalization, and other techniques to mark character or *agency* in objects. The storyworlds of comics might mark

such agency in nonhuman elements, or it might ignore them. Often we are immersed in an environment without any humans, only humanoid animals or other objects, which even in Disney comics may invite us to rethink how we identify Primary World *others* and how ethically we relate to them.[5]

7. *Deictic shifts*, that is, the reader's shifts into and within a storyworld, between different reference worlds. In the July 1968 issue of *Archie*, one story is set in prehistoric times. All the main characters are in cliché cave garb and undertake the usual hijinks in a story about flower power; while Riverdale has regressed to a tropical forest and rocky waste. This jarring and exotic deictic shift to a fictional prehistory highlights, by the very sameness of its world logic to that of modern Riverdale, the abstraction and solipsism of *Archie*'s dream ecology—here calculated, however, to render possible an anti-war message too explicitly political for a Riverdale setting contemporary with the war in Vietnam.

It is now time to put together some of these forms and practices of comics worldmaking to see how diverse imagined ecologies grow out of the manufactured landscapes of the Anthropocene. I will look at examples from 1910, 1920, and 1942 respectively, of ecological worldmaking in McCay's fantasy *Little Nemo in Slumberland*, Herriman's metafictional *Krazy Kat*, and Mills's realist adventure, *Miss Fury*. I will then offer some concluding remarks regarding modernist comics and ecological representation.

ECOLOGICAL COMICS: MODERNIST VISIONS

Winsor McCay was a renowned caricaturist, comics artist, pioneer film animator, and stage performer in early twentieth-century America. *Little Nemo in Slumberland* was one of his most popular achievements, a lavishly drawn strip that ran in the *New York Herald* and was syndicated by Hearst in the decade before the First World War. In the strip, the boy Nemo escapes his dull, regulated world (RW1) every night in dream wanderings in Slumberland (RW2), where he is often accompanied by the Princess of Slumberland, a vaudevillian trickster named Flip, and a burlesque primitive named Impy. The most general world-logic of the strip is that Slumberland's gorgeous, unconventional, creative realms offer alluring, wandering escapes from the monochrome routines of waking life, but they are also subject to internal chaos and volatility which waken the dreamer, always returning him to his boringly programmatic reality. In a sequence of Sunday pages from 1910, Nemo dreams of a journey with Flip and Impy to Mars (RW3). They discover the moon to be composed of giant men on one side and enveloped in giant birds on the other. Their engine is broken, and they fear violence from the giants, but they lasso a bird that draws their ship away toward Mars. The bird is released to return home as they approach the planet. The appearance of Mars is familiar at a distance, but it turns out to be a completely built environment whose "canals" are actually giant passageways between buildings. This fanciful beginning to the story exemplifies the logic of Slumberland (RW2) as a whole: depending on no physical or natural properties of reality as we know it, yet rearranging and rescaling the elements of that reality to the ends of wonder and delight; embedding these elements in an Escheresque architectural complexity of repeating figural outlines and spatial frames made superflat with striking color. Slumberland is not Darwinian. Its beings exist in order to be themselves and to protect their mysterious autonomy, without predation, competition, or struggle. Each species often seems absurd or empty of purpose in itself, but sensational and sometimes knowledge-altering in juxtaposition with others. It is a wandering, planetary ecology crowded with iterative simulacra yet divided by extravagant differences, life pursuing life as dull society or as exotic palimpsest, the latter only accessible in the ungrounded spatial mobility of dream. It is a powerful wish-fulfillment in which the anthropocratic strictures of a mimetic Primary World (naturalistic RW1) dissolve, along with the human traces and consequences of Anthropocenic nature, into the primordial, heterocratically planetary ecology of a fantastic Secondary World (absurd and magical RW2). For a moment, in every strip, the reader may escape not only what the human has made, but what the human has become. The represented Primary World is a dystopian monoculture in which literally nothing new ever emerges, while the genealogy of Slumberland offers an idealized biodiversity, an aesthetic refuge for all that has been, and will be, indifferently lost. This is *Nemo*'s ecological unconscious.

Those of McCay's episodes set in Slumberland's Mars, however, also offer a manifestly ecological worldmaking in its allegory of the global. The planet is unified by one humanoid species, one natural geography, one economy, and one ruler; it comprises a single, continuous city that extends so far above the planet's geological surface that the city's lower reaches are commercially lit or fogged chasms that extend, observed from Nemo's perspective, beyond any vanishing point.

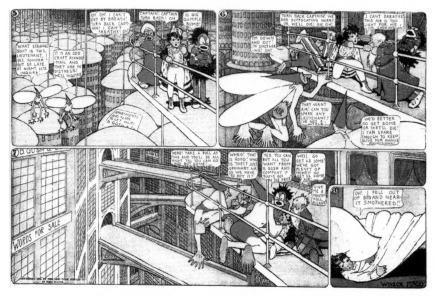

Figure 9.1. The Martian cityscape of Winsor McKay's *Little Nemo in Slumberland* (1910).

Thus, Mars is a spatial and thematic allegory of deterritorialization: the planet has completely disappeared into a modular globalization of urban life. And what is such life like? A series of panels shows the planet upon closer and closer approach, using scale shifts to mark its boundaries and the continuity of its internally iterated features (McCay 2000, 245). At a distance it resembles the familiar globe of scarred red desert, but this surface is revealed to be a built layer above which are posted colorful signs reading "Keep Off This Air," "Private Property," and "B. Gosh & Co." The circumglobal atmosphere has been appropriated by a corporation. It is not surprising that closer in, just above the layer of rooftops, the atmospheric space reveals itself to have been divided into numerous "Lots For Sale" by the same business. Nemo and his friends find the air too thin to breathe, but they are rescued by a friendly constabulary patrol that gives them enough air to last them until they may buy their own supply from B. Gosh and Co. As the episodes continue, we learn that not only built housing, unbuilt atmosphere, and oxygen require money to secure, but so too do sunlight (stored and sold to lower-chasm dwellers), the right to use any word to communicate, and bare life itself (requiring a license). Thematically, the globalization of life on Mars is the total commodification of its planetary nature, humanoid and nonhumanoid, by a monopoly capitalist and de facto global ruler, B. Gosh. Thus, McCay develops the prescient allegory of commercial globalization as a deterritorializing power—a circumglobal transformation of nature into commodity manufacture, without any visible roots in local place or history. It is a totally plastic, re-makeable world, in which every property of life is subject to the power of an obscure autocracy.

Despite this dystopian allegory, Mars appears quite cheerful. Nemo and his friends are unconcerned, happy to pay for their needs; just as the police are happy to share their private air supply with them. For those with sufficient wealth, this global experience is a joy. The condition of alienation from any planetary nature—any nonhuman agency or reference points apart from the peculiar, historical power of B. Gosh—is expressed in the dizzying failure of spatial perspective within its horizonless walls to capture differences in up and down, this way and that. Gravity itself is capricious: Nemo and his friends have trouble not floating upside down and sideways, and they take swimming lessons in a fog (McKay 2000, 246, 248). It is not surprising that they are often disoriented or lost. The feeling of a horizonless sense of possibility, of freedom from any grounding conditions in a continuously topsy-turvy world, may be euphoric, but also has a troubling flipside in anxiety. The dream of freedom liberates the self from gravity, nature, and destiny. But its purposelessness can be anxious, expressed in the threat of subjection—the remaking or loss of self—governed by the agency of others. The amoral danger of the world is figured in the depiction of criminal "pirates"—thieves and kidnappers—who are interchangeable with the power elite. "What will they do with that pirate?" the starship Captain asks, "Fill him full of bullets or yank him up by the neck?" "No," their Martian guide assures them, "Mr. B. Gosh, who owns this whole planet of Mars, will make him a member of his Advisory Board! Don't say I told you, but old Gosh is a robber himself or he'd not own everything!" (McCay 2000, 251). This topsy-turvy world undoes not only moral identity but the very self: the risk of losing one's selfhood is figured variously in getting lost (by chance or, as in Nemo's kidnapping, by unpredictable force); in scenes of vehicular traffic and public transit whose churning masses threaten to swallow and divide the Earth visitors; and in violence to the bodily integrity of the self that can be as ecstatic as it is disturbing. The latter is most darkly expressed in the global sport of the Martians, which involves two teams competing to catch balls flung by a weird creature, the Whang Doodle. The team members are hypnotists who try to hypnotize the Doodle into throwing the ball to them—suggesting, it seems, an allegorical agency for the unpredictable, barely masterable force of others in a world in which all properties of life are contested. If the ball is caught, the player's team wins a point. If the ball is not caught, the player is "torn into small souvenirs to be carried home by the audience" (McCay 2000, 257). Yet on the Fourth of July, mysteriously celebrated on Mars, Nemo, Flip, and the Martians become "sky bombs" that explode scarily against a starry night, unexpectedly revealing new pleasures and new friends (McCay 2000, 255). Across all these panels and pages, McCay uses complex, modular interlocking geometries and vibrant colors to evoke the euphoric interconnectedness of this world, and in this very drive to abstraction, a less sanguine dehumanization of persons as mutually malleable, unpredictably exploited beings.

Slumberland is the allegory of an ecology whose individual creatures are insignificant to its collectively driven life patterns, to vibrant, fractal blossomings of figure and form. In this imaginary cosmos, biophysical transformation wrought by individuals upon the world always exceeds intention, and pleasure and wonder arise from sheer accident, like the discovery of the moon birds, or from accidental, fractal, aggregate spin-offs from intention, like the shadowy architectural chasms of Mars. In *Modern Animalism*, I have argued that there is no lack, so no desire in a Freudian sense, in Slumberland; hence no drive to consume either, or rivalry for other creatures or things. Nature is limitlessly abundant and giving, yet also destabilizing and disorienting. Persistently sustaining yet ubiquitously exotic and occult, this planetary nature— one way of apprehending our own Primary World, as a refusal (escapist or subversive?) of the Anthropocene—offers a humbling, sublime wealth, rather than a masterful, appropriative one.

The planetary sublime of Slumberland not only brackets its inverted image in the allegory of globalization on Mars, but also leaks into its cracks and fissures, breaking up its world vision from the inside, in a more disparate, collage aesthetic that resists allegory and conveys the infinite partial autonomy of persons and events. This is felt in the abruptly shifting perspectives from panel to panel and episode to episode, and in the partial unreadability of every figure and form—of just how human is a humanoid, for example, or how familiar is a house. This undecodable autonomy is exemplified in the creatures Nemo visits at the Martian zoo, which diversely defy expectations based on their outward appearance, and may even be unknowable (McCay 2000, 259). The collage effect is also felt in the logic general to the strip itself of contrasting inner logics of dream and waking worlds. Every episode ends with a panel that belongs not to Mars and Slumberland, but to Earth, where the child is jarred awake by the pleasure or fear of the dream; so the difference between Earth and Mars—here between a bourgeois private domestic regime of restorative sleep for the dull work of the day, and a bourgeois global commercial regime of euphoric/terrifying plasticity—are allegorically incommensurate rather than contradictory, and are held in uneasy, graphic apposition as coexisting perspectives on Anthropocenic modernity, alike immersed in the imagination of ecologies to which they are blind. Thus, the reference worlds of Nemo, both marked as distinct and seen together in composition, stylistically and thematically invade each other. Uncertainties echo among them: Must life be this way? Might it be different somewhere else? What do I really want in this world? For a child, is it too late? (Here the reader's first deictic shift, to the fictional world of the child, has its poignancy.) These are the simple waking questions made strange by McCay's worldmaking art.

Are unconventional ecologies found only in fantasy comics? Certainly, heterodox worldmaking is associated with fantasy genres. For example, the kind of ecological unconscious that McCay expresses in the planetary joys and fears of *Nemo* is unfolded with more knowing, metafictional irony in the funny animal landscape of George Herriman's *Krazy Kat*, a strip that ran in the *New York Evening Journal* and other Hearst syndicate newspapers during much of the same period, from 1913 to 1944. The daily strip reproduced here is from 1920.[6]

Figure 9.2.   The desert world of Kokonino in George Herriman's *Krazy Kat* (1920).

The *Kat*'s storyworld is a desert region, Kokonino, that is identical to Slumberland in its world logic of genealogical volatility and heterocratic anarchy. Here, however, the narrative purpose of the strip does not aim for surprising action and events, as does McCay's adventure, but instead for surprising interpersonal exchanges between creatures and for unexpected commentaries on mundane things in its world.

In the worldmaking of Kokonino, iterability of recognizable forms and hence default recognition of objects and spaces is kept to a stark minimum: storyworld coherence is largely held together by our iconic recognition of the wandering figures of Krazy Kat (whom Herriman's serial readers will associate with a blithe creative sympathy) and Ignatz Mouse (associated with a nihilist creative violence). Otherwise, the forms and elements of the space—even the tone of the sky—have a life of their own, metamorphosing unpredictably. A sense of global coherence is created by the continuity of Herriman's style and by the thematic unity of the desert world. Yet this style is a sketchy one that calls attention to its own performance by hand, fraying at the edges and sometimes disintegrating into illegibility (Ignatz's feet, terrain lines) or barely figurative abstraction (Krazy's tail, tree foliage); while the unity of the desert location is one ironically secured only by highly abstract figures and emptiness. This apparent exposure of the creative hand and the compositional page in the storyworld allows for a continuous deictic indeterminacy between the inferred world of Kokonino and the inferred world of the production of the *Kat* strip. This deictic indeterminacy is echoed iconographically from panel to panel by the wayward emergence, transformation, or vanishing of non-story background objects, as well as formally by panels with and without frames (marking their own fragmentation as units and focalizations), including a striking, full-height panel interrupting the narrative in the middle, thus bringing to the reader's foreground, as equal to or more important than the mere narrative gag, the (normally consciously subordinated) worldmaking performativity and focalization that are here lived, metafictional constituents of the *Kat*'s storyworld, as Krazy and Ignatz wrangle over the nature of the thing on his head, and the words to describe it. Herriman's worldbuilding focuses on dialogue conflicts and ambiguous representations of locations and objects in order to reveal dissonances of idea and feeling among perspectives of the characters and reader—and their diverse ethical responses (here, sympathetic play or frustrated violence). What makes a hat properly a hat? The pun on bean (anatomical or vegetable) allows words to shapeshift in reference and purpose, here justifying Krazy's creative interaction with the bean plant silently figured at the strip's spatial center, a creative object in its own right, as if it generated or motivated the narrative spiraling out from it.

Kokonino's modernist ecology invites us to perceive Krazy's head (mind, personhood) as born of a mundane plant, an imaginative kinship that depends on felicitous mistakes in language and an openness to outrageous self-refashioning; yet this is more attractive, somehow, than Ignatz's censorious and categorical defense of a more familiar ecology of proprieties of character (self, personhood) and word, which do not seem to apply in Kokonino. Kokonino invites subversive ideas of what constitutes modern scarcity and wealth (Herriman 2007, 65–68). Its primitivist, animalized, and desert storyworld is poor in the enjoyment of material goods, technological capacities, or institutional complexity, but rich in the performative pleasures—of curious meditations and interlocutions among its heterogenous denizens, and in these denizens' mysterious freedoms to be what they may. Its natureculture is a planetary utopia, modestly nonhuman and purely anarchic, with which the human reader may authentically identify, while holding a modernist Darwinian nihilism at bay, only in its personifications of creative pleasure and wandering empathy.

One does not have to immerse oneself in fantasy genres, in dream worlds and animalized utopias, to find an ecological unconscious at work in comics, though when it comes to overtly environmental comics, it is rare that one does not. It is true that today's realist comics sometimes use the braiding of nonhuman figures to imply mysteriously alive yet barely glimpsed folds in the spatial perspectives sequenced by the plot—such as the trees in Jillian and Mariko Tamaki's *Skim*, the birds in Kevin Huizenga's *Wild Kingdom*, or the insects in Nate Powell's *Swallow Me Whole*. But in the first half of the twentieth century, comics that are more realist tend to reduce their storyworlds to merely functional or iconic extensions of human social life (whether progressive or not in other respects), such as Frank King's *Gasoline Alley* or Harold Gray's *Little Orphan Annie*. An instructive, borderline example is Tarpé Mills's adventure series for Bell syndicated newspapers, *Miss Fury* (1941–1952), in which an action heroine travels the world defeating bad guys. Miss Fury has no superpowers, and there is nothing more supernatural than fanciful technological innovation in her stories—with the exception, perhaps, of her costume. She wears a skin-tight, full-body, masked outfit made from black puma skin, supposed to have been created by an African witch doctor (Mills 2013, 24). The costume *never* manifestly provides supernatural powers, only naturalistic "blessings in disguise" in "accursed" exchange for which sacrifices are exacted upon the wearer. Yet we comprehend that this costume, an animalized image, somehow works outside of mere human plotting, literally and figuratively occult to it, yet acting upon plot from some Archimedean point of cosmic "justice" (Mills 2013, 84, 95).

Worldmaking in *Miss Fury* is more ecologically interesting than may be expected from a plot-driven action romance. In the last six panels of an episode from 1942, Miss Fury is stranded in Brazilian backcountry, trying to help a group of Euro-American and Indigenous resistance fighters foil the plot of a Nazi army hidden in the jungle.

The panels are themselves identically iterated to generate unity of narrative space and perspective in the storyworld. The mimetic drawing style, though cartoon simplified, avoids caricature and abstraction (diverse human bodies and faces, skin tones, manufactured and natural objects). The spatial organization of the "establishing" panel is conventional vanishing point perspective, gridding its contents into discrete locations in a continuum. Continuity of space is also indicated by the iteration of figures through the first five panels, with a disorienting shift to the space of the sixth panel, directly connected only by the iteration of a word reference to unrepresented "trees." Objects in the establishing panel are inert unless motivated by human plot action. Thus, the global allegory initially appears to be conventional anthropocentric naturalism—at least until spatial fragmentation interferes and generates a more complex world space.

The second panel iterates a transection or slice of the conventional space of the first, but only as a flattened middle ground, bathed in monochrome purple shadow, against a rosy ether without horizon. Mimetic depth is replaced by

Figure 9.3. The modernist worldmaking of Tarpé Mills's *Miss Fury* (1942). From *Miss Fury: Sensational Sundays 1941–1944*, edited by Trina Robbins, courtesy of the Library of American Comics/IDW Publishing.

a flat ontology of character and objects (the costume, the most illegible, both a fabricated thing and an animate entity). Miss Fury's words, having shifted their reference from the immediate, present location to an African past, anchor what is again, as in *Krazy Kat*, a kind of multi-deictic double vision, a synoptic recognition of two reference worlds, one naturalistic and discretely categorized for human use, and the other supernatural, animalized, and distant, which weirdly permeate each other. In short, a "strange" animal power both subtends and exceeds human power, just as the "witch doctor" and the "scientist" are unexpectedly akin (and as we learn elsewhere, alike in knowing the risks of trying to master nonhuman agencies). The donkey that watches Miss Fury move toward the house is pure excess, having been bizarrely placed among her other bags in the car two episodes prior with her explanation: "I certainly don't want to leave *anything* for those Nazis!" (Mills 2013, 93). Its image braids semantically with the animal word and animal vials skin image of the second panel, revealing only another skin, an animal surface and hidden gaze, inscrutable. In these ways are diverse races and species both iconographically individuated and spatially rendered kindred; all genealogies intersect.

In the last three panels, three faces look directly at the reader. In panel four, perspective becomes sheer quality—the rosy sensation as pure sign of the intersectional spaces and incommensurate focalizations of the human and the nonhuman meeting in Miss Fury's transformation. In her look we are addressed from that very interstitiality, seduced into crossing the boundaries of its animalized storyworld, nakedly interpellated. In panel five, the mask replaces the eyes: we arrive, but are addressed without reciprocity, and her ears, which leap from one space to another, now prove more powerful than our and the other eyes (in panel six) watching her. The fully accessible, global Cartesian space of the establishing panel has given way to the chiaroscuro collage of space and sense of the animalized one. As in our other early comics by McCay and Herriman, a biodiverse planetary vision that subordinates human emplotment, here expressed as a wish-fulfillment of justice in the Anthropocene, is the subtle utopian fantasy subtending its storyworld. And akin to those more idiosyncratic strips, too, in its rejection of normative realism, its paratactic work of fragment and totality, its reality shifts and superpositions, and its reaching after primitivism and eroticism as uncanny forms of reader interpellation, the worldmaking of Mills's strip offers an exemplary modernism.[7]

MONOCULTURE VERSUS SYMBIOCULTURE

In conclusion, I would like to propose the relevance to modernism, and, in particular to the emergence of modern comics, of Donna Haraway's distinction between historical concepts of the Anthropocene and of what she calls the Chthulucene—a term she invents by up-rooting the posthuman Cthulhu ontology from the weird horror of H. P. Lovecraft (and from its abject racism and misogyny), and re-planting it in a more ethically generous notion of the chthonic. Haraway does not deny the validity of the Anthropocene concept to modern life, but she is wary of any implication that one species determines planetary futures. She develops Anna Tsing's view of the Anthropocene not as an historical period, but as a historical boundary event or turning point defined by "the wiping out of most of the refugia from which diverse species assemblages (with or without people) can be reconstituted after major events (like desertification, or clear cutting, or, or, . . .)," thus entailing the loss of a heretofore "rich cultural and biological diversity." But subtending this process is, was, and will be a "chthulucenic" one, which refers to "the dynamic ongoing sym-chthonic forces and powers of which people are a part, within which ongoingness is at stake," and which "entangles myriad temporalities and spatialities and myriad intra-active entities-in-assemblages—including the more-than-human, other-than-human, inhuman, and human-as-humus" (Haraway 2015, 159–60). What better description of modern comics is there than of an art of worldmaking in which such rich, myriad, entangled beings may find spaces of hopeful, creative *refuge*, and may flourish?

The art of comics, against the solipsistic machinery of an anthropocentric *monoculture*, yet while parodying the latter's global ambition in its own worldbuilding *style*, sets out to draw the contours of alternative, planetary *symbiocultures*.[8] Comics revel in, even as they worry over, the generative volatility, mutual permeability and mutability of human and nonhuman biotic identities, unfolding their interleaved spaces and times. Haraway's insistence on the monstrously "tentacular," hybrid bases of life finds generic expression in the grotesque tradition—ludic and caricatural—of comics iconography, a tradition that comics extends beyond its tradition of marginal ornamentation into wholly stylized environments.[9] This stylistic tradition is itself embedded in the unique interplay of spatial fragment and worldmaking totality that is comics form. In the stylized and collaged, modernist landscapes of comics, the relentlessly artefactualist representation of a global life tends both to heroicize and to compromise the human figures caught in its storyworlds. Hence, for its readers, comics both express the anxiety masterfully to appropriate nature for a transcendentally autonomous, orthodox image of human reproduction, and also express the seduction of losing oneself among more sustainable, but mortal and wayward, genealogies.

Modernist comics are then, ironically, monocultural images of symbiocultural worldmaking: hubristically reproducing the actual historical invasion of human styles into global conditions, yet playfully or seductively unfolding the myriad planetary vitalities that reinvent lives and refuges despite us, that question what may be kindred, and that expose to the wandering eye ethical challenges always lying in wait.

NOTES

1. On the poetics of gaps in comics, see Postema 2013.
2. See also Herman 2010.
3. The written text in comics uses an alphabetic language form that may be read according to two semiotic modes, one associated with conventional print, and the other with visual art and design. So too, under different protocols, with its graphic images.
4. This sense of an implied world is part of the peculiar meaning of the panel. McCloud has persuasively argued that the panel is an iconic form indicating a division of time or space (McCloud 1994, 98–99), a claim I would here adapt to suggest that the panel is an icon with an always dual signifying function, acknowledging the implication of what it explicitly frames in a larger unseen world attainable only by

imaginative inference; as such the panel is both representational (of a unit of time or space) and performative (of a worldmaking action).

5. Baker argues that any animalized character, even of the most conservative commercial provenance or narrative employment, is always grasped, in part, as radically animal and so "disturbs the logic and consistency of the whole" text, "*bringing to light* the disruptive potential of the story's animal content" and "limit[ing] the extent to which the narrative can patrol and control its own boundaries" (Baker 2001, 139).

6. See Herriman 2007, 71.

7. Enlisted in Mills's realist adventure are ideologies of primitivism (internalized animal powers, white leadership, white stereotypes and appropriation of African magic) and eroticism (for which the strip was notorious, and once censored); yet Mills, one of the rare leading female artists in a male-dominated industry, offered for her time, both a relatively progressive iconography and individuated characterization of indigenous Brazilians, and a more sensitive and individuated portrayal of women and of significant relations among them. Eroticism functions here the same way that the ludic does in the humor strips, and is suggestively queered rather than strictly heteronormative. The romance *plots* of the strip are conventionally heterosexual, but the sexual *interaction* is more ambiguous, as when Era silently watches Miss Fury getting dressed (Mills 2013, 91) or when Baroness Von Kampf commands Miss Fury to undress before her, leading to an extended semi-naked fight (Mills 2013, 35). Whether this plays into a "queer ecology" (Mortimer-Sandilands and Erickson 2010) in the strip seems uncertain, though it is surely the case in the ludic gender play with "nature" in *Krazy Kat* and, more elaborately, in the later *Skim* (Tamaki and Tamaki 2008). Perhaps the ludic and posthuman heritage of comics will always exert a tug upon its storyworlds away from sexual definition and regulation.

8. I use symbioculture to name the general ecology that corresponds to what Haraway historicizes as the Chthulucene.

9. See Haraway 2004, where she unfolds this image. On the grotesque in comics, see Willmott 2014 and 2017.

WORKS CITED

Baker, Steve. 2001. *Picturing the Beast: Animals, Identity, and Representation*. 2nd ed. Chicago: University of Illinois Press.

Bal, Mieke. 1985. *Narratology: Introduction to the Theory of Narrative*. Toronto: University of Toronto Press.

Beaty, Bart. 2015. *Twelve-Cent Archie*. New Brunswick, NJ: Rutgers University Press.

Groensteen, Thierry. 2007. *The System of Comics*. Translated by Bart Beaty and Nick Nguyen. Jackson: University of Mississippi Press.

Haraway, Donna. 2015. "Anthropocene, Capitalocene, Plantationocene, Chthulucene: Making Kin." *Environmental Humanities* 6: 159–65.

———. 2004. "The Promises of Monsters: A Regenerative Politics for Inappropriate/d Others." In *The Haraway Reader*, 63–124 New York: Routledge.

Heise, Ursula K. 2008. *Sense of Place and Sense of Planet: The Environmental Imagination of the Global*. New York: Oxford University Press.

Herman, David. 2002. *Story Logic: Problems and Possibilities of Narrative*. Lincoln: University of Nebraska Press.

———. 2013. *Storytelling and the Sciences of the Mind*. Cambridge, MA: MIT Press.

———. 2010. "Storyworld." *Routledge Encyclopedia of Narrative Theory*. Edited by David Herman et al. London: Routledge. Digital edition.

Herriman, George. 2007. *The Kat Who Walked in Beauty: The Panoramic Dailies of 1920*. Edited by Derya Ataker. Seattle: Fantagraphics.

Lyytikäinen, Pirjo. 2012. "Paul Ricoeur and the Role of Plot in Narrative Worldmaking." In *Rethinking Mimesis: Concepts and Practices of Literary Representation*, edited by Saija Isomaa et al., 47–71. Newcastle upon Tyne: Cambridge Scholars Press.

McCay, Winsor. 2000. *Little Nemo 1905–1914*. Köln: Evergreen/Taschen.

McCloud, Scott. 2006. *Making Comics: Storytelling Secrets of Comics, Manga and Graphic Novels*. Toronto: HarperCollins.

———. 1994. *Understanding Comics: The Invisible Art*. New York: HarperCollins.

Mills, Tarpé. 2013. *Miss Fury: Sensational Sundays 1941–1944*. Edited by Trina Robbins. San Diego: IDW Press.

Mortimer-Sandilands, Catriona and Bruce Erickson, eds. 2010. *Queer Ecologies: Sex, Nature, Politics, Desire*. Bloomington and Indianapolis: Indiana University Press.

Postema, Barbara. 2013. *Narrative Structure in Comics: Making Sense of Fragments*. Rochester: RIT Press.

Ranta, Michael. 2014. "(Re-)Creating Order: Narrativity and Implied World Views in Pictures." *Storyworlds: A Journal of Narrative Studies* 5: 1–30.

Richardson, Brian. 2012. "Narrative Worlds: Space, Setting, Perspective." In *Narrative Theory: Core Concepts and Critical Debates*, edited by David Herman et al., 103–10. Columbus: Ohio State University Press.

Tamaki, Mariko, and Jillian Tamaki. 2006. *Skim*. Toronto: Anansi.

Willmott, Glenn. 2017. "The Animalized Character and Style." In *Animal Comics: Graphic Agents in Multispecies Storyworlds*, edited by David Herman, 53–76. London: Bloomsbury Academic.

———. 2014. "Comics as a Cross-Writing Tradition." *Jeunesse: Young People, Texts, Cultures* 6 (2): 97–103.

———. 2012. *Modern Animalism: Habitats of Scarcity and Wealth in Comics and Literature*. Toronto: University of Toronto Press.

Wolf, Mark J. P. 2012. *Building Imaginary Worlds: The Theory and History of Subcreation*. New York: Routledge.

Chapter Ten

Modernism on Ice

Marianne Moore and the Glacial Imagination

Julia E. Daniel

On July 25, 1922, the Moore family made their way to Paradise Inn in Mt. Rainier National Park, home to the geologic marvel of a glacier-capped volcano. Marianne Moore and her brother joined a small hiking group to traverse the glacial ice. This was no small feat, and involved some considerable dangers, even under the watch of a careful guide. The experience deeply impressed the poet. When Moore began to write "An Octopus," she not only turned to her Mt. Rainier Park guidebook as a source, but also composed passages in the margins.[1] And yet, the long poem that resulted from this trip barely testifies to her firsthand experience. Rather than a lyric engagement with the space, "An Octopus" presents us with sprawling, entangled rhetorics arising from the guidebooks published by the National Park Service (NPS), unofficial travel brochures for the Pacific Northwest and beyond, landscape painting, gemology, taxonomy and taxidermy, cartography, law, nutritional science, not to mention odder sources, such as Cardinal Newman's *Historical Sketches* or words overheard at a circus. The result is a poem not about the nearly incomprehensible reality of the glacier but about the difficulty involved in attempting that cognitive feat.

"An Octopus" is an exercise in failed ways of imagining the hyperobject of the glacier, particularly failures of comprehending time, scale, strength, and movement, though all these terms are inevitably entangled. Moore presents us with an endless snow of quotes (both attributed and unattributed) and metaphors, each of which attempts to gain a toe-hold on the sheer face of the glacier. She then highlights the inevitable slips and trips of each, as those multiple discourses result in inevitable discords in the massive echo chamber of Moore's icy poetics. Significantly, "An Octopus" does not critique these failed arctic fantasies by juxtaposing them against the reality of the glacier, as has often been argued. Rather, the hyperobject of the glacier, gigantically diffused across spacetime, never makes an immediate, material appearance in the poem. As one kind of metaphor slips through the cracks, another one comes to replace it, only to slip again and then be replaced by yet another mode of fantasy. Rather than existing as an object within the poem, the physical reality of the glacier dwells as an amorphous pressure beyond the limits of verse, one that causes language to rupture while always exceeding it. Moore constantly withholds the vigorous intimacy with the ice so longed for by reader and hiker alike.

This is not to say that Moore presents every stumble of the language as a failure to be bemoaned; even in their missteps, some linguistic attempts to scale the glacier rise to heroism. Moore's technique in this poem—her bricolage, ironies, and fractured allusiveness (and illusiveness)—comes not primarily from the technologies, art forms, and the atmosphere of newness we attribute to modernism, but from an Anthropocenic modernism that pushes against and is pushed by geologic realities both ancient, distant, still and dangerously current, present, mobile. If the Anthropocene posits that human impact on the global environment comprises its own geologic epoch, Moore's "An Octopus" reminds the modern reader that there is no "outside" to geo-logic chronology for human communities. And if modernism is an animal of the city and the machine, Moore insists it is also a creature of the glacier and the volcano. If anything, the absenting hyperobject of the glacier inspires the hyper-abundance of the verse. It invites poet and public to constantly brave new attempts with new tools. It is the hike itself, the athletic and inexhaust-ible imaginative feats the poem embodies, that is the ultimate reward.

OCTOPI AND ICE: THE HYPEROBJECT IN THE ANTHROPOCENE

In his attempt to enact a post-human, post-Nature materialism, Timothy Mor-ton famously defines a hyperobject as that which is "massively distributed in time and space in ways that baffle humans and make interacting with them fascinating, disturbing, problematic, and wonderous" (Morton 2013, 58). Our most common examples of such hyperobjects are usually ones entangled in environmental harms, such as pollution or radioactive fallout. These objects have real material lives and are finite in their way, but our human sense of scale and time renders them nearly incomprehensible in their relative mas-siveness. Morton catalogs the uniquely weird properties of such hyperobjects. For example, their amazing nearness and constant remoteness renders them both viscous and nonlocal. Their sweeping scale, far too vast for the eye to take in at a glance, also means that hyperobjects are "genuine nonhuman objects that are not simply the products of a human gaze" (Morton 2013, 199). Their hugeness and diffusion through time also results in temporal undulations that unsettle our human-scale chronologies. (The afterlife of a casually discarded Styrofoam cup boggles the mind.) And in the face of the hyperobject, the human becomes freshly frail: "The time of hyperobjects is a time of weakness, in which humans are tuned to entities that can destroy them" (Morton 2013, 176). Morton captures the wondrous monstrosity of such gigantic beasts in language Moore would recognize. The hyperobject is at once a kind of iceberg that hugely encapsulates us (such as graces the cover of Morton's book) and an octopus always receding into the blackness of its own ink plume, at times Cthulhu-like in its tentacled, menacing spread.[2]

And yet, in terms of Morton's taxonomy, Moore's glacial octopus is a somewhat erratic animal. It possesses the prerequisite qualities of a massiveness in time-space that threatens the human creature who cannot begin to see, let alone comprehend, all of it. What I have called *a* glacier is actually an interconnected network of twenty-eight glaciers, snow packs, ice fields, and melt systems, all sprawled across the top of Mount Tacoma, a 14,400-foot-tall episodically active volcano in the Cascade Range in Washington State.[3] This younger volcano burst out of the range roughly five hundred thousand years ago, relative to the twelve-million-year-old peaks in the vicinity. And it is a dangerous creature. More than four hundred people have died on the glacier or in the park since rangers began tracking these fatalities in 1897, including the highly publicized death of a young hiker only a year before Moore attempted her own hike.[4] Even for those not tempted to hike the ice, the glaciers' melt cycles are volatile and can result in highly dangerous mud slides and flash-flooding that imperils park-goers, as well as human habitation downstream. As the NPS warns visitors today: "only you can decide if you want to spend time in this unpredictable and changing landscape" (NPS 2015).

However, the scale of Tacoma's glacial system makes it an odd hyperobject, one that's a little young and a little small. The ice fields cover only about thirty-five square miles of land. And the ice does not originate in a pre-human past: it settled during the Little Ice Age, somewhere in roughly the 1600s, which makes it a creature of, not before, the Anthropocene—at least according to its earlier datings. However, it is not simply the glacial fields, but their situation on top of Tacoma that make them uniquely resistant to human viewing and encroachment. Although the glacier covers only a handful of miles, its fractal spread over and against the imposing peak of the mountain's topography means that the glacial system can never be easily captured at a glance or traversed in an afternoon. The glaciers also present a smooth face that mask varying densities, ranging in fifty to five hundred feet in depth, as well as treacherous fissures that can swallow entire hiking companies. Scale and scope become more than a question of bare millage as the margins of the glacial pack defy human encapsulation along several axes. And while barely a breath in a wide timescale, the history of the ice also still impresses at the human level. Moreover, it is the weird futurity of the glacier that captivates Moore. Its uncanny frozenness suggests massive permanence far beyond the hiker and yet its freakishly slow, powerful registers of movement constantly hack away at the mountain, then burst into horrific events of suddenness that defy attempts to anticipate them: avalanche, mudslide, flood, and fissure. Moore's vacillations between incredibly static images and rapid-fire shuffling through kinetic metaphor after metaphor capture the difficulty of a human mind as it grapples with the inevitably warped perception of the glacier's forever-and-yet-horrifically-now qualities.

If referring to Tacoma's glacial expanse as a hyperobject stretches, or, rather, shrinks our typical definition, the use of "hyperobject" as a critical term also presents some odd, though potentially fruitful frictions in a book about the Anthropocene. As Ursula Heise has argued, the two seem to be antithetical: "The Anthropocene as defined by Paul Crutzen and Eugene Stoermer actually prioritizes human agency in the wholesale transformation of the planet over the last two hundred years in ways that are diametrically opposed to Morton's approach," precisely because Morton shifts us away from the centrality of human agency (Heise 2015, 461). However, this divide is only insurmountable if the Anthropocene posits that human agents are the *only* geologic force in this era (which it does not) and if Morton argues that there is *no* possibility for human agency within the age of the hyperobject (which he does not). Indeed, Moore's octopus testifies to the bizarre life of the hyperobject in and of the Anthropocene. In emphasizing the mediating role of the National Park Service, Moore presents an Anthropocenic glacier that is literally shaped by human activities: the planned paths around and across the ice, the built structures of shelters, the feet and picks that pock the snow, occasionally resulting in the crescendo of an avalanche. But she also presents us with a monstrous ice field that limits human bodies. The poem boasts lists of what you should and should not touch, look at (and how), eat, as well as recommendations for managing the real risk of bodily harm or death, all taken from the official park guidebook.

What follows here is a glacially slow close-reading of the first and last images of ice in the poem. Both attempt to achieve an aerial view and on-the-ground perspective of the glacier, resulting in dizzying telescoping of failing points-of-view. Both passages also utilize and discard an abundance of sources, quotes, maps, and figurative language in an attempt to understand the glacier. The most prominent of these, as we will see, is the metaphorical equivalence between the glacial fields and a monstrous octopus. Rather than providing a felicitous ground to engage with the hyperobject, Moore's octopus constantly writhes away from or mercilessly constricts the mind that struggles to understand it.

"AN OCTOPUS"

From the very title of the piece, Moore sets her readers on unstable ground. As with several of her poems, the title functions in tandem with the opening line. We move from "An Octopus" to the first line: "of ice" (Moore 1994, 71). However, unlike her title "The Fish," which moves into a line describing their movement in the water, or "The Jerboa," which announces the animal under consideration, "An Octopus" is a feint. This is not an aquatic poem, nor is it really an animal piece per se. The octopus of the title is only the first of several metaphors that will be used and discarded in an attempt to imagine the glaciers. Nor is the octopus image one of Moore's own creation. This first major image immediately engages with the rhetorics of the guidebook that the Moore family received upon their arrival to Mt. Rainier National Park. The first of several notes provided by Moore alerts her reader that "Quoted lines of which the source is not given are from the Department of the Interior Rules and Regulations, The National Parks Portfolio (1922)" (Moore 1994, 273).[5] While early responses to "An Octopus" often attributed this monstrous metaphor to Moore's own zoological imagination, contemporary criticism has identified the top-down image of the octopod glacier as a reference to the prominent aerial map in the guidebook and *Parks Portfolio*. Here, the rendering of the glaciers is particularly octopoid, as the cartographer depicts tentacle-like snow appendages trailing down the sides of the volcano. *The National Parks Portfolio* explicitly guides the would-be hiker into engaging with this map as if it were octopus: "Seen upon the map, as if from an aeroplane, one thinks of an enormous frozen octopus stretching icy tentacles down upon every side among the rich gardens of wild flowers and splendid forests of firs and cedars below" (Yard 1921, 85).[6] The second line in Moore's poem, "Deceptively reserved and flat," points us to the deception of this two-dimensional attempt to render the mountainous, icy terrain. What is provocative here is that the speaker does not engage in a unique, immediately sensuous imagining of the glacial hyperobject on which she hikes (and Moore could have drawn from her own firsthand experience). From even beyond the official margins of the poem, the title drops us squarely into the landscape of official NPS language. There is no dreaming of the space beyond the controlling rhetoric of the park, even as there is no real hope that these languages can accurately ensnare the real contours of the glaciers in our minds.

But the deception is not just an issue of scale and depth. It is also one of "reserve," a loaded word in a National Park context, one that also brings questions of time and movement into play. On the one hand, the map presents a deceptively tame octopus, a politeness Moore will soon blast away in the following lines. On the other hand, the deception of reserve also has legal, land-management valences. The earliest acts of nature preservation on the national level used the term "reserve" to protect key flora and fauna, such as the Forest Reserve Act of 1891. As Roderick Frazier Nash has demonstrated, even prior to the official creation of the National Park Service in 1916, land reservation language shifted from materials management (save the trees because we need the lumber) to transcendentally-infused historic preservation efforts (save the trees because we need this beautiful, pre-frontier scenery to soothe our urban souls). At root, the word "reserve" is about setting aside, delimiting and protecting a space. In an American context, this most often meant setting aside national reserves as managed chronotopes: a kind of nature museum designed to freeze a landscape into our ideal of a pre-settled wilderness. However, as Moore reminds us here, the harder we try to imaginatively freeze the frozen octopus, the more it oozes out from between our fingers. Chronologically stabilizing the glacial fields by maintaining them as a pre-human arctic wilderness is an untenable deception. Beyond the shaping imposition of even the most careful hiker, who leaves footprints in her wake, and the impact of human managers, as they place signs and trails to control the hiker, the glaciers themselves are constantly raking across the volcano below them. The very definition of glaciers, the way we distinguish them from ice fields, is that they *move*. As you read this, the glaciers on Tacoma are dragging their weight across the rock below, moving up to a foot or so a day. The map, the guidebooks, and the very management of the physical parkscape by the NPS engages in ecologically bizarre deceptions of a frozen timeline that valorizes a kind of immobility that the glaciers actively frustrate: their lack of reserve makes them nearly impossible to reserve.

Moore underscores this bizarreness not by giving us the real ice as a counterforce, but by sinking deeper into the meat of the metaphor, which causes the octopus to receded father from our view. What exactly is the tenor of the octopus vehicle? Just when the map proposes to offer this creature to us at a glance (or, rather, as the product of a glance), Moore plunges us down the z axis: "it lies 'in grandeur and in mass' / beneath a sea of shifting snow dunes;" (Moore 1994, 71). What one sees on the map, and even sees when viewing the mountain in person, isn't quite the glaciers or, by extension, the octopus. While the octopus at first seemed to be all surface and borders on the map, Moore now reveals that isn't the octopus at all. If anything, the surface is an untrustworthy environment, as the marine imagery of the sea smashes against terrestrial snow dunes. The only way the eye registers the movement of the glaciers is through the shifts of these dunes, and so octopus and sea, glacial fields and snow, creature and environment become hopelessly confused in human attempts to comprehend the terribly slow and dangerous kinetics of the hyperobject. Such confusion registers on the level of functionally vague word choices: "It" sends us scattering, as does "lies." The glacier reclines beneath the snow; the metaphor gurgles falsehoods. Specifically, in quoting "in grandeur and in mass" from the Rainier guidebook, Moore readies us for the juxtaposition between two modes of NPS rhetoric to remind us that both are a form of deception.[7] The admiring, transcendental wilderness language of "grandeur" and its humbling, scenic value is one way of engaging with the glacier, a mode frequently turned to in the Rainier guide. A corrective to this often purple prose and its imaginative excess might be a more scientific discourse, one that helps us conceive of the glacier in terms of mass, mileage, density, and temperature. Here is a potential node of real engagement with the physical fact of the octopus.

But Moore is quick to keep us from falling into that deception as well. As Morton reminds us, hyperobjects invite a kind of data glutting that reveals, rather than relieves, our inabilities to comprehend them: "The more data we have about lifeforms, the more we realize we can never truly know them" (Morton 2013, 56). Moore performs the failings of such quantitative fantasies as she braids them together with the octopus imagery:

> beneath a sea of shifting snow dunes;
> dots of cyclamen-red and maroon on its clearly defined pseudopodia
> made of glass that will bend—a much needed invention
>
> (Moore 1994, 71)

While her fierce, detailed extension of the vehicle makes the octopus come into clearer focus, that same feat tosses us into weird vacillations in scale that make the glaciers impossible to hold in view. We now see an octopus beneath the sea, its sharply outlined tentacles flecked with red. The large tentacles and their sure outlines pull us back to that aerial, cartographic view. Moore here culls information from one of her repeated sources for quotes in the poem: Clifton Johnson's *What to See in America*: "Often there are seen on the snow mysterious patches of pink or light rose color, commonly spoke of as 'red snow.' Really each patch represents a colony of billions of microscopic plants" (Johnson 1919, 535). These maroon patches are *Chlamydomonas nivalis*, otherwise known as Watermelon or Blood Snow. These colonies of artic algae thrive in the cold and take on a pinkish hue in the spring, resulting in red patches where the snow has melted or been compacted under foot. Moore zooms us vertiginously from the very massive to the impressively small, from the aerial to the microscopic. As Morton argues, hyperobjects are composed of huge quantities of such organisms, one of the weird qualities that make them difficult to see with the human eye. Moore takes up the inconceivable, miniature biomasses of the hypernumerous algae and transmutes them into anatomical features of the octopod's embrace in an attempt to negotiate such difficulties of scale.

To make matters even weirder, the speaker also turns us to the hot-house blooms of the tropical cyclamen to understand the rosy coloration of these hugely tiny algal ice plants. In trying to gain specificity of pigment, the metaphor flails again, as the octopus now carries armfuls of tropical flowers blooming in a dessert of snow. And despite the speaker's assertion to the contrary, it becomes harder, not easier, to see those reddened appendages. Because the octopus sinks out of our view beneath the snow, the only way the pseudopodia, or tentacles, are "clearly defined" is through the definitional activities of the map and guide rhetoric that attempts to delimit those glacial appendages through measurements, facts, and figures. But Moore has already cautioned us away from trusting how mass lies. As such, the glacial tentacles remain *pseudo*podia—literally, a false foot. Taking up the seemingly precise languages of taxonomy and invertebrate anatomy offers no escape from metaphor, nor does it get us closer to the glacial hyperobject. If anything, the word choice again emphasizes the falsehood of our linguistic contortions: we define glaciers as if they were tentacles, we define tentacles as if they were human feet. Moore makes sure that the as-if-ness of these equivalences always comes to the fore by constantly shuttling back and forth between nodes of always provisional language.

For a moment, we receive some relief from the evasive fictions of the octopus image, as we land on seemingly firm ground: "made of glass that will bend—a much needed invention— / comprising twenty-eight ice fields from fifty to five hundred feet thick" (Moore 1994, 71). Here is the language of science stripped from figuration: industrial applications of glass fabrication, bare facts regarding quantity and depth. Moore's note on the line directs readers to Sir William Bell, who proposed several inventions that would revolutionize the modern world, including "a smooth road surface that will not be slippery in wet weather; a furnace that will conserve ninety-five percent of its heat" and bendable glass (Moore 1994, 273). By likening the ice to bendable glass, "a much needed invention," the glacial octopus transforms into its own feat of modern engineering, as Moore links it to acts of human ingenuity and construction. We might say that the glacier preempts human industry and so upholds the glacial hyperobject as an ante/anti-human marvel. However, bendable glass is yet another fallible way of capturing the glacier. On the material level, ice *isn't* glass, so before we even receive the Bell quote in full, the speaker has taken up yet another human-scale object as a potentially more useful vehicle for the glacial fields. Yet, as soon as the mind drifts in that direction, an entire discourse of applied science, industrial practices, and modernity itself pops to mind. "Glass that bends" sends us away from the always reclusive ice and back to ourselves, reminding reader and vacationing hiker that the world beyond the park, and all its emphatically moderns needs and marvels, inevitably shapes our interaction with the space.

Even when we have what feels like firm, real contact with the ice, what we have in actuality is most often just another quote from yet another book, an unattributed line pilfered directly from the Rainier guidebook: "comprising twenty-eight ice fields from fifty to five hundred feet thick" (Moore 1994, 71). Here we have a clean articulation of spread and depth without the figurative stumbling blocks of lines prior. And yet, in the Macmillian edition, the scientifically exact line is so long that not even the page can accommodate it. The line snaps, as "feet thick" must fracture off below. The excessive length of the brittle line warns of the uselessness of glutting oneself on these facts and figures, the likes of which stuff the NPS guide and portfolio. The materiality of type and page, as well as the poetics of language and line, lack the very flexibility of the ice itself that was praised in the line above. If real ice bends, words break before it, as we receive yet another false foot: a piece of text (about feet) that looks like its own spondaic line, and yet is really just the dangling, amputated bit of the excess that precedes it. Even worse (or better), the entire poem is an assemblage of such pseudopodia. As Patricia Willis has expertly demonstrated, the irregular lineation and syllabification of "An Octopus" arises from twenty-eight uneven sentences, one for each glacial appendage down the volcano's slopes. While Willis clearly identifies the correspondence between sentences and glaciers, we should also be wary of how *pseudo* these *podia* are. In "An Octopus," Moore breaks from her usually exacting syllabic verse structures and creates a jagged metrics that splinters across her sentences. This poetics perfectly captures the imperfections of attempts to utter the truth about the hyperobject beyond the poem.

The precision of the ice field statistics gives way to the final thought of the sentence: "of unimagined delicacy." As before, the line points away from us and toward us simultaneously. It gestures to a tensile quality of the absenting hyperobject, delicate in ways we can't comprehend, while also shaking a fist at our failures to imagine it. And it's true: the poem has yet to imagine such delicacy, busy as it has been in listing qualities of grandeur and mass, all while admiring the apparently unbreakable hardiness of the ice. Registers of movement and strength collide, as the glacial hyperobject is simultaneously inconceivably strong and slow, fragile and fast in comparison to human registers. The language attempts to keep up as the speaker hops from image to image, leaving incongruous figures in its wake:

"Picking periwinkles from the cracks"
or killing prey with the concentric crushing rigor of the python,
it hovers forward "spider fashion . . ."

(Moore 1994, 71)

We receive an image of fragility, "Picking periwinkles from the cracks" only to swiftly pivot to an alternative in the next line: "or killing prey with the concentric crushing rigor of the python." The ticklish alliteration and general girlishness of "picking periwinkles" delights with delicacy—a relief from the octopus as we shift to the gathering of little blossoms—until one goes to the notes. There, Moore sends us to M. C. Carey's article "The Octopus in the Chanel Island." In this short travel piece, Carey explicitly meditates on the octopi's "amazing strength combined with extreme delicacy of touch" (Moore 1994, 282). The image Moore crafts here is not of a human carefully plucking periwinkle flowers out from rocky spots, like those she describes later in the alpine flower meadows around the base of Tacoma. Rather, Moore quotes Carey's description of how muscular octopods can suck periwinkles, little mollusks often found in tidal pools, right out from underwater crevasses. What seems to be fragile is in fact strong, and we have mistaken the image in part due to our terrestrial biases and lurking anthropocentrism, our inability to distinguish periwinkles from periwinkles. Here, delicacy is unimagined largely because it has been misinterpreted.

So it seems that Moore then abandons the article, with its decontextualized floral romps, to build her own image of strength: the glacier as a python constricting its prey. And yet, again, the quotes lie. The next line is still from Carey, even though Moore has closed the quotation: "It can pick a periwinkle out of a crack, and yet crush a larger prey with the grip of a small python" (Carey 1923, 282).[8] The tension Moore builds here is not between the misguided language of travel literature and the firsthand wisdom of the hiker, cautious before the crushing power of the sublime: it is all secondhand figurations, ones that Moore presses together until the seams show. For example, even if we have no access to her source, Moore leaves us wondering who or what is the "prey" of this python-like beast? While the python equivalent makes some sense in Carey, as he is investigating the predatory behaviors of octopods, the serpentine twisting of the glacial octopus lacks a clear referent. Is it that the ice strangles the mountain beneath it? This seems uncomfortable, as the in-turned twist of the python rubs against the out-spreading, hovering forward of the glacier as depicted in the next line, as Moore abruptly moves

from centripetal to centrifugal forces. Perhaps the prey is the tourist behold-
ing or hiking upon the ice? This again feels odd, as there is yet no actual body
located in the world of the poem. Nor will there ever be. Moore takes up the
bodiless imperatives and conditional language of the guide throughout, es-
chewing firsthand travel narrative in favor of the familiar, official tone of the
guides directed at a hypothetical hiker: continue along the path, one should
pack light, leave your address at the ranger's lodge. Ultimately, there is no
obvious analogous prey in this landscape for the metaphor to coil about. By
withholding the referent, Moore creates an atmosphere of tense uncertainty
about the dangers involved in engaging with this metaphorical octopus, the
aura of danger that Morton associates with life in the time of hyperobjects but
lacking the specificity of where and how that danger is deployed.

Here also is a slow-motion wink at the associative workings of the mind.
The glacier is an "unimagined delicacy" in an entirely different sense: a tasty
morsel, an object of human consumption. "Delicacy" sends the speaker's
mind to a new set of materials: food articles about calamari and seaside vaca-
tion travelogues. Both "spider fashion" and "ghostly pallor changing / to the
green metallic tinge of an anemone-starred pool" originate from articles in
The Illustrated London News. The first quote is taken from W. P. Pycraft's
essay "Good News for the Gourmet" (1924), in which he describes a new
dining craze: calamari.[9] The article provides close anatomical descriptions
of a variety of marine creatures often mistakenly taken for octopi in order
to guide both diners and chefs in procuring a tasty and nontoxic morsel:
"When 'sauntering' along it walks on these arms in a spider-like fashion, very
'creepy' to behold" (Pycraft 1924, 1224). The second quote is an elaborated
paraphrase from Francis Ward's "'Poison Gas' in Nature: The Lesser Octopus, A Summer Seaside Visitor to be Avoided" (1923). Ward describes the
physiology and habits of *Eledone Cirrosa*, a kind of octopus known to cause
difficulties for fishermen and swimmers in some coastal regions of England.
He provides two pages of illustrations and a full paragraph on *Eledonae* col-
oring: "If frightened, an intense ghostly pallor passes right over the animal.
. . . Then rapidly the pallor passes off, and the cephalopod is again a deep
terra-cotta red" (Ward 1923, 270). A layer of iridescent tissue below the upper membrane results in a "delicate green metallic tinge" (Ward 1923, 270).
Both sources treat the octopi relative to human needs as either restaurant-
goers or beachside vacationers, linking proper acts of zoological investigation
with successful acts of human playing and eating. In even these emphatically
scientific biological metaphors, Moore presents Rainier's glacial octopus as
an object of human recreational consumption.

While at first this octopod crushed its vague prey like a python, demonstrating its strength, delicacy creeps in again when we find the full context

of Moore's quote: the cephalopod turns white when it is afraid. The ever-pale (and sometimes pink) covering of the glacial octopus suggests that this creature is now startled prey, blanching before the face of danger. But what has frightened it? Again, we are left searching for a referent that the image withholds. Does this glacial octopus fear us, the reader-hiker-fisherman-chef that threatens it? But scale again baffles, as it seems impossible that such a gigantic, hardy snow monster would have any cause to fear us, especially as "we" aren't really there. This vacillation between perceived strength and fragility captures the difficulties of imagining the hyperobject, a problem often captured in the guide rhetoric Moore parodies. The NPS materials constantly warn of the dangers involved in hiking the glacier while simultaneously alerting visitors to the various ways their encroachment might dangerously mar the parkscape. Octopus and hiker, both fictive creations of the guide, are poised as predator and prey of each other at once.

By the fourth sentence, Moore begins disentangling us from the octopus as the poem moves down to consider the forest environment below the snowline. The shift down into the tree line marks a similar shift away from the controlling octopus metaphor, as hereafter Moore picks up new tools to imagine the forests and rocks, ranging from gemology to Ruskin's treatise on Alpine landscape paintings. While veins of ice run throughout the piece, it is not until the final moments of the poem that the octopus returns again in full force, a Cthulhu-like bookend to this sprawling work. It returns at an odd, familiar crawl: "'Creeping slowly as with meditated stealth, / its arms seeming to approach from all directions,' / it receives one under winds that 'tear the snow to bits'" (Moore 1994, 76). Though five pages of poetry intervene between these two images, the imagining mind returns again to the same tools, figures, and even sources in a last attempt to comprehend the glacial fields. The strange, omnidirectional undulations of the octopus come at one from every vector, an image that creates the same sense of diffuse, omnipresent threat that characterize the glaciers in the first sentences. Or, rather, they *seem* to, and this small qualification signals a more acute awareness of the mind's warping effect when considering the glacial hyperobject that, while very large, cannot in fact approach from all possible directions at once. The perceived boundlessness and huge scope of motion presented here has everything to do with the struggles of human-scale perception.

While performing the hesitant limits of that perception, Moore also foregrounds the present absence of the imagined "one" who hikes the similarly imaginary glacier. While it is true, as Robin Schulze argues, that "The mountain's true nature . . . lies beyond language itself," it is not because, "[l]ost in the mountain's strange and mindless whiteness, the poet lacks the power to express what she sees" (Schulze 1996, 60). The bodiless speaker has seen nothing, has been nowhere. There has been zero immediate contact with the ice in the fiction of the poem. Immediately prior to this windy moment, Moore relies on the familiar conditional and imperative language of guide rhetoric: "one must do as one is told" "if one would 'conquer the main peak'" (Moore 1994, 75). We know this "one." It is the placeholder for ourselves in these travel fantasies, while also the stand-in for all hikers, as well as the legal fiction of the regulated and prosecutable agent who may or may not adhere to the rules. And yet, hyperobjects do not admit of hypothetical bodies: they are massive realities, not abstractions. As Moore's obtuse language, borrowed from the guide, constantly reminds us, we are not on the mountain, nor is the speaker. We cannot play hiker on an imagined glacier because once it is imagined, it is no longer truly glacial. Thus, Moore makes sure our hike is permanently forestalled, especially during what should be the final summiting of this sublime peak. In emphasizing how the imagination fails in grasping the hyperobject, Moore must withhold human embodiment as well, unless we fall into the snow trap of thinking physical contact generates firm knowledge and mastery.

Even when considering the avalanche that concludes the poem, Moore keeps us at several frustratingly safe removes. A metaphorical curtain closes on the imagined performance of hiker-on-glacier, as a long-distance view of the avalanche suspends rather than resolves the same issues of scale, scope, and movement that troubled the poem from the beginning. "[T]he glassy octopus symmetrically pointed," and what it points to is an avalanche of figurative language: "its claw cut by the avalanche / 'with a sound like the crack of a rifle, / in a curtain of powdered snow launched like a waterfall'" (Moore 1994, 76). A glacier like an octopus, an ice mantle like glass, a sound like a rifle, a curtain that is launched, a launch that is like a waterfall. As in the first image of the octopod glacial system, Moore emphasizes the not-quite-ness of these equivalences. Most worrisome is the appearance of an unexpected claw. While squid do have toothy, clawish appendages on their harpoon tentacles, octopi have none. Has this entire imaginative venture been one of failed animal identification? And how could we miss a claw? As Pycraft's article on calamari would remind us, failing to properly identify octopods might end in death for the hapless traveler.[10] The metaphorical monster from the first lines now becomes hopelessly odd in the moment of greatest danger here as the avalanche appears.

Even stranger, what does it mean to have the claw cut by an avalanche? The glacier becomes both squid and knife that cuts the squid as the metaphor impales itself. The oddity arises from a human desire to split the perceived static and kinetic registers of the glacier. From the perspective of the guide and the hiker, the ideal state of the glacial animal is reserved stillness, so the active and unpredictable movement of the avalanche gets cast in terms of dismemberment and violence. Of course, the glacier is always moving and an avalanche is as much part of the motile life of the glacial fields as is its inch-by-inch creeping. Time similarly slices and is sliced in this moment. We tend to read the final passage as an immediate shift from symmetry to asymmetry, as the peak fractures before our very eyes. However, instead of reading the line as, "the glassy octopus symmetrically pointed, [then] its claw [is] cut by the avalanche," we might also parse it as, "the glassy octopus [is] symmetrically pointed [because] its claw [was] cut by the avalanche." From certain at-ground angles, the mountain has a double hump, or the tips of a claw that has symmetrically opened wide, with the glacial fields pouring out below it. Is the avalanche the kinetic destroyer of symmetry or the honed tool that creates it? Because of the way the line withholds the verbal specificity we crave, there is no clear answer. And fittingly so. If, as Morton says, time is "an emission of objects themselves," then there can be no emanation of geologic time in the poem as the hyperobject is massively, densely absent (Morton 2013, 67). Without such a lodestone, the weird times in Moore's poem undulate not from the hyperobject but radiate out from the mind that struggles to perceive it.

Moore here braids together unstable temporalities with unimaginable spaces. Our inability to pin down the time in the line directly relates to confusion about how we should visualize the mountain in our minds: symmetrical or asymmetrical? Moving or still? So too does Moore make strange chains of cause and effect in the largely imperceptible history of how the landscape shapes and is shaped. Elizabeth Gregory links the sound of the crack to an actual shot from a rifle, and so the avalanche is "the wound the earth felt at the fall" in Eden, a result of human harm (Gregory 1996, 176). Perhaps. Unfortunately, the cause of the avalanche is permanently withheld. It is the sound of the fracturing snow and ice, just moments before gaining violent momentum, which registers in the human ear *like* a gunshot. Just as we cannot locate the source of the marmot's alarm in an earlier, lightly comedic moment, here we are completely cut off from cause and effect. What we do know is that the mind turns us to human tools of sport, leisure, and violence in order to comprehend the magnitude and consequences of the avalanche, trapping us again in the scale of the human. Moreover, the avalanche episode exists in the constructed past of the quote, something that happened once-upon-a-time that we hear about only now. We have resolved the danger in the safety of travelogue while emphatically freezing the reader within the temporality of quotation and storytelling, far away from the real, chilling hyperobject.

In Morton's words, "we are always in the wrong" against the hyperobject (Morton 2013, 173). Moore captures that always-in-the-wrongness, which is why the poem never proffers us a materially immediate experience of the mountain. In the words of her epigraph: "Omissions are not accidents." In omitting the glaciers entirely, Moore purposefully and playfully engages an Anthropocenic hyperobject by performing the impossibility of such interaction. The glacier exceeds our capacities for fact, our abilities to comprehend its scope in spacetime, its infinitely slow and massively deadly movements, and thus the poem is constantly taking up, testing, and abandoning ways of imagining this octopus of ice. But this, ultimately, becomes the achievement of the poem. As the speaker says, "it is the love of doing hard things" that turned the American public against the works of Henry James. As Moore shows us, the coyness of the hyperobject invites the strenuous imaginative exploration that it will always outstrip. In contrast, the poet and reader here have taken up such athletic, creative acts of hard-doing, inexhaustibly trekking ahead even when the slick ground of our fantasies prevents us from real progression.

NOTES

1. Margaret Holley provides a rich description of Moore's composition process: "What Moore's own underlined copy of the pamphlet shows us is that not only did she copy into her poem numerous phrases from the pamphlet's text, tables, notes, and even its bibliography, but also that she actually composed some portions of her poem in the margins of the pamphlet" (Holley 1987, 67).

2. For example: "Or we discover that the space we inhabit is . . . the interior of a gigantic iceberg whose seeming transparency was simply a matter of our less than adequate eyes" (Morton 2013, 160); "Without a background, without Nature, without a world, the iceberg haunts us" (189); "It is as if we were inside a gigantic octopus" (64); "By understanding hyperobjects, human thinking has summoned Cthulhu-like entities" (64).

3. The NPS currently refers to both the mountain and the park as "Rainier," the title given to the peak by George Vancouver in honor of a military compatriot. It was ratified by the United States Board of Geographic names in 1890, even though a variety of native names were still in use at the time, including Tacoma and Tahoma. Following the restoration of "Denali" as the designation of the former Mt. McKinnely, there has been some discussion of officially recuperating "Tacoma" as the title of the mountain, though there are several other possible native terms currently under consideration as well. (See, for example, the 2015 opinion piece written by *The Seattle Times* editorial board.) In keeping with Moore's polyvocality, I will refer to the mountain as Tacoma, unless I am analyzing the poem and its National Park materials, most of which use Rainier as the official place name.

4. Jack Meredith died while hiking on Little Tacoma in August of 1921. Interestingly, the first recorded death had everything to do with human technology and

clumsiness and little to do with the environment: "Gun fell from pocket. Struck in neck" (NPS 2015).

5. Moore quotes heavily from both the individual Mount Rainier guidebook given to visitors and the NPS *Parks Portfolio*, a collection of such guides from numerous parks. Because there are textual differences between these two documents, I will refer to the former as the Rainier guidebook and the latter as the *Portfolio* throughout. As I have argued elsewhere, Moore engages primarily with these NPS materials throughout the poem. For more on her NPS archive, see Daniel 2017, 119–154.

6. The controlling metaphor of the frozen octopus is also a recurrent image found throughout the several official and unofficial guidebooks that Moore references in her notes. Similarly, Clifton Johnson's scenic tour guide that Moore mentions in a later note, *What to See in America* (1919), states: "From the snow-covered summit twenty-eight rivers of ice pour down . . . like the tentacles of a huge octopus" (Moore 1994, 534). In Snow Sentinels of the Pacific Northwest, Joseph Hazard also describes Columbia Crest, the chief peak of Mount Rainier, as "the eye of a glacial octopus" (Hazard 1932, 177).

7. "'Easily King of all is Mount Rainier,' wrote F.E. Matthes, of the United States Geological Survey, reviewing that series of huge extinct volcanoes towering high above the skyline of the Cascade Range. 'Almost 250 feet higher than Mount Shasta, its nearest rival in grandeur and in mass, it is overwhelmingly impressive both by the vastness of its glacial mantle and by the striking sculpture of its cliffs'" (*Rainier Guide* 7).

8. Carey's article is largely a menagerie of such metaphors. He likens anatomical structures of the octopi to pythons, woodpeckers, parrots, and calves in just this paragraph.

9. "The merit of the octopus as food for man—as well as whales—has lately been very freely discussed, and the verdict, on the whole, is greatly in its favour" (Pycraft 1924, 1224).

10. Like Moore, Pycraft is not optimistic about the ability of the layman to make the correct identification. The article concludes: "I must end as I began. How are we to know which is the 'octopus' which we are to eat 'fried to a golden brown'? We have a bewildering variety to choose from and as like as not we shall choose the wrong one" (1224).

WORKS CITED

Carey, M. C. 1923. "The Octopus in the Chanel Island." *The Graphic; An Illustrated Weekly Newspaper*, August 25, 1923: 282.

Cronon, William. 1996. "The Trouble with Wilderness, or, Getting Back to the Wrong Nature." In *Uncommon Ground: Rethinking the Human Place in Nature*, edited by William Cronon, 69–90. New York: Norton.

Daniel, Julia E. 2017. *Building Natures: Modern American Poetry, Landscape Architecture, and City Planning*. Charlottesville: Univ. Virginia Press.

Gregory, Elizabeth. 1996. *Quotation and Modern American Poetry: "Imaginary Gardens with Real Toads."* Houston: Rice University Press.

Hazard, Joseph T. 1932. *Snow Sentinels of the Pacific Northwest.* Seattle: Lowman and Handford Co.

Heise, Ursula K. 2015. Review of *Hyperobjects: Philosophy and Ecology after the End of the World*, by Timothy Morton. *Critical Inquiry* 41 (2): 460–61.

Holley, Margaret. 1987. *The Poetry of Marianne Moore: A Study in Voice and Value.* Cambridge, UK: Cambridge Univ. Press.

Johnson, Clifton. 1919. *What to See in America.* New York: Macmillian.

Ladino, Jennifer K. 2005. "Rewriting Nature Tourism in an 'Age of Violence': Tactical Collage in Marianne Moore's 'An Octopus.'" *Twentieth-Century Literature* 51 (3): 285–315.

Moore, Marianne. 1994. *Complete Poems.* New York: Macmillian.

Morton, Timothy. 2013. *Hyperobjects: Philosophy and Ecology after the End of the World.* Minneapolis: University of Minnesota Press.

Nash, Roderick Frazier. 2001. *Wilderness and the American Mind.* New Haven, CT: Yale University Press.

National Park Service, US Department of the Interior. 2015. "Fatalities at Mt. Rainier National Park." Accessed December 8, 2015.

National Park Service, US Department of the Interior. "Mount Rainier: Frequently Asked Questions." November 25, 2015.

Pycraft, W. P. 1924. "Good News for the Gourmet." *The Illustrated London News*, June 28, 1924: 1224.

Riley, Kate, Frank Blethen et al. 2015. "After McKinley, it's time to consider remaining Rainier." *Seattle Times*, September 1, 2015.

Rules and Regulations: Mount Rainier National Park Washington, Season from June 15 to September 15. 1922. Washington, DC: Government Printing Office.

Schulze, Robin G. 1996. *Web of Friendship: Marianne Moore and Wallace Stevens.* Ann Arbor: University of Michigan Press.

Ward, Francis. 1923. "'Poison Gas' in Nature: The Lesser Octopus, A Summer Seaside Visitor to be Avoided." *The Illustrated London News*, August 1, 1923: 270.

Willis, Patricia C. 1984. "The Road to Paradise: First Notes on Marianne Moore's 'An Octopus.'" *Twentieth-Century Literature.* 20 (2/3): 242–66.

Yard, Robert Sterling. 1921. *The National Parks Portfolio.* Washington, DC: Government Printing Office.

Chapter Eleven

The Poetics of Modernism's Plastics

Michael D. Sloane

Recently, Patricia L. Corcoran, Charles J. Moore, and Kelly Jazvac found a new "stone" on Kamilo Beach in Hawaii (Corcoran et al. 2014, 4). What they call "plastiglomerate" is a Frankenstein's monster. Composed of melted plastic, beach sediment, basaltic lava fragments, and organic debris, plastiglomerate is "an indurated, multi-composite material made hard by agglutination of rock and molten plastic" (Corcoran et al. 2014, 4–5). After combing twenty-one sample locations on Kamilo Beach, the scientists discovered a total of two hundred and five samples of both in situ and clastic, or deposited and fragmented, plastiglomerate that exhibited varying combinations of coral, plastic, basalt, and woody debris like charcoal, nuts, seeds, and sand (Corcoran et al. 2014, 6). Although much of the specimens' plastic parts were melted beyond recognition, the team was able to identify a number of discrete objects like bottle caps, fishing nets and ropes, lids, partial containers, packaging, pellets, pipes, tubes, and rubber tires (Corcoran et al. 2014, 5–6). Based on their findings, Corcoran and her colleagues propose that plastiglomerate is "the first rock type composed partially of plastic material that has strong potential to act as a global marker horizon in the Anthropocene" (Corcoran et al. 2014, 7). Plastiglomerate is a hybrid registering our impact on the earth and a harbinger of what is to come in the Anthropocene, especially if we continue consuming plastic at our current clip. Over the course of half a century, for instance, the average North American has increased their annual consumption of pounds of plastic by 900 percent, much of which has ended up in the ocean (Frienkel 2011, 7, 119).[1] Like nonbiodegradable plastic sticking to stones, the human species is irrevocably stuck as actors in and contributors to the Anthropocene, but this is not necessarily news.

Paul J. Crutzen and Eugene F. Stoermer use "Anthropocene" to describe our current epoch. Starting alongside James Watt's 1784 steam engine, the

Anthropocene marks how human activities—industry's carbon dioxide and agriculture's methane—have indelibly affected the earth (Crutzen and Stoermer 2000, 17–18). Yet, as Donna Haraway notes, humanity has always made a mark on the environment: "[t]here is no question that anthropogenic processes have had planetary effects . . . for as long as our species can be identified" (Haraway 2016, 99). For her, the Anthropocene is "more a boundary event than an epoch," and she is eager "to make the Anthropocene as short/ thin as possible and to cultivate with each other in every way imaginable epochs to come that can replenish refuse" (Haraway 2016, 100). Advocating for "a big new name," or "more than one name," Haraway acknowledges "Anthropocene," "Plantationocene," and "Capitalocene" while adding her own: "Chthulucene," or that which "entangles myriad temporalities and spatialities and myriad intra-active entities-in-assemblages—including the more-than-human, other-than-human, inhuman, and human-as-humus" (Haraway 2016, 100, 192n28). The Anthropocene is not a write-off just yet. The "Anthropocene is temporally fuzzy, not absolutely indeterminate" (Morton 2016, 76); moreover, the "Anthropocene has to be named before people can try to take responsibility for it" (Purdy 2015, 4). Haraway's skepticism is important, but I would like to dwell on the Anthropocene to understand and learn from humanity's conscious and unconscious cultural and aesthetic responses to a sea change that has been underway, a sea changed by plastic.

Timothy Morton's remarks on the Anthropocene and hyperobjects help facilitate my analysis of the poetics of plastic. He challenges the ostensible denial, racism, colonialism, speciesism, and hubris of the Anthropocene and argues that when "we scale up to Earth magnitude very interesting things happen to thinking" (Morton 2016, 24). He contends that the "*Anthropocene' is the first fully antianthropocentric concept* . . . because it enables us to think the human species not as an ontically given thing . . . [one] can point to, but as a hyperobject that is real yet inaccessible" (Morton 2016, 24–25). Elsewhere, Morton explains that "hyperobjects" refer to "things that are massively distributed in time and space relative to humans," which can include black holes, oil fields, the biosphere, nuclear materials, Styrofoam, and plastic bags (Morton 2013, 1). Conceived of in this way, the Anthropocene and hyperobjects recalibrate the thinking of things like plastic to small and large scales. The Anthropocene has shaken up how we make sense of the world, let alone life, and it appears in the everyday (Clark 2015, 9). Indeed, we can consider how "distinct types of material thinking emerge and might yet be invented in relation to the specificities of plastics" (Gabrys et al. 2013, 7). In fact, Christian Bök proposes that this is well underway with the very invention of plastic giving rise to a "celluloid spectacle" (Bök 2001, 93). For him, the unified imagination of the Romantics has been displaced by an "injection-moulded mentality" that is "pliable and durable as any blob of polypropylene" (Bök 2001, 93). He even suggests that the very act of writing is the production of a complex polymer put together with syllables rather than molecules (Bök 2001, 93).[2] With this in mind, we can—and should—analyze the material history and poetics of plastic and plasticity in search of different modes of thought, even ecological, plastic ones. After all, Roland Barthes knew what is now a reality: "the whole world *can* be plasticized" (Barthes 1972, 99). And yet we have not fully explored how the "Plastic Age radically transmuted the cultural values attached to the natural and the artificial" (Bensaude Vincent 2013, 25), one that exhibits the stirrings of an artificial ecology involving plastic that formed and informed early twentieth-century literature in subtle ways. Typically put to use in the production of consumer goods, plastic also plays a part in the creation of art.

"The new plastics made one, above all, modern" (Brown 2009, 151), writes Judith Brown in *Glamour in Six Dimensions*. Discussing designer, artist, and poet Florine Stettheimer's use of cellophane for Gertrude Stein and Virgil Thompson's 1934 production of *Four Saints in Three Acts*, Brown considers cellophane to be modernism's objective, material correlative (Brown 2009, 151). With its crisp, smooth, clear, hygienic, icy, superficial, impersonal, and pure form with or without content, she suggests cellophane as a metaphor for modernism's formal ideals, let alone the period's approach to the plasticity and possibility of language (Brown 2009, 151–52). Yet, she notes how "[w]e've lost, in the intervening decades, the ability to read the early-century semiotics of plastics" (Brown 2009, 145). Here, I will continue Brown's smart start in scratching the surface of the semiotics of plastic and plasticity with other forms that manifest themselves in modernism. To borrow from Carl Rakosi, what else can we find in the "city wrapped in cellophane" (Rakoski 1967, 20) that is modernism? How can we think about "the plastic parts of poems" (Stevens 1954, 197), as Wallace Stevens put it? If plastic is "less a thing than the trace of movement" (Barthes 1972, 97), then what about the poetics of plasticity in modernism, one that considers the materiality of mutability, change, exchange, morphing, metamorphosis, and transformation in and around object matter? In response, I argue that modernism registers the stirrings of an artificial ecology due, in part, to the emergent Plastic Age. Here, the line between natural and unnatural is blurred, which writers pick up on in different ways. The production and proliferation of plastic in the first half of the twentieth century influences writers who are experimenting with content and form. Whether they knew it or not, modernist writers tapped into a culture that was on the cusp of a material revolution. This seems anachronistic because they did not have a name for what we now know as the Anthropocene. Yet, their artworks still responded to material conditions.

I argue, then, that modernist writers' work presciently points to and focalizes the Anthropocene in and through plastics and plasticity, which yields other forms of thought. From here, then, I offer a history of the Plastic Age in order to contextualize modernism's backdrop. Then, I sample, explore, and analyze plastic literatures by turning to Futurism, Gertrude Stein, Mina Loy, William Carlos Williams, The Baroness, and Abraham Lincoln Gillespie. Paying close attention to a number of texts, I offer close readings that help us to learn more about the nature of the Anthropocene through modernism's plastics and plasticity.

"Plastic has been naturalized," writes Jeffrey L. Meikle (Meikle 1995, 1). We have been living in the Plastic Age for some time. Plastics proliferated around the mid-twentieth century. For instance, in 1939, American companies made 213 million pounds of synthetic resins, and by 1951, their output reached 2.4 billion (Meikle 1995, 125). The emergence of the Plastic Age between the world wars was a novel phenomenon (Meikle 1995, 63–64), one that did not go unnoticed in modernism. And even before this interwar period, semi-synthetic prototypes like celluloid appeared. Specifically, during the nineteenth century, natural plastics like shellac and rubber appeared. Then, in the early 1860s when the firm Phelan & Collender solicited a new substance to substitute for ivory and billiard balls, the experiments began. In 1869, John Wesley Hyatt stumbled upon celluloid, which could be heated, softened, compressed, and molded into a shiny, strong solid (Meikle 1995, 11). Celluloid was used to produce brush and knife handles, combs, harness fittings, piano keys, and small novelties as a substitute for and imitation of ivory, tortoiseshell, and horn (Meikle 1995, 11). The rhetoric around the production of celluloid was paradoxical, utopic, and hyperbolic. In an 1878 advertising pamphlet, celluloid was described with words like "new," "unchangeable," "uniform," and "perfect" (Meikle 1995, 11). Yet, celluloid could appear in "a thousand forms" (Meikle 1995, 11). This contradiction was a symptom of the collective unconscious experiencing frisson in response to changing material production practices at the turn of the century. Yet, celluloid's ability to imitate the old helped to neutralize fears of innovation (Meikle 1995, 12). And despite the "[m]odernist disdain for imitation as dishonest and immoral" (Meikle 1995, 13), industrial development was embraced: "[i]mitation became one more sign of increasingly precise human control and thus, paradoxically, a sign of innovation. Far from indicating shoddiness or dishonesty, imitation offered provocative evidence of the extension of human artifice through new technology" (Meikle 1995, 13–14). From a Celluloid Company's brochure in 1890 to the *DuPont Magazine* in 1921, celluloid was touted as a convincing counterfeit for coral, ivory, malachite, tortoiseshell, amber, turquoise, lapis lazuli, agate, carnelian, mother of pearl, abalone pearl, ebony, mahogany, and oak (Meikle 1995, 15). Modernity's ambivalent response to plastic counterfeits registers a tension between superstructure and base that would make its way into modernist artworks, and the strange stirrings of an artificial ecology were made more apparent by Bakelite.

In 1907, Leo H. Baekeland invented the "first chemically synthetic plastic," or what he called "Bakelite," which was "a substance distinct from its reactive parts, a substance with no direct analogue in nature" (Meikle 1995, 5, 33). In 1909, referred to as "the father of plastic," Baekeland boasted that his Bakelite was "far superior to . . . all plastics" (Meikle 1995, 5). Yet, Bakelite was not like the plastic we know today "because its chemical reaction rendered it permanently hard, infusible, and insoluble" (Meikle 1995, 5). Nevertheless, at the outset of the new century, people knew things were changing at the chemical level. For example, in 1890, *The Century Dictionary* defined plastic as that which is "'capable of change or modification'" (qtd. in Meikle 1995, 4) whereas in 1910, the *Century Dictionary Supplement* described it as "the commercial name for any one of a class of substances, such as celluloid or viscose, which are worked into shape for use by moulding or pressing when in a plastic condition" (qtd. in Meikle 1995, 4). Bakelite was used for insulation and the production of pipe stems, billiard balls, knobs, buttons, knife handles, radios, cars, appliances, and jewelry, and it prospered soon after its appearance: between 1911 and 1916, Bakelite increased by 1,900 percent (Meikle 1995, 45, 49, 60).[3] What was the response to plastic flooding the market in modernity? How was semi-synthetic and synthetic material understood, interpreted, and aestheticized in a cultural context, especially if someone like Baekeland "discarded imitation of any particular natural substance as a goal and invited people to make of Bakelite what they wanted" (Meikle 1995, 48)?

Plastic subtly permeates modernism. Take, for instance, e. e. cummings' reference to a "celluloid collar" (cummings 1991, 986); William Faulkner's description of Southern California as "the plastic asshole of the world" (qtd. in Baldwin 2001, 35); Allen Ginsberg's exclamation that we are "Slaves of Plastic!" (Ginsberg 2007, 548); Hope Mirrlees's "Scentless," "Icy," and "Plastic" roses (Mirrlees 1920, 8); Marianne Moore's "plastic animal" (Moore 2016, 68); Gary Snyder's "plastic spoons" and "PVC pipe" (Snyder 1974, 67); or how Louis Zukofsky's representation of the "bear / on / the ashtray" (Zukofsky 1991, 170) might just be made out of Bakelite.[4] To further explore the poetics of plastic, I will begin with Futurism, which was born from F. T. Marinetti's 1909 manifesto, two years after the first synthetic plastic and forty years after the origin of celluloid.

In an essay entitled "The Plastic Foundations of Futurist Sculpture and Painting" from 1913, Umberto Boccioni sought to "achieve the plastic state of mind" (Boccioni 2009, 140). Two years later, in 1915, Giacomo Balla and Fortunato Depero offered a shopping list for "The Material Construction of a Plastic Complex," one that includes "celluloids" (Balla 2009, 210). Then, in 1917, the patriarch of Futurism, Marinetti, wrote "Manifesto of Futurist Dance," which describes a number of dances including "Dance of the Aviatrix" where human meets machine in a sexualized scene: "[t]he danseuse will dance on top of a large, violently colored geographical map. . . . On her chest, like a flower, a large celluloid propeller constructed so that it vibrates with every bodily movement" (Marinetti 2009, 239). In these excerpts, it becomes increasingly clear that the appearance of plastics and plasticity started to make their mark on modernism; moreover, modernists drawn to dance seem to be thinking through human plasticity in and of itself, which Gertrude Stein picks up on around this time, too.

While Stein knew what celluloid and cellophane was, plastics do not really appear in her work;[5] however, plasticity as form affects the nature of her writing. Consider how *Orta or One Dancing* (1911–1912)—a portrait of the American dancer Isadora Duncan (Stein 1993, 120)—illustrates the poetics of plasticity through the gradual and consistent morphing of words and phrases. Stein writes:

> She was dancing in being that one believing that thinking in having meaning in meaning being existing. She was dancing in this thing. She was dancing. She was dancing in moving in every direction being something having meaning. She was dancing in this thing. She was dancing. She was dancing, she was using then being one believing in meaning being existing. She was dancing in being one having feeling of anything being cheering. (Stein 1993, 129)

The word "dancing" appears in every sentence in the passage above. As we read through it, we find it paired with other combinations of words like, "being," "believing," "cheering," "existing," "thinking," "meaning," and "thing." Over the course of this sixteen-page portrait, the dancing woman changes, and how her mutable body exists means different things at different times, which appeals to our understanding of plasticity as such. As Ulla E. Dydo puts it, Duncan's "free, expressionist dancing is shaped into the rhythmic repetitions and permutations of the portrait, which embodies what it says in what the language does" (Stein 1993, 120). The emergence of discourses in and around the Plastic Age obliquely made their mark in Stein's work, which turns to more than just linguistic play.

In *Geography and Plays* (1922), under the section "EVIAN WATER," Gertrude Stein writes that "Evian water is very good. Sometimes I am not sure it is put up by them at least now when there is a war. I say it is fresh. When I do not like a bottle I throw it away. I throw the water away" (Stein

1922, 346). Eerily anticipatory of today's disposal of polyethylene terephthalate (PET) plastic bottles, Stein's speaker is cognizant of the natural resource she wastes. Also, for her time, a time for which the phrase "global warming" would not enter discourse for another twenty-nine years after Stein's death in 1946,[6] Stein surprisingly sees and situates the self and the environment as symbiotic rather than separate, each one affecting the other. For instance, in 1911's *Bon Marche Weather*, the juxtaposition of the weather with consumerism asks us to consider the ways in which we appropriate and absorb our environs and the effect or delayed effect that our consumptive practices can and will have on the environment; Stein writes:

> Very pleasant weather we are having. Very pleasant weather I am having. Very nice weather everybody is having. Very nice weather you are having. . . . There are a very great many things everybody is buying. There are a very great many things you are buying. There are a great many things they are buying. There are a great many things I am buying. (Stein 1993, 149)

Dydo notes that "bon marché" means "reasonably priced, a good buy" and refers to a Parisian department store; for her, Stein's piece studies the connection between the weather and shopping by the way in which the colloquial phrase "Very pleasant weather we are having" not only fills the void of everyday life, but also triggers how one banal conversational topic or observation leads to another (Stein 1993, 149). Following this, *Bon Marche Weather* suggests that thoughtlessness lends itself to consumption for consumption's sake, let alone how we are interpellated to desire to consume. And there is an ecological element and Anthropocene moment to this, too, given that what and how we consume and waste affects climate control. Stein did not know this, of course, but the sheer proximity of consumption and climate in *Bon Marche Weather* places the small and the large—the self and the surrounds—in dialogue with one another. Stein does, however, slightly shift from description to prescription toward the end of her piece when she subtly offers up a socioeconomic commentary by reminding us that there is a contingency or class of people who cannot or will not continually consume or buy into buying when she writes, "There are a great many things not any one is buying. There are a great many things I am not buying. There are a great many things you are not buying. There are a great many things some are not buying" (Stein 1993, 149–50). To buy or not to buy? Being and buying come together in Stein's *Bon Marche Weather* to emphasize our coexistent relationship with the environment, the earth. Consciously or not, the outside enters into Stein's work, which Mina Loy's "Gertrude Stein" gestures to with the titular person figured as physicist Marie Curie investigating experiential knowledge and materiality in the laboratory of language "to extract / a radium of the word" (Loy 1997, 94). And Loy herself was also drawn to natural and unnatural things.

From the celluloid parrot she owned to the trash she collected from New York's Bowery district (Zelazo 2006, 65), Loy was creatively participating in an artificial ecology. Ten years after the appearance of the first fully synthetic plastic, Bakelite, Loy published "Songs to Joannes," which reveals plastic and plasticity through four frames: innovation, perception, paradox, and limitlessness. Historically, a shorter version of Loy's poem was first published in *Others: A Magazine for the New Verse* in 1915 under the title "Love Songs" (Parmar 2013, 34). Then, in 1917, *Others* published the thirty-four section poem, which, along with the first iteration, resulted in both popularity and scandal given its experimental and erotic nature (Parmar 2013, 34).[7] Often read as an account of Loy's love affairs with Futurists F. T. Marinetti and Giovanni Papini (Parmar 2013, 30), "Songs to Joannes" is so much more—indeed, "Loy was a semiotician," Suzanne Zelazo suggests, one whose "poetry mobilizes an array of signifying systems, all of which aim to concretize consciousness" (Zelazo 2006, 51). Loy's "Songs to Joannes" also engages with the semiotics of plastic in the Plastic Age. In her poem, she leaves literal room for speculation of another kind of nature when she writes,

> And the most of Nature   is green[.]
>
> (Loy 1997, 66)

What about the nature that is not green?[8] Is it unnatural? The negative or white space between "Nature" and "is green" signifies an absent, yet present unexplored notion of nature in an artificial ecology that appears in Loy's four frames.

First, Loy writes about a new formation that points to the plasticity of innovation; part of section XIII reads as follows: "Something taking shape / Something that has a new name / A new dimension" (Loy 1997, 57). This excerpt reveals an intimate relationship in the works with the speaker's command and secrecy, but with the Plastic Age in the background, the poem also evokes innovation, emergence, and malleability. Moreover, the "Something taking shape / Something that has a new name" is left unformed and unnamed, which points to a potentiality in process not unlike the production of plastic. And Loy's paradoxical rhetoric of an untold telling points to an elusive and illusive changing materiality.

Second, perceptually speaking, section XVIII of Loy's poem reveals the surrounds moving away from discrete parts ("the severing / Of hill from hill") and toward an emergent middle ("The interim / Of star from star") leading to a stillness ("The nascent / Static / Of night") (Loy 1997, 59). Here, the scenery is seen with eyes that understand how the in-between is something.

The speaker's description of the environs frames perception as a gradual transformation of consciousness. Moving from one short, sharp line to the next, the night scene is slowly moulded into stillness, like the concretization of thought or the cooling of plastic.

Third, section XXVII of the poem employs scientific discourse to wonder about the paradoxical tangibility and ephemerality of objects relative to human interaction. The section begins with the distanced conjunction of "Nucleus" and "Nothing," in the opening line, which contains a slightly enlarged space between the two words. Then, there is the juxtaposition of the human with the artificial: "The hands of races / Drop off from / Immodifiable plastic" (Loy 1997, 63). This section of Loy's poem foregrounds a scene of nonreproductive sexual intercourse within a metaphysical register, which gestures to the paradoxical nature of plastic states. Specifically, the alliterative juxtaposition of "Nucleus" and "Nothing" not only pits the energy and life of the atom or cell against nothingness, but also sets up a bathetic narrative when nothing comes after or from what could be a kernel of life. Reading this section of "Songs to Joannes," Rachel Blau DuPlessis suggests that "[t]here is angry mourning for the washing away of their sperm and cyprine mixture, a 'plastic' substance that was not allowed to do anything" (DuPlessis 2001, 68). Additionally, Loy's poem understands plastic to be a formless substance that can take another shape, like the malleability of celluloid or Bakelite; however, it is, ultimately, "immodifiable"—here, we have a paradoxical representation of a substance that cannot be what it is.

Fourth, seemingly without limit, plastic is and is not plastic—a strange synthetic that appears in section XXVIII:

> Forever
> Coloured conclusions
> Smelt to synthetic
>
> (Loy 1997, 64)

In this section of "Songs to Joannes," there is a sort of synesthesia as the speaker experiences the color of whiteness and emerges anew while nearing a "climacteric" orgasm. Rather obliquely, plastic's unnatural nature appears in a scene where the speaker ecstatically steps out of the self and into an "[i]llimitable monotone," which can be read as an experience of *la petit mort*, or a temporary return to an inorganic—perhaps synthetic—state. With the rhetoric of natural and unnatural chemical syntheses and substances in the backdrop, Loy's poem points to how unreal a human experience like an orgasm can be—it is plastic transcendence. And so as the presence of plastic started to make its way into human history and cultural expression, writers like

Loy consciously and unconsciously picked up the emergence of an artificial ecology. Through micro and macro plastic transformations and experiences, Loy's poem not only helps us to see that there has been and is another nature always at work, but also suggests that cognitive change and enlargement in intimate relations can reach planetary proportions.

In 1927, William Carlos Williams published "Paterson," which contains the now famous line, "no ideas but in things" (Williams 1998, 1: 263). Later, parts of this poem would make up Williams's long poem *Paterson* (1946–1958). Yet, well before Williams's succinct articulation of his aesthetic philosophy in "Paterson," he was immersed in the everyday, like in the "The Red Wheelbarrow" from *Spring and All* (1923). In the time of the Anthropocene, this poem takes on another resonance. The answer to our current crises is not pastoral nostalgia. Rather, it is, in part, a matter of recognizing the significance of relationships of scale between the universal and the particular, or the global and the local, which reveals itself here as the world weighs down on a tool left outside to rust. Encouraging more than just a move away from inattention and inactivity, Williams's poem points out how perspective can call us to action, especially when "so much depends / upon" something so simple. We encounter, engage, and effect the Anthropocene and its unknown future daily. What else can we learn from Williams's attention to detail, to ideas in things?

In this regard, Poem X of *Spring and All*, "The Eyeglasses," has not been looked at closely enough. Offering an overview, one critic explains how the poem exhibits a constantly shifting focus, accumulates sensory data, yields a tension between absorption and detachment, features modes of natural and artificial imitation, and blurs the line between the imagination and the world (Ahearn 1994, 106–07). Another critic notes Williams's experimentation with "ungluings and re-connection" with "various ways of concentrating inside a small arena a potentially over-diffuse feeling for the larger, sensuous universe" (Swigg 2012, 61–62). A number of these themes are useful for thinking through the Anthropocene, especially the poem's fluid focalization, adherent absorption, and larger little. Yet, more can be said about the framework for the work of frames—namely, a pair of celluloid tortoiseshell eyeglasses in a "practical frame" (Williams 1998, 1: 204–05).

Real tortoiseshell was treasured. Meikle notes how "[t]ortoiseshell, a richly mottled yellow-brown material prized for large decorative combs used to restrain Victorian dresses, was perhaps the most scarce" (Meikle 1995, 16–17). He notes how in 1920, the hawksbill turtle's shell ranged from $2 to $25 a pound, and long before celluloid imitations, cattle horns were used by ranchers up until 1900 when packinghouse practices changed (Meikle 1995, 17). With the advent of celluloid, species survived or suffered a little less; the earlier discussed 1878 pamphlet notes how "celluloid [gives] the elephant, the tortoise, and the coral insect a respite in their native haunts; and it will no longer be necessary to ransack the earth in pursuit of substances which are constantly growing scarcer" (qtd. in Meikle 1995, 12). Conveniently forgetting about poaching, let alone the aura around the authentic in capitalism, this pamphlet nonetheless contains a conservationist sentiment. So, how are we to understand the nature of Williams's "celluloid made to / represent tortoiseshell"? With a celluloid production plant nearby—the Arlington Company of New Jersey (Meikle 1995, 19)—Williams's had his eyes on plasticity.

First, with the "favorable / distortion of eyeglasses," Williams's poem paradoxically presents the clarity of corrective lenses as that which is twisted, out of shape, or misleading, yet still "favorable." Mediated vision points to a modified reality, which allows us to "see everything" and near objectivity, or "remain / related to mathematics." Yet perhaps there is another way of seeing the details of our surrounds, or the "universality of things." After all, the speaker is looking at eyeglasses rather than wearing them: "But / they lie there with the gold / earpieces folded down."

Second, ironically, without wearing the glasses, the speaker can see them for what they really are—a thing that is not just itself, but something else, too. Bringing together animal and object, Williams's poem enfolds species and substance in a way that plasticizes nature, which gestures to a burgeoning artificial ecology. With this mutation, a reptilian humanity rears its head as one wears tortoiseshell glasses on his, her, or their face. As spectacles and species join, humanity can see itself in another scale. Here, the "practical frame" is productive as plastic imitation points to something that cuts across organisms in the "Mimeocene": the copying and "emergence of self-replicating molecules" (Morton 2016, 70).

Third, the speaker's interest in and drive toward the "universality of things" collects that which is small and large, near and far including a flower, waste, farmer, daughter, skin, eyeglasses, math, letter, linen, typewriter, and lake. This litany emphasizes the importance of being cognizant of entities and events in the surrounds. While it includes mostly the local, there is a leap with the poem's reference to Titicaca, a lake in South America. Going global, Williams's poem brings the mundane and the remote together without hesitation. With the Plastic Age in the backdrop, there is a sense of expansion, extension, and enlargement as new forms are formulated out of what seems like nothing, as plastics point to how "matter and form are generated in one single gesture" (Bensaude Vincent 2013, 20). Within reach, Williams's celluloid tortoise shell eyeglasses are there for us if we want to see things a little differently. And to see things a lot differently, we can turn to one of Williams's acquaintances, the Baroness.

The German-born Baroness Elsa von Freytag-Loringhoven walked the streets of New York during the early twentieth century (Gammel 2002, 3). The Baroness was William Carlos Williams's lover, but attacked him on more than one occasion and, compared to Williams, has been historically placed at the margins of modernism.[10] From June 29, 1910, to April 18, 1923, the Baroness spent most of her time living in New York, where she made her mark as the "first American dada" (Gammel 2002, xvii, xix; Heap, qtd. in Gammel and Zelazo 2011, 331). Often living in squalor, her work was borne out of waste.[11] In his misogynistic account of an encounter with the Baroness,[12] Williams describes her place on Fourteenth Street close to the Hudson River where she lived for several years at "the most unspeakably filthy tenement in the city" (Gammel 2002, 231; Williams 1967, 11). "Romantically, mystically dirty, of grimy walls, dark, gaslit halls and narrow stairs," writes Williams, "it smelt of black waterclosets, one to a floor, with low gasflame always burning and torn newspapers trodden in the wet. Waves of stench thickened on each landing as one moved up" (Williams 1967, 11). Williams could not stomach it because he did not have the guts: "you lack entrails," writes the Baroness to him in an undated letter, "you have all your life been disemboweled" (Freytag-Loringhoven 2014, n.p.). Dwelling in debris, in modernism's melting pot tenement living, the Baroness lived in a room full of ironware, tires, gilded vegetables, hungry dogs, celluloid paintings, and ash cans (Gammel and Wrighton 2013, 796). And she wore plastic.

From wrist to shoulder, the Baroness wore celluloid curtain rings around her arms, ones she stole from a furniture display. Adorned with plastic, the Baroness took to collecting, sculpting with, and writing on and about celluloid (Gammel 2002, 182, 184, 201, 209, 390). This plastic appears in the Baroness's poem "A Dozen Cocktails—Please" from 1927.

> Always eat them————
> They have dandy celluloid tubes—all sizes—
> Tinted diabolically as a baboon's hind complexion.

(Gammel and Zelazo 2011, 48)

It is clear how the Baroness's "rebellious, highly sexed howls and counter-cultural Dada gestures made her a forerunner of the Beat poets of the 1950s" (Gammel and Zelazo 2011, 8)—consider the sexually explicit rubble of Ginsberg's "Sunflower Sutra." A poem presenting a "carnival of oral sexuality" (Gammel 2002, 377), "A Dozen Cocktails—Please" is especially playful and provocative with its reference to "celluloid tubes." The Baroness's celluloid tube is a tube of lipstick, one that is the color red like a "baboon's hind complexion," which expresses the speaker's animal nature. Moreover, the celluloid tube is a condom: "the Trojan condoms [were] first produced in New York in 1920 and legalized in 1923" (Gammel and Zelazo 2011, 340). As both lipstick and condom, the celluloid tube brings together images of oral sex, anal sex, and bestiality—the plasticity of species means so much more in the Anthropocene. And as the Baroness degenders the phallus (Gammel and Zelazo 2011, 42), she assembles a human, animal, and object relation that is open to many different, intersecting lines of desire that generate several sexual scenarios. Here, plastic yields the plasticity of interpretation, and nature is more unnatural than we imagined.

Little is known about Abraham Lincoln Gillespie (1895–1950). Writing on the experimental poet, Cary Nelson notes how he is a postmodernist *avant la lettre* (Nelson 1989, 74). Gillespie's work exhibits a number of traits including the combination of pop culture with references to the nature of language, the self-conscious collapse of phrases into words, and the creation of new words through collage-like combinations (Nelson 1989, 74).[13] His aesthetic is motivated by a desire to reveal the way language shapes consciousness, which is a part of his satirization of the unconscious power of verbal culture (Nelson 1989, 74). Given his countercultural work, he distrusts how language is received and works to challenge the assumptions of his readers by way of his witty, yet difficult style (Nelson 1989, 75). Gillespie's strange style reveals a form of plasticity, too. Indeed, the power of plastic to unconsciously affect material culture shapes his way of thinking and writing. In "ABSTRAKTIDS," Gillespie offers a poetic collection to illustrate "a style of Word-Phrasing," or "barely-covert continuity in minimized grammar-sequence," in order to make the politics of language more pedestrian and evoke a wide range of provocative aesthetic affects ("a broader-gamuted JOLT-POSSIBLE, like to that given Plastic Color by Pointillism") (Gillespie 1980, 8). "ABSTRAKTIDS" begins as follows: "infradigit-enunceColor Plastic / nowhere-within-Space transcendCommand Nirvana / nowhere-within-handy-Space Chinese FloatInfinity" (Gillespie 1980, 7–8). Aware of the mutability of plastic, Gillespie's "ABSTRAKTIDS" exhibits this very process on the page with its peculiar portmanteaus. What appears to be automatic or associative writing is, rather, methodically thought out. With his hybrids, Gillespie strings together syllables like polymers, to borrow from Bök. With words like "clean" and "slobber" entering into the string "fragile-cleanslobber-purity" or other combinations like "lewdtalk," "sewerquiet-underflow-residue," "fartsootMurmurs," "oozeddry," or "Minddecree-droolsput-leakLipsSPEAK" (Gillespie 1980, 7–8), Gillespie's messy assemblage registers a tension in its clean, efficient thoughts sullied by aesthetic entanglements affected by the very nature of plastic properties.

From Futurism to Stein to Loy to Williams to the Baroness to Gillespie, it is apparent that there is a thematic and formal attention to the modernist semiotics of plastics. Indeed, we could even consider F. Scott Fitzgerald's poem "A Slave to Modern Improvements" from 1914 as an early form of plastic surgery, where the speaker's father is a physician who wants to become a celebrity by replacing his son's "parts with junk" like a silver chest, crystal eye, platinum lung, aluminum fingers, asbestos toes, and trash (Fitzgerald 1971, 7–8). Focalized and reified through plastics and plasticity, the Anthropocene appears obliquely in a number of texts by these authors who teach us a number of different things. Specifically, Futurism foregrounds a techno-corporeality; Stein shows us gradual transformation situated within an environ; Loy highlights another unnatural nature always at work interpersonally; Williams gives us new insights into the scale of sight itself, let alone what is seen in species; the Baroness voices an understanding of an unavoidable immersion in embodiment of nonhuman things and phenomena; and Gillespie reveals how language is the practice of plasticity. Through parts of modernism's poetics of plastic, we can start to see how the yet-to-be-named Anthropocene appeared. Indeed, the activity of and actors within modernism's artificial ecology mark the nascent stages of the thought and impact of scale and species today.

NOTES

1. My calculation of 900 percent is based on Susan Frienkel's observation that, in 1960, the average American consumed thirty pounds of plastic per year; today, one devours three hundred pounds per annum (Freinkel 2011, 7). While Freinkel notes that 1.6 billion pounds of plastic per year ends up in the ocean, her statistic dates back to 1981 (Freinkel 2011, 119, 272). More recently, the United Nations estimated that 7 million tons of trash ends up in the ocean, and 5.6 million tons of which is plastic (Humes 2012, 134).

2. For an interesting discussion of Russian modernist philosopher poet Lucian Blaga's notions of the "plastic metaphor," see Jones 2006, 177.

3. This is my calculation based on how "[p]roduction rose sharply from about 100,000 pounds in 1911 to more than two million pounds in 1916. The General Bakelite Company prospered" (Meikle 1995, 49).

4. Frienkel's *Plastic: A Toxic Love Story* makes reference to the fact that Bakelite was used to make ashtrays (Freinkel 2011, 23).

5. In Stein's *A Bouquet. Their Wills* (1928), the word "celluloid" appears in an interlude (Stein 2002, 412).

6. See Broecker 1975.

7. For a discussion of the experimental and erotic nature of "Song to Joannes," see Quartermain 2013, 147, 149–50, 152n9.

8. See Cohen, 2013.

9. See Williams 1967a, 164–66, 168–69.

10. One of the earliest publications on the Baroness is Robert Reiss's "'My Baroness': Elsa von Freytag-Loringhoven" from 1985. Since then, just over a dozen critics have written about the Baroness, and Irene Gammel has authored a majority of the publications.

11. The Baroness used everyday refuse to make sculptures; take, for instance, the following description of one of her artworks: "under a glass bell, a piece of sculpture that appeared to be chicken guts imitated in wax" (Williams qtd. in Gammel 2002, 264).

12. For a discussion of Williams's sexism and misogyny in the New York Dada avant-garde, see Jones 2004, 10ff.

13. Secondary criticism on Gillespie is scant at best; peripheral references are common with some slightly longer discussions. For instance, see Zaniello 1979 "The Thirteenth Disciple of James Joyce: Abraham Lincoln Gillespie" in (1979): 51–61 or Delville 1998, 50–51.

WORKS CITED

Ahearn, Barry. 1994. *William Carlos Williams and Alterity*. New York: Cambridge University Press.

Baldwin, Doug. 2001. "Putting Images into Words: Elements of the 'Cinematic' in William Faulkner's Prose." The Faulkner Journal 16 (1/2): 35–64.

Balla, Giacomo, and Fortunato Depero. 2009. "Futurist Reconstruction of the Universe." In *Futurism: An Anthology*, edited by Lawrence Rainey, Christine Poggi, Laura Wittman. New Haven, CT: Yale University Press.

Barthes, Roland. 1972. *Mythologies*. Translated by Annette Lavers. New York: Hill and Wang.

Bensaude Vincent, Bernadette. 2013. "Plastics, Materials and Dreams of Dematerialization." In *Accumulation: The Material Politics of Plastic*, edited by Jennifer Gabrys, Gay Hawkins, and Mike Michael, 17–29. New York: Routledge.

Boccioni, Umberto. (1913) 2009. "The Plastic Foundations of Futurist Sculpture and Painting." In *Futurism: An Anthology*, edited by Lawrence Rainey, Christine Poggi, and Laura Wittman, 139–42. New Haven, CT: Yale University Press.

Bök, Christian. 2001. "From *Poetry Plastique*." *Open Letter* 11 (2): 93–102.

Broecker, Wallace. 1975. "Climate Change: Are we on the Brink of a Pronounced Global Warming?" *Science* 189 (4201): 460–63.

Brown, Judith. 2009. *Glamour in Six Dimensions: Modernism and the Radiance of Form*. Ithaca, NY: Cornell University Press.

Burke, Carolyn. 1996. *Becoming Modern: The Life of Mina Loy*. New York: Farrar, Straus, and Giroux.

Cohen, Jeffrey Jerome, ed. 2013. *Prismatic Ecology: Ecotheory beyond Green*. Minneapolis: University of Minnesota Press.

Corcoran, Patricia L., Charles J. Moore, and Kelly Jazvac. 2014. "An Anthropogenic Marker Horizon in the Future Rock Record." *GSA Today* 24 (6): 4–8.

Clark, Timothy. 2015. *Ecocriticism on the Edge: The Anthropocene as a Threshold Concept*. New York: Bloomsbury.

Crutzen, J. Paul, and Eugene F. Stoermer. 2000. "The 'Anthropocene.'" *The International Geosphere-Biosphere Programme Global Change Newsletter* 41: 17–18.

cummings, e. e. 1991. *Complete Poems 1904–1962*. Edited by George J. Firmage. New York: Liveright.

Delville, Michel. 1998. *The American Prose Poem: Poetic Form and the Boundaries of Genre*. Gainesville: University of Florida Press.

DuPlessis, Rachel Blau. 2001. *Genders, Races, and Religious Cultures in Modern American Poetries, 1908–1934*. Cambridge: Cambridge University Press.

Fitzgerald, F. Scott. 1971. *In His Own Time: A Miscellany*. Edited by Matthew J. Bruccoli and Jackson R. Bryer. Toronto: Popular Library.

Freytag-Loringhoven, Baroness Elsa von. "Letter to William Carlos Williams." *BaronessElsa*. Edited by Tanya Clement. Encoded by Eleanor Dickinson. http://www.baronesselsa.org/teibp/content/Williams-2-1-38.xml. Accessed 3 August 2021.

Frienkel, Susan. 2011. *Plastic: A Toxic Love Story*. Boston: Houghton Mifflin Harcourt.

Gabrys, Jennifer, Gay Hawkins, and Mike Michael. 2013. "Introduction: From materiality to plasticity." In *Accumulation: The Material Politics of Plastic*, edited by Jennifer Gabrys, Gay Hawkins, and Mike Michael, 1–14. New York: Routledge.

Gammel, Irene. 2002. *Baroness Elsa: Gender, Dada, and Everyday Modernity, a Cultural Biography*. Cambridge, MA: MIT Press.

Gammel, Irene, and John Wrighton. 2013. "'Arabesque Grotesque': Toward a Theory of Dada Ecopoetics." *ISLE* 20 (4): 795–816.

Gammel, Irene, and Suzanne Zelazo. 2011. *Body Sweats: The Uncensored Writings of Elsa von Freytag-Loringhoven*. Cambridge, MA: MIT Press.

Gillespie, Abraham Lincoln. 1980. *The Syntactic Revolution*. Edited by Richard Milazzo. New York: Out of London Press.

Ginsberg, Allen. 2007. *Collected Poems 1947–1997*. New York: Harper Perennial Modern Classics.

Haraway, Donna J. 2016. *Staying with the Trouble: Making Kin in the Chthulucene*. Durham, NC: Duke University Press.

Humes, Edward. 2012. *Garbology: Our Dirty Love Affair with Trash*. New York: Penguin.

Jones, Amelia. 2004. *Irrational Modernism: A Neurasthenic History of New York Dada*. Cambridge, MA: MIT Press.

Jones, Michael S. 2006. *The Metaphysics of Religion: Lucian Blaga and Contemporary Philosophy*. Madison, NJ: Fairleigh Dickinson University Press.

Loy, Mina. 1997. *The Lost Lunar Baedeker: Poems of Mina Loy*. New York: Noonday Press.

Marinetti, F. T. 2009. "Manifesto of Futurist Dance." In *Futurism: An Anthology*, edited by Lawrence Rainey, Christine Poggi, Laura Wittman. New Haven, CT: Yale University Press.

Meikle, Jeffrey L. 1995. *American Plastic: A Cultural History*. New Brunswick, NJ: Rutgers University Press.

Mirrlees, Hope. 1920. *Paris: A Poem*. London: Hogarth.

Moore, Marianne. 2016. *Observations*. Edited by Linda Leavall. New York: Farrar, Straus, and Giroux.

Morton, Timothy. 2016. *Dark Ecology: For a Logic of Future Coexistence*. New York: Columbia University Press.

———. 2013. *Hyperobjects: Philosophy and Ecology after the End of the World*. Minneapolis: University of Minnesota Press.

Nelson, Cary. 1989. *Repression and Recovery: Modern American Poetry and the Politics of Cultural Memory*. Madison: University of Wisconsin Press.

Newcomb, John Timberman. 2012. *How Did Poetry Survive? The Making of Modern Verse*. Urbana: University of Illinois Press.

Parmar, Sandeep. 2013. *Reading Mina Loy's Autobiographies: Myth of the Modern Woman*. New York: Bloomsbury Academic.

Purdy, Jedediah. 2015. *After Nature: A Politics for the Anthropocene*. Cambridge, MA: Harvard University Press.

Rakosi, Carl. 1967. *Amulet*. New York: New Directions Press.

Snyder, Gary. 1974. *Turtle Island*. New York: New Directions Press.

Stein, Gertrude. 1922. *Geography and Plays*. Boston: The Four Seasons Company.

———. 2002. *The Gertrude Stein Reader: The Great American Pioneer of Avant-Garde Letters*. Edited by Richard Kostelanetz. New York: Cooper Square Press.

———. 1993. *A Stein Reader*. Edited by Ulla E. Dydo. Evanston: Northwestern University Press.

Stevens, Wallace. 1954. *The Collected Poems of Wallace Stevens*. New York: Vintage.

Swigg, Richard. 2012. *Quick, Said the Bird: Williams, Eliot, Moore, and the Spoken Word*. Iowa City: University of Iowa Press.

Quartermain, Peter. 2013. *Stubborn Poetries: Poetic Facticity and the Avant-Garde*. Tuscaloosa: University of Alabama Press.

Williams, William Carlos. 1967a. *The Autobiography of William Carlos Williams*. New York: New Directions.

———. 1967b. *Contact, Numbers 1–5, 1920–1924*, edited by Williams Carlos Williams and Robert M. McAlmon. New York: Kraus Reprint Corporation.

———. 1988. *The Collected Poems of William Carlos Williams*. 2 vols. Edited by A. Walton Litz and Christopher MacGowan. New York: New Directions.

Zaniello, Thomas. 1979. "The Thirteenth Disciple of James Joyce: Abraham Lincoln Gillespie." *A Journal of Modern Literature* 7 (1): 51–61.

Zelazo, Suzanne. 2006. "'Altered Observation of Modern Eyes': Mina Loy's Collages, and Multisensory Aesthetics." *Senses & Society* 4 (1): 47–74.

Zukofsky, Louis. 1991. *Complete Short Poetry*. Baltimore: The Johns Hopkins University Press.

Chapter Twelve

Sky and Smoke

Literary Atmospherics in Cary and Ibuse

Stuart Christie

A contrastive analysis of literary atmospherics in Joyce Cary's *The Horse's Mouth* (1944) and Masuji Ibuse's *Black Rain* (*Kuroi Ame*) (1962) presents sharply differing accounts as characters in these novels look skyward, careening between representations of a world of artistic possibility and threats of contamination. This dramatic shift, alternately fulfilling and fearful, provides a greatly altered scope for aesthetics in relation to the modernist Anthropocene. In *The Horse's Mouth*, the delivery of a moral aesthetic relies mainly upon Cary's "art-organized experience" (Case 1959, 119), the painterly representation of the skies above London which, canvas-like, serves artistic freedom and independence as a background for the human story. In *Black Rain*, by contrast, the horrific sculpting of the Japanese lifeworld by unseen atmospheric agents renders the putative perfectibility of art obscene. New atomic-era diseases (*genbakubyō*), like the communities they at once disfigure and enunciate (*hibakusha*), make a mockery of the painterly sky, and radically re-impose as radioactive the world-forming climate (*fūdo*) Ibuse's contemporary, Japanese philosopher, Watsuji Tetsurō, theorized. Such atmospheric bivalency—humanist in Cary and denaturing in Ibuse—is constitutive of a shared epistemological horizon within the modernist Anthropocene that differentiates, even as it connects, London and Hiroshima, Gulley Jimson's antics and the voiceless collective of Hiroshima's irradiated dead. I conclude with some provisional assertions about how our contemporary understanding of this shared horizon is also changing, as the stress of the Anthropocene requires the heuristics of world-consciousness to accelerate beyond the logic of juxtaposition (Here/Not-Here) and toward convergence (Everywhere Here). While the accelerating convergence of the modernist Anthropocene may create more opportunities for the singularity of imaginative experience, it also threatens the epistemological basis of alterity proper, the means by which any locality, experience, or individual action may be recognized as different from others.

Distinct from the philosophical nuances of contemporary debates around the Anthropocene, human geographers of the future will doubtless reference the heavy ecological demands made upon our species by converging skies.[1] While true of our own meteorological moment, it may be worth remembering that blank vellum has always afforded an outlet to heaven. Lacking solid form and any intrinsic content, air and sky have always constituted the upper reaches, even the attenuation, of a heavier, earthly "Nature." If atmosphere has always been contiguous with *terra firma*, actively shaping and sculpting our earthly state, it also has offered access to a divine realm that, by definition, excludes us. Before undertaking their earthly dispatch, Alexander Pope's sylphs frolicked because "whoever fair and chaste Rejects mankind, is by / some Sylph embrac'd: For Spirits, freed from mortal laws, with ease Assume what sexes and what shapes they please" (Pope Canto 1: lines, 898–900). Subsequently, this celestial realm also housed a darkening critique of human progress, in the guise of William Blake's Urizen brooding, gazing earthward with pity. With the advent of modernist literature, the sky has been considered a compositional surface reflecting the wonder (or decay) of our own human designs. Or their absence: as in Wallace Stevens's "Evening without Angels," where the atmosphere offers rebuttal, deflecting all poetic designs: "Air is air, / Its vacancy glitters around us everywhere / Its sounds are not angelic syllables" (Stevens 1982, 136–37). Here Stevens invokes "vacant" air to deflect the threat or promise of a celestial ("angelic") invitation which, in fact, is not there. Stevens's poem denies atmosphere any agency to deliver, on behalf of angels, portents.

Yet even when considered variously, literary atmosphere in itself encompasses and bounds nothing. Instead, atmospheric mimesis nominalizes the presence of something that remains shrouded apart from words. Signifying the poverty of the human—whatever it is we cannot comprehend—skies house sites of imaginative potential but that is all, the faulty premise (and promise) of the human-built environment projected upward. By contrast, as in Tōmatsu Shōmei's stunningly beautiful cloudscape, the truth of atmosphere is that it simply is (Fig 12.1).

Such contrasting, yet constitutive, depictions of literary atmosphere—as equally human-inspiring and human-deflecting—give renewed urgency to the reconsideration, as in the ensuing analysis, of poetic convergence: that is, whether skies care for us or not. Much as Blake's "Contraryes" once augured, the modernist Anthropocene collapses differences in space and place, enabling contrastive logic at an aesthetic level. Notions of cosmology and

Figure 12.1. The vacancy of the skies glitters everywhere. Hateruma Island, Okinawa [波照間島] Platinum palladium photograph, 1971. Tōmatsu Shōmei © Shōmei Tōmatsu —INTERFACE.

life-world formerly determined contrastively are now converging as a function of global predicament.

Bounding human existence so variously, the figurative skies of the modernist Anthropocene, as I view them, depend upon the exegesis of two related claims. First, modernist writers continue to use atmosphere to signify the long-standing reduction of the human condition to a correlate of an as-yet-fallen divine nature that, nevertheless, portends artistic possibility. As such, the problem of writing the atmosphere emerges as a function of the "fall" of human nature, which is readily commuted to the problem of artistic representation itself. Signifying subjects are "fallen" doubly: first, into the necessity for writing the ineffable, an attempt which must inevitably fail and which provides further evidence for that original failure. We sin, therefore we must write; we write, therefore we add to the freight of sin.

Second, the advent of twentieth-century philosophical humanism ensured that the simple fact of naturalist correlation to human existence, even in the interests of redemption, would be challenged if not overturned outright. Admittedly, this finding disputes the exceptionality of the Anthropocene as a category unique to our own time and extends its totalizing claims backward across a far longer event horizon. Humanist exceptionalism, this argument runs, has always imposed its own image upon the world to whichever effects.

Armed with skeptical hermeneutics, Heidegger not only attacked the subordination of the human category to nature in principle—a riposte to *fin de siècle*
literary naturalism—but reversed it.[2] Since Auschwitz and Hiroshima, the
results have remained catastrophic: vengeful skies have persisted, rendering
pathetic the fallacy that the Anthropocene could be in any way distinct from
the human world that called forth the fiery apocalypse upon itself. Even so,
literary skies have remained sites of immanence challenging the bounding
function of human perception whether of individual perspective or scientific method. Troping upon the "ex" (outside) of *ex-sistere*, Watsuji Tetsurō
termed this function a "climactic limitation," forcing humanity to the very
margins of being—atmosphere (*fūdo*)—a constitutive liminality that at least
initially centers the modernist Anthropocene positively, as the subordination
of the species to nature while rejecting empiricism.[3]

How, then, could the painterly heavens of a Joyce Cary novel frame the
smoking hells of Masuji Ibuse's? How dare they? The Anthropocene is the
how and the why. Juxtaposing the atmospheres of these novels, at one time
seemingly so far apart, puts stress upon the model of planetary relationality
Eric Hayot has described as "worldedness," dependent as it is upon the toggle
"between the world inside and the world outside the work" (Hayot 2012, 134,
139). I suggest here that not only does the Anthropocene necessarily refigure
and displace the human category of existence distinct from the work, but it
also requires all humanist texts, epistemologies, and heuristics to be translated as a function of eco-phenomenological convergence radically disruptive of the delimiting, prepositional logic of bifurcation (whether "inside" or
"outside"). To speak or write of the inside and outside of the "worldedness"
of the Anthropocene posits no heuristic worth pursuing, even as emerging
planetary frames themselves are remapping traditional coordinates of the
"globe" (globality) in terms recent critiques have provided.

For example, while the juxtaposition of Cary and Ibuse's atmospherics
provides direct evidence for what Jennifer Wenzel has, in a striking analysis,
called "world-imagining from below" (Wenzel 2014, 19), any underlying
juxtapositional premises ("below"/"above") also converge. Wenzel's newer
metrics, spaces, and scalars for the planetary must assuredly produce alternative geographies for understanding subalterneity in any local context. Still,
as every locality is now increasingly impinged upon by the planetary atmosphere, addressing the question of what constitutes any "local" aesthetic for
our time—text, canvas, sky—should involve aligning the Anthropocene's
differing scalars with increased ecophenomenological urgency. Distinct from
its skies, the "world" can no longer prefigure or predict a human future. Nor
can this latest "worlding" constituted by the Anthropocene—reframing the

term as Gayatri Chakravorty Spivak seminally asserted it—simply move its humanist presumptions and epistemologies off-planet. Instead, we must confront the shocking recognition that we can no longer consider humanity—even, or especially, a brutalizing, neo-imperial, and globalized one—as in any way privileged by the power Wenzel's "planetarity" now exercises over us. The Anthropocene is de-privileging us all, although the scale and tempo of its devastating effects are certain to harm subaltern peoples and other species first.

Grim as the foregoing may seem, and suspending questions of comparative aesthetics for the moment as prurient, all skies of the Anthropocene are converging. So long as it remains diffident to such convergence, "worldedness" will remain an empty signifier until alternative geographies of connection, fueled by predicament, populate our planetary philosophies. The falling-short of literary theory at the present time, as we seek to address challenges pertaining to ecophenomenology—including what may be thought of as the "Anthroposcenic" content for contemporary forms of existence—urgently requires all scholars to query the moral capacity of modernist aesthetics and literatures to speak or write any longer for the "world." As we now enter a more "mature" and denaturing Anthropocene, distinct from the human world and rapidly elevating away from it, the liminality, even fragility, of contemporary theorizations of world and planetary discourse based upon the human prerogative and the bare life seems obvious.[4]

All too clearly, this power of the Anthroposcenic is now totalizing and re-writing physical and geographical spaces at heretofore inconceivable speeds. The Maldives will soon enough be no longer, except at an ebbing tide; Antarctica serves increasingly as a summer species habitat. The dream of early modern explorers, the Northwest Passage, is to become a reality after all, thanks to global warming and Russian ice-breakers. Extreme meteorology is our planetary dispositif now, and subaltern species everywhere, human and not, will know this planetary truth most severely: first, by the material facts and aggression of subalterneity itself, which makes subaltern communities most vulnerable to climate crisis; and second, by their relative powerlessness in seeking voice to reply, to resist, or even to denounce Wenzel's still crucial question for the late Anthropocene: "what would it mean to think more like a planet, less like a person?" (Wenzel 2014, 24). Wenzel's question astutely addresses the binary between planetarity and subjectivity as false; it also highlights the problem that planetary consciousness, like the subaltern, *cannot speak*. The Anthropocene not only risks abstracting the human category as we currently understand it, but makes inevitable the emergence of a subsequent, and uniquely weathered, *humanitas* in forms few can predict. The threat of extinction returns us brutally to our species self; even as this remains a threat that the subaltern classes of the world, and all species and ecologies distinct from the subaltern human, have always faced. Species privilege no longer means what it once did.

SKIES

For Joyce Cary, skies establish ground for the underlying determinism of the creative mind which, as Cary believed, "sums up" human problems for imaginative action. In this aspect, Cary's debt to William Blake—whom he read askance the received Arnoldian, and later Symbolist, critical traditions (Larrissy 2006, 100; Case 1959, 117)—is clear. Additionally, Cary's masterpiece, *The Horse's Mouth*, expresses idiosyncratic, if indirect, homage to literary inheritances from his own Anglo-Irish background: first, to James Joyce (the protagonist in Cary's novel, the failed painter, Gulley Jimson, is the portrait of the artist as a jaded and utterly dissolute man); second, to Blake himself, whose dissenting antinomianism Cary cherished (Larrissy 2006, 101) as the corrective to an ensuing tradition that, since Matthew Arnold and T. S. Eliot, had presumed to overlook the devourer in the prolific, and the defiler in the beauty. It is entirely to Cary's credit that, in Jimson's journey through Greenbank, London, we find a bourgeois *Künstlerroman* recast as a satanic descent into darker truths of genius and embodiment made all the more glorious—and notorious—because it is at once foreordained and chosen.

Edward Case sums up Cary's contrarian difference apart from his own critical era nicely: "Cary avoided the knowledge-problem. It was as a painter that he looked at the world. [A painter's] concern is its nature and rendition" (Case 1959, 120). Thus redoubtable in defense of the material aesthetic, Cary opens almost every chapter of *A Horse's Mouth* with an upward glance, offering outlet onto the infinite via Jimson's decidedly humanizing perspective:

> It was half-past six, too dark to paint, turning very cold. Clouds all streaming away like ghost fish under the ice. Evening sun turning reddish. Trees along the hard like old copper. Old willow leaves shaking up and down in the breeze, making shadows on the ones below, reflections on the ones above. Need a tricky brush to give the effect and what would be the good. (Cary 1944, 21)

"Too dark to paint," Jimson's multitudinous mind (and Cary's ekphrasis in writing it) paints anyway. Expansive and never estranging, Jimson's perception of the sky is familiar and certain. His answer to Hitler is the old mahogany clouds above (Cary 1944, 63) and the moonlit Thames "before somebody thought of dirt, and colors, and humans" (Cary 1944, 82). Jimson does not require the sky to appear to be anything other than that which it appears to him to be. As such, it grounds reliably the particularity of his perspectivalism, vision, and experience of the "world" in any weather and mood:

> And I went out to get room for my grief. Thank God, it was a high sky on Green-bank. . . . Under the cloud-bank. Sun was in the bank. Streak of salmon below. Salmon trout above soaking into wash blue. River whirling along so fast that its skin was pulled into wrinkles like silk dragged over the floor. (Cary 1944, 56)

Jimson's painterly atmospherics are a reliable index of his own being, whether in agony or ecstasy, as well as of his willful and defiant urge to make existence, however false, beautiful:

> The sky feels too big. . . . But I liked it. I swam in it. I couldn't take my eyes off the clouds, the water, the mud. And I must have been hopping up and down Greenbank hard for half an hour grinning like a gargoyle, until the wind began to get up my trousers and down my back, and to bring me to myself, as they say. Meaning my liver and lights. (Cary 1944, 5)

Here skies return Jimson to himself, the celebrant of his "liver and lights." The epiphany, at least as Cary depicts it, allows Jimson to adopt, for one miraculous moment of infinitude, the pose of Walt Whitman ("I swam in it").

What is remarkable about Cary's skies is their clarifying and steadying aspect. The skies above Greenbank inevitably return Jimson to his better—that is, aestheticizing—self. The question then remains: For whom does Gulley Jimson burn? What being or worldview does his trouble propitiate? To my mind, Jimson is the Job of high modernism, "born to trouble as the sparks fly upward" (Barnes 1998, 5:7).[5] But with a difference: there is ecstasy in his agony. His trouble breeds a determination to defy ugliness. Such aesthetic redemption may be found in Jimson's peculiarly agonized appreciation of creative independence; his pursuit of aesthetic truth on the lam comes to rest upon a set of interactions he rather crudely, yet remarkably, describes as located "inside" and "outside" existence. Confounding "Old Bill" (Blake) with "Ben" (Spinoza) allows Jimson to map the inside onto the outside of being:

> Yes, I said to myself, I've got something. Contemplation, in fact, is on the OUTSIDE. It's not on the spot. And the truth is that Spinoza was always on the outside. He didn't understand freedom. . . . Freedom, to be plain, is nothing but THE INSIDE OF THE OUTSIDE. (Cary 1944, 124)

To Jimson, contemplating the beauty of the skies out there (God, eternal verities, truth uncompromised by representation) must align with the individual's freedom to search for the corresponding aesthetic down here (will, artistry, self-love). Admittedly, "freedom" can be a vague term upon which to align the two. Edward Case defines Cary's freedom, and that of his characters, as "that inward autonomous realm where man knows his own needs and yearnings, and ponders their realization. Freedom, above all, is *human power*" (Case 1959, 117; emphasis in original). Such a powerful alignment of the "outside" and "inside" is best embodied by re-centering the human.

Still, Jimson's metaphysical fancies are, mostly, passing ones. Metaphysics does not trouble his faith in hand and eye to capture beauty amidst a variety of planes, lines, and perspectives. If Blake's poetry seeks to transform mere observation into eternal vision—noting his distinction between cognitive perception and intuitive apperception (Trigilio 2000, 15; 31, 80)—then Jimson's canvasses invert the claim by returning visionary immanence back to the dimensional world, by imposing forms upon ineffable truths. The diverse imaginary and aesthetic expanses wherein Jimson takes refuge are actually homologies, linking the determinations of his imagination (percepts) to their externalization on canvas and, again, to the painterly skies above. Sky, percept, painting: the succession (metalepsis) of negative expanses never adds up to pay dirt, financial or metaphysical, for Jimson. Still, we see that he appreciates the difference between seeing and feeling the aesthetic enough to propound it to others. And the painterly skies, one realizes, afford shelter from harm in ways the bleak realities of Jimson's material existence cannot.

Less visionary than workaday aesthete, Gulley Jimson survives jail each time, recanting nothing, and scrabbles at the Blakean requirement—that infinity be perceptible—without ever really achieving more than a momentary exaltation. But these moments are enough. This is, perhaps, why Jimson's noxious character eventually becomes so likeable. Irredeemable yet resolute, he takes his epiphanic truth any way he can, the Blakean avatar of Dionysian ecstasy, embodying excess to the very aesthetic system that at once nourishes and excludes him (Larrissy 2006, 9), on the "inside" and "outside" of the eternal moment. His love of the sky, now, makes more sense: by subordinating celestial skies and their metaphysics to the canvas, Promethean imagination may assert a false primacy over eternity; it also serves as an ecstatic outlet into history.

To recap: Cary's painterly skies depict his crystalline ideological commitment to artistic freedom, even as they illustrate far older aesthetic principles reminted in *A Horse's Mouth* for modernist literature. Cary's skies are, mainly, evidence for ekphrasis, words as paint and paint as words, *materia media* for a presumptive vision ("outside") in support of humanist creation ("inside"). That such exercises must by more recent philosophical definitions fail in principle—since Edmund Husserl ontology has been required to serve phenomenology—does not bely the power, necessity, and jubilation by which Jimson's torrid career (as pauper, thief, and miscreant) serves his search for artistic beauty, a search that enables the refusal of Cary's art to worry over the "epistemological problem" and, instead, to embrace metaphysical potential: "not the problem of whether reality can be *known*, but how it is constituted, and how it may be re-created" (Case 1959, 120). Holes in the night-jar, Jimson's skies offer negativity to the world as it is, an outlet by which the artist may achieve *ekstasis*. This, then, is an important discovery: Cary's skies are not merely reflective of a humanist narcissism —of Jimson or Plantie or Coker or any other human being. They are also determining, and catalytic, of an otherwise salutary and self-obliterating impulse toward alterity proper. They recall to us an ascent toward our more beautiful selves, even as they inevitably return us, plummeting, to our fallen state.

SMOKE

Famously, Erich Auerbach recognized the shift from godly externality to innate nature as a constitutive difference in narrative figuration. Reading the seemingly mundane fact of Odysseus's scar askance the Pauline gospels, the first chapter of *Mimesis* contrasts the absence of background in Homer ("procession of phenomena" in an eternal foreground) with the telos, culminating in Christian redemption, imposed on St. Paul's road to Damascus. Auerbach goes on to recognize, in Homer, a "retarding element . . . opposed to any tensional and suspensive striving toward a goal" (Auerbach 2013, 5). The Christian gospels, by contrast, "seek to subject us [to interpretation] and if we refuse to be subjected we are rebels" (Auerbach 2013, 15). Of course, both types of figuration—processionally suspended and interpretively masterful— are always-already subjected to language; and the rewriting of skies for modernism allows for our reconsideration of the co-articulation, or alignment, of different epistemological frames. Having considered Cary's use of the sky in an English literary context, we now shift our figuration, in time and space, to a Japanese rendering. The comparative treatment of literary atmosphere shifts from sky to smoke.

As retrospectively recounted by its narrator, Shizuma Shigematsu, the plot motif of Ibuse's *Black Rain* is elegant enough. Having survived the bombing of Hiroshima on August 6, 1945 along with his niece, Yasuko, and his wife, Shigeko, Shizuma compiles (and then diversely integrates) several journal accounts, including his own, of the bombing and the struggles to survive during the week following. In compiling these for the historical record, Shizuma has only one ostensible motive: to assure potential suitors that Yasuko, having survived the bombing, carries no evidence of radiation sickness and as a consequence is marriageable. Almost incredibly, the entire family survives the bombing, even though all three are in separate locations. Each bears different symptoms or injuries, with Yasuko bearing strange "marks" (*māku*):

> The sky was dusky with the smoke from the fires. There was no water from the taps, so I made Yasuko wash her hands at the pool in the garden, but the marks would not come off. She said they were made by the black rain, and they were firmly stuck on the skin. They were not tar, nor black paint, but something of unknown origin. (Ibuse 2012, 92)

Marked by apocalypse, Yasuko's "unknown" and indelible marks remain untranslatable.[6]

This illegible and unknowable rain signifies the boundary in signification between the sacred and the profane, the heavenly and the mundane. Such marks cannot yet serve an epistemological purpose. All that is certain is that they came from the sky and, like atmosphere, offer sites of translation and contiguity between formerly (and presumably absolutely) distinct realms of knowing. Shizuma and his family, like all other victims of that monstrous event, become knowing of something essential, even (or especially) when they cannot understand it. The enemy's bomb has dropped, followed by black rain; it has instigated the procession of events in a foreground. But the mastery of interpretation has not yet arrived to impose the certainty of a *telos* attributing meaning to such a powerfully destructive event. It is a *novum* which, in a momentary flash, created a new paradigm within the Anthropocene. But even this is not yet known.

As we have seen, Cary's painterly sky served mainly as the ground for Jimson's frantic conflation of agency and transcendence. Western skies serve the humanist and painterly aesthetic. In *Black Rain*, rather, skies emerge as the site of transitivity: conveying all human offerings, yet only selectively responsive to oracular necessity and the human propitiation of the divine. In ancient Greece, the ἑκατόμβη (hekatómbē)—translated as the flaying and burning of one hundred ritually prepared oxen—was not just socially symbolic but also designed to stimulate divine pleasure by means of the ascent of smoke (Gr., *thuein*) to the heavens (Naiden 2013, vii, 263–65). Once sniffed by capricious gods, laden vapors rising from ritually prepared sacrifices instigated partisan struggle on Olympus, as smoke signals called forth different godly parties and coalitions to action. Ancient Greek gods grew accustomed to hecatombs, the trails of rising smoke serving to suture sacred and profane realms.

In *Black Rain*, smoke rising into the sky emerges as the fugitive critique of an empirically rendered materiality. Only three days after the blast on August

6, the smoke of holocaust rises from burning pyres of bodies all along the banks of the toxic river running through central Hiroshima:

> On both sides of the river, the dried up part of the bed had the aspect of a crematorium. Wherever I looked, upstream or downstream, the columns of smoke were rising. Here, the blaze would be fierce and the smoke thick; there, mere wisps of smoke would be rising from still smoldering embers. . . . From the top of the embankment, countless holes were visible, dug in the sand. I could see bones in most of them, and the skulls especially stood out with strange clarity. . . . In olden times, I suddenly recalled, they used to refer to skulls as "the unsheltered ones." (Ibuse 2012, 137–38)

In *Black Rain*, skies can no longer shelter humanity, if they ever did, from the wrath of the gods humans would propitiate. Smoke rising from the corpses of tens of thousands of Hiroshima's dead signifies not only a uniform destruction but its procession over time. Radiating outward from the epicenter, burning pyres offer a scatter-plotting, which correlates not only to actual loss of life but to an existential pattern of despair—where surviving humans learned they would not, dropped, and died.[7] (By contrast, at ground zero there is no smoke, only silence.) As such, the radioactive skies of Hiroshima did indeed *communicate* the "freedom" of human agents to imagine newer forms of the aesthetic and to experience them differently. But, in Ibuse, this new language for humanity is not yet understood. And the difference the bombing makes to existence occurs in the form of a horrific condemnation of the kind of humanizing aesthetic Cary, for example, is so determined to believe in.

Directly influenced by Heidegger, Ibuse's contemporary, Watsuji, regarded atmosphere as an object of philosophical inquiry rather than as an artifact of scientific method (i.e., climatology). For Watsuji, climate (*fūdo*) constitutes interstitiality—in matter, time, and signification—rendering the figure-ground distinction liminal. *Fūdo* bears a purposive, even functional, relation to the human experience without being subordinated to time, which Watsuji viewed as an unnecessary and over-determining value in Heidegger's classic. (Watsuji had read *Sein und Zeit* as early as 1927 while pursuing postgraduate studies in philosophy in Berlin.) *Fūdo*, by contrast, allows "a means for man [sic] to discover" being (Watsuji 1961, 8), such that "the apprehension of the self in climate is revealed as the discovery of such measures" (Watsuji 1961, 6).

Climate, one recognizes, is Watsuji's third term when seeking to triangulate human possibility and nature. Additionally, *fūdo* allows a Japanese-centered theory of existence to exist "outside" Western individualism, time, and narrative as he supposed Heidegger to have framed it: "Climatic phenomena show man [*sic*] how to discover himself as 'standing outside' (i.e., *ex-sistere*)." Such "outsidedness" of being is extrinsic to the natural totality, yet also affords, for Watsuji, an historical inevitability apart from scientific naturalism. Rather than humanity being bound to a haphazard nature, climate and history serve a mutually reinforcing design:

> [The claim that humanity] works on and transforms climate . . . ignore[s] the true nature of climate [which is] that it is in climate that man apprehends itself: [C]limate does not exist apart from history, nor history apart from climate. (Watsuji 1961, 8)

At once distinct from the human, and yet historicized by means of the human, *fūdo* functions as Watsuji's objective correlative, allowing for an external agent (climate) to prompt social interconnectedness and relationality in community: "Thus climate is seen to be the factor by which a self-active human being can be made objective" (Watsuji 1961, 12). Climate, we are made to understand, may be harsh or adversarial, but it is necessarily tailored to the human. It shapes the contours of space as neither vacuum nor background but by sustaining "tangible climatic, scenic and topographical characteristics" (Baek 2013, 589).

Approaching Gulley Jimson's vocabulary, the climatic "outside" serves the humanist inside of Watsuji's argument, with a resulting congruence between the object-person and nature-object:

> The cold, for instance, is not only something that sends us off for warm clothes; it can also be utilized to freeze the bean curd. Heat is not only something that makes us use a fan; it is also the heat that nourishes the rice plants. . . . In other words, [our] self-comprehension through climate . . . leads us to discover ourselves. (Watsuji 1961, 13)

With such climactic "tools" in hand, inevitably shaping human forms and experiences, Watsuji renders his critique of Heideggerian mastery over Nature. Climate proffers a "purpose-relation" to human community:

> It is in our relationship with the tyranny of nature that we first come to engage ourselves in joint measures to secure early protection from such tyranny. The apprehension of the self in climate is revealed as the discovery of such measures. (Watsuji 1961, 6)

Yet, just as clearly, a circularity in Watsuji's thinking emerges. His foundational returning of atmosphere to the question of world-forming, in response to nature's "tyranny," risks collapsing *fūdo* into *weltbildend*: that is, how human existence may eventually seek to master forces inherently more powerful.

In Ibuse, the untranslatable evidence of black rain, indelibly marking Yasuko and other victims' bodies, offers a devastating exegesis, at least in part, of Watsuji's theory that it is through the atmosphere we come to know ourselves. By depicting the aftermath of Hiroshima, Ibuse's novel not only illustrates aspects of Watsuji's argument but extends it forward into the Anthropocene, as *fūdo* imposes newer, postatomic "climactic burdens and impositions" upon humanity (Watsuji 1961, 15). Devastatingly, Hirsohima and Nagasaki—much like the ongoing fallout from the Fukushima nuclear disaster of 2011—made a mockery of the world- and culture-forming aspects Watsuji attributed to *fūdo*. And, mindful of rapidly accumulating evidence for the toxification of the troposphere since then, the skies of the Anthropocene have shifted from being "fit to purpose" for aesthetic and humanizing reasons, to being purposive of wider-scale ecocide. It would seem that the emerging literatures of the Anthropocene, including narratives of the troubling, yet significant, *hibakusha* genre documenting it (Douglass and Vogler 2003, 41–42), have taken us beyond the point where the skies may redeem humanity, even as they all too clearly still determine it. The aesthetic of *weltbildend* collapses, and a new era for the literature of the world un-forming—the denaturing of the Anthroposcenic—is born.

Finally, Ibuse's narrative offers a clear and uncompromising example of Merleau-Ponty's flesh-of-the-world (*chair du monde*) at the very dawn of ecophenomenology. The Japanese civilian population serves as the control group for a horrific experiment. Merleau-Ponty writes:

> The flesh is not matter, is not mind, is not substance. To designate it, we should need the old term "element," in the sense it was used to speak of water, air, earth, and fire . . . *a sort of incarnate principle that brings a style of being* wherever there is a fragment of being. (Merleau-Ponty 2004, 9; emphasis added)

I cite Merleau-Ponty's terms and usages to convey how burning flesh in Ibuse serves an "elemental" purpose on behalf of a new "incarnate principle." Hecatombs to the emergence of the Anthropocene, the burning flesh of the Japanese, too, is "autochthonous, rooted in a corporeal exchange with the world" (Toadvine 2004, 275). Nor is Merleau-Ponty's commitment to anti-empiricist exigency ("adhering" to a here and a now) misplaced in a suddenly denatured world. Succeeding black rain in the procession of events, rising smoke over Hiroshima serves as a collective elegy for the departed. It also rebuts empiricism to the very limits of corporeity itself.[8] Nor is there any redeeming basis for climate (*fūdo*) as Watsuji's anti-naturalism in support of human connectivity had supposed. After Hiroshima and Nagasaki, we are closer to base matter as "substrata" (Nishida 1966) of the human category, than we have ever been; we are doomed by the skies that formerly housed us. There is no longer subsistence or, even, what Agamben called bare life. There is only bare matter.

Heedless of such speculations, Shizuma dutifully carries on his search for a husband for Yasuko, and fruitlessly, once news of her status as *hibakusha* spreads. Attended by white rainbows, the atomic bombings of Japan in early August 1945 are folded into an oracular history, a tradition parallel to (yet subversive of) the history of *humanitas*. Black rain, imposing onto survivors the fate of *hibakusha*, offers simply another atmospheric marker of godly externality, as Auerbach would have it, as the living irradiated parade along the mythic processional of the postatomic age. When the rain subsides, there will be the smoke of pyres burning, the transformation of the flesh-of-the-world into something else. So revised, Merleau-Ponty's flesh-of-the-world becomes elemental of a denatured humanity, the forever altered human subject as a peculiar object of the late Anthropocene. Tōmatsu Shōmei's image captures the contours, neck and shoulders of an aging *hibakusha*, whose patterned scars resemble flesh-rivers (Fig. 12.2).

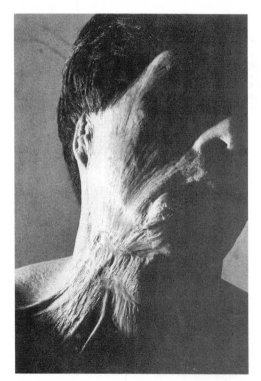

Figure 12.2.   Flesh-rivers. Hibakusha Yamaguchi Senji. Platinum palladium photograph, 1962. Tōmatsu Shōmei © Shōmei Tōmatsu—INTERFACE.

No longer sheltered by the skies of literary modernism, what may be said to be left of human nature as subjects of the Anthropocene? As Toadvine rightly reminds us, the term "human nature" is not so much an oxymoron—although the toxicity of human experience attending planetarity is now woefully clear—as a figurative continuum:

> We arrive here at a deeper ontological dimension of sense [that] can be called "natural" only in a singular way, since this notion of "nature" is no longer defined by the classic opposition with the artificial, the human, or the organic. Rather, the term "nature" here can name only the continuity of being itself. (Toadvine 2004, 279)

Indeed, the horrors depicted in *Black Rain* barely sustain any forward "continuity" of being by the end of the novel. Shizuma does recover meaning in the discovery of a pool of baby eels,[9] even as the aporia constituted by the atomic smoke and skies over Hiroshima was created by the monstrous excess of *weltbildend*—the American correction, in culture and technology, of a Japanese world-in-being that had itself sought to correct the world for others. Watsuji's *fūdo* thesis also returns, as we have seen, but only as a monstrous inversion. *Fūdo* still functions, but it no longer sustains, shapes, or surfaces the contours of a habitable world. The baby eels will most likely die upriver, among the earliest prey of the Anthropocene and its smoking Japanese skies.

The toxicity of atmosphere in Ibuse returns us, at conclusion, to the concept of "worldedness," which seeks, at least in part, to impart to an otherwise abstract world-systems theory the urgency of historical and aesthetic necessity. I have argued that the skies of the Anthropocene serve equally well as ground for human endeavor and its obliteration. It may be worth considering briefly what actually are those differences the *novum* of the Anthropocene makes to literary ecology.

As we have seen, figural convergence is one difference distinct from juxtaposition. If the human impact upon nature has been considered a commonplace consequence of the rise of empiricism and its scientific method, then the *accelerating* convergence of differently situated singularities, from Blake to Cary to Ibuse, expands the flatness of established literary technique and criticism—such as collage or irony—into a multivariate worldedness for literary criticism by which formal boundaries and distinctions *could be* re-enlivened and reinvented on a planetary scale. Could be: the radical foreshortening or failure of poetic juxtaposition—potentially making Cary seem quaint in the age of Ibuse—recalls eighteenth-century universals that once linked the Human to Nature irrevocably; and which, again, permits the consideration of the Anthropocene but only as if all of humanity were truly One, speaking—choking—with only one voice.

It remains to be seen whether or not any putative univocality of the Anthropocene may pose as grave a peril to humanity as the kinds of actual and environmental perils currently facing us. One recognizes that positing planetary universalism creates powerful motivations and opportunities for collective predicament and action. It also re-posits risk, iteratively, as the ever-larger scalars for imagining the Anthropocene require ever-larger compensations and responses, in time and space, which may militate against the wholesome varieties of local existence. Can the Anthropocene be imagined as myriad—imaginatively pluralized—without diminishing its world-organizing force? The accelerating convergence of figures describing the Anthropocene may create newer modalities for "worldedness" nonetheless, as what we think we mean by any singular context or voice is increasingly subsumed by a planetary history. (Hegglund's "metageographies" would appear to amount to one such scaling toward the universality of form, making the singularities of the planetary moment as they appear to individuals in specific places, Shizuma's pleasure at the baby eels, seem all the more precious.) At any scale, imagined "Anthroposcenic" potential—one wants to underline the difference the "s" makes—match the severity and scope of the actual threats posed by the Anthropocene precisely. If the Anthropocene is, simply, a contemporary manifestation of evil, then the devil's foundry is forging eternity each and every ecophenomenological moment, crisis after crisis without end (Fig. 12.3). Worse for us, the impact of the Anthroposcenic makes the question of moral evil seem irrelevant to the grip of material predicament.

Fundamentally, then, any nominal "historical content" for the converging figures I have focused upon here, whether sky or smoke, may not actually matter. It is the acceleration of the Anthropocene toward the total absorption of *any figure* that is recreating singularities which individual readers can recognize, interpret, and pattern even while being utterly oblivious to the larger scales, experiential and existential, at work. The Anthropocene remains diffident to the Anthroposcenic: whichever theories of individualized reflection may eventually emerge—say, epiphanic aesthetics produced by universalizing contexts—will burn with all the rest. And, as we have seen, the Heideggerian *weltbildend* is obliterated by Ibuse's radioactive skies. Disseminating widely different cultural and aesthetic assumptions at origin, Cary's and Ibuse's respective atmospherics must inevitably collide as former human masters over the Anthropocene become its drones, demoted to the status, shared with animals and inanimate objects, of *weltarm* (poverty in world).[10] Nor do Cary's skies and Watsuji's *fūdo* serve human existence as they once did. Searing with white heat any remnants of redemptive realism,

Figure 12.3. "The devil's foundry." Urugami Tenshudo Church, Nagasaki. Platinum palladium photograph, 1961. Tōmatsu Shōmei © Shōmei Tōmatsu—INTERFACE.

Ibuse's postatomic atmospherics corrode the very seam, or suture, joining the "inside" to the "outside" of any aesthetic. The Anthropocene has for some time (probably since August 6, 1945) required us to move beyond the "enunciative space within literary discourse that ironizes the notion of geographical space itself" (Hegglund 2012, 6).

I hope I have demonstrated that the convergence of the Anthropocene's modernist skies may nevertheless be scried in the meantime. Some measurable basis for theorizing the acceleration of contacts between and across Anthroposcenic figures, contexts and histories may be derived as of scholarly consequence for some limited time. But the material consequences of the Anthropocene, morals and philosophies apart, will certainly arrive anyway. *Black Rain* depicts how even the refusal of a compositional aesthetic for the skies constitutes another kind of living within our human atmosphere, a precarious life invoking the sacred and ritualized procession of time as extinction edges ever closer. Obliteration at ground zero (bomb, weather, contagion) all too capably evacuates whichever fructifying modernist spaces and thinking produced the resurgent scientific barbarism that concocted modernity in the first place—falsely, as it has turned out—in the name of the human. After Hiroshima, the Anthropocene's poisoned skies never again offered to shelter human existence from ourselves. And yet, still: the search for an overarching moral framework for planetarity persists. The failure of the Anthropocene aesthetic has, it seems, produced a ghostly remnant, a mortally wounded morality, haunting our dreams of escaping the Anthroposcenic figure, sky, or canvas. This is the brutalized hope with which we declare our as yet *human* refusal to accept the fact of our own destruction.

NOTES

1. Human geographers Jennifer Robinson, Gillian Rose, and Clive Barnett theorize the "demands" of globalization, observing that "The potential for communication and other kinds of interaction across the globe has opened up opportunities for the demands of those living in quite distant places to be brought to our attention, and for our demands to be addressed to others, whether they be relatively close by or quite far away" (Barnett et al. 2008, vi).

2. We cannot dispute that skies, as atmospheric reflectors of "deep ecology," have been diminished by their faithful service in support of humanist exceptionalism. Offering critique of a post-Heideggerian trajectory, Jennifer Wenzel notes that "versions of planetarity that are imagined around the human . . . seem like a reconstructed, post-anthropocentric humanism, [a] more-than-humanism" (Wenzel 2014, 25).

3. Applying Watsuji's philosophy to architecture and design, Baek offers a serviceable definition of *fūdo*: "Literally a combination of two Chinese letters, *fū* means wind, and *do*, earth [grounding Watsuji's] claim that man and natural phenomena are intertwined in such a way that the phenomena operate as the metaphor for human subjectivity, transcending scientific objectivism" (Baek 2013, 589). See Janz 2011.

4. Bifurcating the skies makes for tidy epistemological distinctions and constitutes the historical and juridical bases for exclusions Giorgio Agamben has called *bare life*. The predicament of planetarity is presently eroding the geographical bases for such "states of exception," which sustained ecocide renders unexceptional. See Agamben, *Homo Sacer*.

5. I cite Barnes's commentary on the Hebrew from which the King James translation is derived: "'As the sparks fly upward'—the Hebrew expression here is very beautiful (רֶשֶׁף בְּנֵי [benēy reshep]) [translated as] 'the sons of flame fly'" (Barnes 1998, n p.). The notion of deathly fire producing lively progeny, upward arcing sons of fire, is as ancient as Heraclitus.

6. Trigilio cites evidence of the mark from the Book of Ezekiel in the Old Testament: Jehovah "set a mark upon the foreheads of the men that sigh and cry for all the abominations that be done in the midst thereof" (Ez 9:4).

7. Of the individual body, presumably dead or alive, Goss writes: "There is no "body" as such. [. . . Yet] [b]odies matter, and they matter not because they are inconsequential signs of notable differences but because bodies ground all being in the world, all encounter, and all possibility of thought, reflection, and knowledge" (Goss 2012, 1).

8. Nishida Kitaro's critique of Aristotelian nominalism prophesied postatomic skies: nothingness imposes predicate status upon humanist worldliness: "The array of things which makes a human world is that accidental daylight which in a certain slant [Gr. *Klima*] illuminates the earth" (qtd. in Berque 2004, 392).

9. Discovering a stream full of larval eels to the rear of his factory, Shizuma overhears only eerily displaced fragments of the emperor's surrender, broadcast to the nation over the radio. Barely heeding it, Shizuma finds hope in the struggle of the baby eels: "On you go, on up the stream!" I said to them encouragingly. . . . I wondered where they had been swimming on August 6" (Ibuse 2012, 297).

10. In *Black Rain*, the American occupation's censorship of *hibakusha* stories imposes yet another kind of denaturing, as *mono no aware* (a term Richie first translated in 1961 as the "inescapable sadness of living" or, elsewhere as "sympathetic sadness" [qtd. in Deamer 2014, 11]) banishes metaphysics to the realm of stoicism. Still, the voices of suffering have persisted to tell their tale. See Douglass and Vogler 2003, 41.

WORKS CITED

Agamben, Giorgio. 1998. *Homo Sacer: Sovereign Power and Bare Life.* Translated by Daniel Heller-Roazen. Stanford, CA: Stanford University Press.

Auerbach, Erich. 2013. *Mimesis: The Representation of Reality in Western Literature.* Translated by Willard R. Trask. Princeton, NJ: Princeton University Press.

Baek, Jin. 2013. "Fudo: An East Asian Notion of Climate and Sustainability." *Buildings* 3: 588–97.

Barnes, Albert. 1998. *Notes on the Old Testament.* Grand Rapids, MI: Baker Books.

Barnett, Clive, Jennifer Robinson, and Gillian Rose, eds. 2008. *Geographies of Globalization: A Demanding World.* London: Sage Publishing.

Berque, Augustin. 2004. "Offspring of Watsuji's theory of milieu (*Fûdo*)." *GeoJournal* 60: 389–96.

Blake, William. 2002. *Collected Poems.* Revised ed. Edited by W. B. Yeats. New York: Routledge Classics.

Cary, Joyce. 1944. "The Art of Fiction: Joyce Cary." Interview by John Burrows and Alex Hamilton. *The Paris Review* 7. Accessed March 19, 2021. https://www.theparis review.org/interviews/5071/joyce-cary-the-art-of-fiction-no-7-joyce-cary.

———. 1948. *The Horse's Mouth.* Harmondsworth, UK: Penguin.

Case, Edward. 1959. "The Free World of Joyce Cary." *Modern Age* (Spring): 115–24.

Deamer, David. 2014. *The Specter of Impossibility: Deleuze, Japanese Cinema, and the Atom Bomb.* London: Bloomsbury.

Douglass, Ana, and Thomas A. Vogler, eds. 2003. *Witness and Memory: The Discourse of Trauma.* New York: Routledge.

Goss, Erin M. 2012. *Revealing Bodies: Anatomy, Allegory, and the Grounds of Knowledge in the Long Eighteenth Century*. Lewisburg, PA: Bucknell University Press.

Hayot, Eric. 2012. *On Literary Worlds*. New York: Oxford University Press.

Hegglund, Jon. 2012. *World Views: Metageographies of Modernist Fiction*. New York: Oxford University Press.

Ibuse, Masuji (井伏 鱒二). 2012. *Black Rain* (*Kuroi Ame* [黒い雨]). Translated by John Bester. New York: Kodansha.

Janz, Bruce B. 2011. "Watsuji Tetsuro, Fudo, and Climate Change." *Journal of Global Ethics* 7 (2): 173–84.

Larrissy, Edward. 2006. *Blake and Modern Literature*. London: Palgrave Macmillan.

Merleau-Ponty, Maurice. 2004. *Basic Writings*. Edited by Thomas Baldwin. London: Routledge.

Naiden, F. S. 2013. *Smoke Signals for the Gods: Ancient Greek Sacrifice from the Archaic through Roman Periods*. Oxford: Oxford University Press.

Nishida, Kitarô Zenshû. 1966. *Logic of Place and Religious Worldview.* (*Bashoteki ronri to shûkyôteki sekaikan.*) In *Complete Works.* Vol. 11. Tokyo: Shoten.

Pope, Alexander. n.d. "Concordance of *Rape of the Lock.*" *The Victorian Literary Studies Archive.* Accessed March 19, 2021. http://victorian-studies.net/concordance/pope.

Spivak, Gayatri Chakravorty. 1985. "Three Women's Texts and a Critique of Imperialism." *Critical Inquiry* 12 (1): 243–61.

Stevens, Wallace. 1982. "Evening without Angels." *The Collected Poems of Wallace Stevens.* New York: Vintage.

The Holy Bible. 1993. New International Version [NIV]. New York: Harper/Torch.

Toadvine, Ted. 2004. "Singing the World in a New Key: Merleau-Ponty and the Ontology of Sense." *Janus Head* 7 (2): 273–83.

Trigilio, Tony. 2000. *'Strange Prophecies Anew': Rereading Apocalypse in Blake, H. D., and Ginsberg.* London: Associated University Presses.

Watsuji, Tetsurō (和辻 哲郎). 1961. *A Climate: A Philosophical Study.* (*Fūdo ningen-gakuteki kōsatsu* [風土 人間学的考察]). Translated by Geoffrey Bownas. Tokyo: Ministry of Education/Japanese National Commission for UNESCO.

Wenzel, Jennifer. 2014. "Planet vs. Globe." *English Language Notes* 52 (1): 1–30.

Index

Abraham (biblical), 47
Abram, David, 24
"ABSTRAKTIDS" (Gillespie), 203
Achilles, 41
Ackerley, Chris, 60, 65
Adam, Barbara, 138
"Adonais" (Shelley), 49
aesthetic of entanglement, 23–25
affective geology, 146
Agamben, Giorgio, 226n4
Allen, Thomas, 146
American Indians, 6–8, 11, 42
American sublime, 39
Anderton, Joseph, xv, 73n2
Angus, Ian, 12
Animal Ecology (Elton), 119, 129n9
animals, Lawrence on, 4–8, 10, 13–16
Anthropocene: anthropocentrism and,
    60, 62, 153; art and daemon in, 41;
    Beckett and, 59–62, 72–73; *Blast*
    and, 22–23, 26, 31, 33–35; Bonneuil
    on four grand narratives of, 128n3;
    as Capitalocene or Corporatocene,
    55, 192; Chthulucene and, 169,
    192; climate change, infrastructural
    unconscious and, 41; Crane and,
    39–40, 54; "dream of mastery" and
    "dream of naturalism" responses
    to, 5–6; Earth and, 24, 97–98, 101,

105, 111–12; ecocriticism and,
23–24; ecologies of comics and, 160,
164, 169; emergent, xiii, xv–xvi,
xviii; genre fiction on, 140–41; as
geological epoch, xi–xii, xv–xvi,
5, 59, 97, 100, 135–36, 191–92;
"good Anthropocene," 67, 116; the
Great Acceleration in, xi, 39–40,
54, 135; historicity and, 93, 135–36;
human and nonhuman in, 59–60,
62, 153; human nature and, 223;
human species and, 79, 81, 91–92,
103, 120–21, 213–14; hyperobjects
and, 174–77, 187, 192; Lawrence
and, 3–5, 11–13, 16–18; in literary
studies, 23; misanthropocene,
12; modernist, xvii, 137–38, 153,
209–12; modernity and, 97, 135;
Moore, M., and, 174, 176, 187;
naming, 59–62, 72–73, 146–47;
natural and human forces in, 23–24,
26, 31; natural sciences and, 59;
nature in, 9, 40, 223–24; noosphere
and, xvi, 84; planet and modernism
in, 98–99; as planetary problem,
102–3, 112; plastic and, 191–92,
194; plastiglomerate in, 191; *The
Science of Life* and, 120; skies of,
210, 221, 223, 226; Stapledon and,

116–17, 124, 126; start of, dating, 134–35; Stein and, 197; stratigraphy and, 135; timescales of, 146–47; un-naming, 72–73; Vorticism and, 23, 32; Wells, H. G., and, 116–17, 120, 123, 127; Williams, W. C., and, 200; worldedness and, 212–13, 224; worlding and, 212–13

Anthropocene Fictions (Trexler), 117

Anthropocene lyric, 15, 40–41

Anthropocene Working Group, xi

Anthropocenic modernism, xvii, 134, 174

anthropocentrism, xiii–xiv, 12–13, 16–18, 21, 182; of Anthropocene, 60, 62, 153

anthropogenic climate change, 12, 79, 116, 123, 125

anthropomorphism, 9–10

anthropos, xv–xvi, 11–12

the anthroposcenic, 213, 221, 224–26

Apocalypse (Lawrence), 18

Archie comics, 159–60

Arlington Company of New Jersey, 201

Arnold, Matthew, 28, 214

artificial ecology, plastic and, xvii, 193, 195, 198–201, 204

Athena, 41, 49

Auerbach, Erich, 217

Auschwitz, 212

automobiles, 39–40, 44–45

avant-garde movements, 21–22, 25, 27–28

Baek, Jin, 226n3

Baekeland, Leo H., 195

Bair, Deirdre, 61

Bakelite, 195, 198–99, 204nn3–4

Baker, Steve, 171n5

Bal, Mieke, 154

Balla, Giacomo, 196

Balog, James, 147

Barad, Karen, xiv

Barnes, Albert, 226n5

Barnett, Clive, 226n1

The Baroness (Freytag-Loringhoven, Elsa von), xvii, 194, 201–4, 205nn10–11

Barthes, Roland, 193

Bate, Jonathan, xiv

Battle of Ypres, ix

Beck, Ulrich, 136–37

Beckett, Samuel: Anthropocene and, 59–62, 72–73; on human and nonhuman, 60; *The Unnamable* by, xv–xvi, 60–73

Bell, William, 180

Bennett, Jane, xiv, 148

Bergson, Henri, 118

Berlin: Symphony of a Metropolis, x–xi

Berry, Wendell, 35n2

Between the Acts (Woolf), 115

Bezos, Jeff, 143

biocentrism, 4, 9–12

bio-engineering, 116, 126

biosphere, 12, 15, 40; Earth and, 99–100; ecosphere and, 17; noosphere and, 84, 100–101

Black Rain (Ibuse), xvii–xviii, 209, 227nn9–10; skies in, 218–19, 221–25; smoke in, 217–23

Blake, William, 210, 214–16

Blast: Anthropocene and, 22–23, 26, 31, 33–35; on climate and geography, 22, 26–27, 29–32; on entanglement of natural and human forces, 25; Lewis, W., and, 21–23, 26–34; as mesh, 26–33; on nature and art, 25, 31–32; on nature and culture, 31–32, 34; on nature and industry, 22–23, 26, 32–33; "storm from the North" symbol in, 27, *27*, 29; Vorticism and, 21–23, 26–31

Blast 1, 21, 26–32, *27*

Bloom, Harold, 41

Boccioni, Umberto, 195–96

Boer, Inge E., 62

Boes, Tobias, 141

Bök, Christian, 192–93

Bon Marche Weather (Stein), 197

Bonneuil, Christophe, 128n3
Brand, Stewart, 142–46
The Bridge (Crane), xv; on automobiles, 44–45; on fossil fuels, 42–46; Genesis and, 45–46; on Love, 49–50; on Nature, 40–42, 44, 55; on Pocahontas, 42, 44–46; on US Civil War, 44–45; on Whitman, 44–46
The Bridge of San Luis Rey (Wilder), x
Briscoe, Lily, 137
Bristow, Tom, 40
British imperialism, 10
Brown, Judith, 193
Buell, Lawrence, xiv, 25, 35n3
Burke, Kenneth, 41

capitalism, xiii, 140–41, 146, 162, 201; materialism and, 9
Capitalocene, 55, 192
Carey, John, 119
Carey, M. C., 182
Carroll, Hamilton, 140–41
Çary, Joyce: *The Horse's Mouth* by, xvii, 209, 214–18, 220; Ibuse and, xvii, 209, 212, 218–19, 223–24; on skies, 214–18, 220, 224
Case, Edward, 214, 216
celluloid, 192–96, 198–203, 204n5
Center for Research on Environmental Decisions (CRED), 133, 144
Chakrabarty, Dipesh, 23, 62, 79–81, 92, 123
Chaplin, Charlie, xi
Chasing Ice, 147
Chester, Emily, xv
Christie, Stuart, xvii–xviii
Chthulucene, 169, 171n8, 192
city symphony film genre, x–xi
Civil War, US, 44–45
Clark, Timothy, 93n1
climate: *Blast* on geography and, 22, 26–27, 29–32; as *fūdo*, Watsuji on, 219–21, 223–24, 226n3; humanity and, 220; Vorticists on, 22, 32

climate change, xii–xiii, 115; anthropogenic, 12, 79, 116, 123, 125; canon of literature on, 117; infrastructural unconscious and, 41; uneven distribution of harms, 133
"The Climate of History" (Chakrabarty), 79
climatological time, xii–xiii
Clock of the Long Now (CLN), xvi, 134, *142*, 142–46, *143*
clocks, modernism and, 134, 136–39, 142, 147
coal, 10–11, 124–25
Cohn, Ruby, 60–61, 64
Colebrook, Claire, 40, 54–55
colonization, European, xi
comics: ecological unconscious and, 153, 158, 161, 165–66; ecology and, xvii, 153–69; fantasy, 154, 159–60, 165–66; modernism and, 169–70; realist, 157, 160, 166–67, 171n7; semiotic modes of, 156, 170n3; storyworlds in, 154–60, 165–67, 169–70; worldbuilding in, 154–60, 166, 170; worldmaking in, xvii, 153–58, 160–61, 165–67, *168*, 169–70; worldreading in, 154–57
comparative planetology, 98–101, 106–7
The Concept of Modernism (Eysteinsson), 6
Conrad, Joseph, ix
"Convergence of the Twain" (Hardy), ix
Corcoran, Patricia L., 191
Corporatocene, 55
cosmic mind, 106–7, 109
cosmic scale, 80–83, 86–91, 93, 105, 107
cosmic time, 82, 88–90
cosmology, 99, 102, 104, 210–11
cosmopolitanism, 28, 89
Costello, Bonnie, 22, 25, 35n5
Coupe, Laurence, xiv
Cowley, Malcolm, 46

Crane, Hart: Anthropocene and, 39–41, 54; *The Bridge* by, xv, 40–46, 49–50, 55; daemons and, 41, 49–50, 54; in the Great Acceleration, 39–40, 54; on machines, 39–40, 44–45; "Modern Poetry" by, 39–40; "O, Carib Isle!" by, xv, 40–41, 46–55; technological sublime and, 39–40; *White Buildings* by, 49; Whitman and, 44–46, 54–55

creative evolution, 118

CRED. *See* Center for Research on Environmental Decisions

Crossley, Robert, 82–83, 94n5

Crutzen, Paul, xi, 121, 134–35, 176, 191

Cthulhu, x, 169, 175, 184, 187n2

Cubism, 21

culture: ecology and, 28; monoculture *versus* symbiocultures, 169–70; nature and, 22, 31–32, 34

cummings, e. e., 195

Curie, Marie, 197–98

daemons, 40–41, 49–50, 54

Dahlem Conference, 134–35

Daniel, Julia, xvii

Darwin, Charles, 83–84, 87, 94n6

The Day of the Triffids (Wyndham), 15

deep ecology, 226n2

deep-historical temporality, xv, 23

Depero, Fortunato, 196

Derrida, Jacques, 112n2

Descartes, René, and Cartesianism, 59–60, 65–67, 69, 169

digital utopia, 145

Disney comics, 158, 160

Duino Elegies (Rilke), 14–15

Duncan, Isadora, 196

DuPlessis, Rachel Blau, 199

Dydo, Ulla E., 196–97

Dyson, Freeman, 143

Earth: Anthropocene and, 24, 97–98, 101, 105; atmosphere of, 68–69; biosphere and, 99–100; cosmos and, 82, 88–89; humanity and, 11, 17, 121, 125; humans and, 110, 126–27; modernity and, 97; as planet, 98–99, 101–2, 110–12; *Solaris* on, 110–11, 112n3; space and time scales, 85; stratigraphy of, human subjectivity and, 59

Earthmasters (Hamilton), 123

eco-cosmopolitan perspective, 98

ecocriticism, xiv–xv, 12, 60, 62; first-wave, 23–24, 35n3, 69; modernism and, 115; second-wave and third-wave, 24

Ecocriticism in the Modernist Imagination (Sultzbach), xiv

ecological and environmental management, 116, 121, 123–24, 126–27

ecological unconscious, 153, 158, 161, 165–66

ecology: artificial, xvii, 193, 195, 198–201, 204; deep, 226n2; environmental imagination of, xv; human, 121–24, 126–28, 129n9; human culture and, 28; human energy consumption and, 119–20; indigenous, 22; of Lawrence, 17–18; nature and, xiv, 55; Stapledon on, 116, 126–28; Vorticists on, 22; Wells, H. G., on, 116–24, 126–28, 129n9

ecology, comics and, xvii; Anthropocene and, 160, 164, 169; ecological unconscious, 153, 158, 161, 165–66; modernist visions, 160–69; storyworlds, 154–55; theory and form, 154–60

The Ecology of Modernism (Schuster), xiv

ecomodernism and ecomodernists, 116–21, 124, 129n8

"An Ecomodernist Manifesto," 5, 17, 35n5

ecophenomenology, 128n1, 212–13, 221, 224

ecosphere, 17
Edwards, Paul, 26–27
ekstasis, 40, 217
Eledone Cirrosa, 183
Eliot, T. S., ix, xiii, 214
Elton, Charles, 119, 129n9
emergent Anthropocene, xiii, xv–xvi, xviii
Emerson, Ralph Waldo, 25
England, climate and geography of, *Blast* on, 30–32
English Futurism, 26–27
English industrialism, 29, 32–33
Enlightenment humanism, 59–60, 65–66
entanglement, aesthetic of, 23–25
environmentalism and environmentalists, 98, 120, 153
environmental thinking, 115–16
eroticism, 169, 171n7
European colonization, xi
"Evening without Angels" (Stevens), 210
Evian water, 196–97
evolutionary scale, 87, 94n6
experiential or embodied time, xii–xiii
"The Eyeglasses" (Williams, W. C.), 200–201
Eysteinsson, Astradur, 6

Fabians, 29
fantasy comics, 154, 159–60, 165–66
fascism, 82–83
The Fate of Homo Sapiens (Wells, H. G.), 127
Faulkner, William, 147, 195
Fiasco (Lem), 112
Le Figaro, 21
film technology, x
Fitzgerald, F. Scott, 204
Fletcher, Angus, 40–41
Ford, Ford Madox, 3
Forest Reserve Act of 1891, 178
Forty Signs of Rain (Robinson, K. S.), 141
fossil fuels, 11, 40–46, 55, 116, 119–20, 124–25

Four Saints in Three Acts, 193
Freud, Sigmund, 41, 104–6, 109
Freytag-Loringhoven, Baroness Elsa von, xvii, 194, 201–4, 205nn10–11
Friedman, Susan Stanford, xiv, 97–98
Frienkel, Susan, 204n1, 204n4
Frost, Robert, 35n5
fūdo (climate), 219–21, 223–24, 226n3
Fukushima nuclear disaster, of 2011, 221
Futurism, 28, 32; anthropocentrism and, 21; English, 26–27; Italian, xvii, 26, 29, 33; Lewis, W., on, 26–27, 29, 33, 35n9, 36n14; on machines and technology, 21–22; of Marinetti, 6, 21–22, 26–27, 29, 34, 195–96, 198; plastic and, 194–96, 204
Futurism of Place, 26–27
"Futurist Manifesto" (Marinetti), 21–22, 195

Galison, Peter, 136
Gammel, Irene, 205n10
Gasiorek, Andrzej, 36n14
Gasoline Alley (King), 167
Genesis, 45–46, 48–49, 51
geochronology, 135
geoengineering, 122–24, 129n11
Geography and Plays (Stein), 196–97
geological epoch, Anthropocene as, xi–xii, xv–xvi, 5, 59, 97, 100, 135–36, 191–92
geological sublime, 40, 55
geology, 147; affective, 146; biosphere, earth and, 99–100; fossil fuels and, 42–44, 55; Freud on, 105; humanity and, 127; timelines of, Woolf on, 115; timescales of, humans and, 42–43, 79–80, 83–84, 93, 115, 125
geopsychoanalysis, 112n2
"Gertrude Stein" (Loy), 197–98
Gillespie, Abraham Lincoln, xvii, 194, 203–4
Ginsberg, Allen, 195, 202
Glamour in Six Dimensions (Brown), 193

globalization, 162–64, 226n1
global warming, 197, 213
The God Species (Lynas), 121
Gontarski, S. E., 59
"good Anthropocene," 67, 116
"Good News for the Gourmet"
    (Pycraft), 183
Goss, Erin M., 227n7
Granofsky, Ronald, 11
Gray, Harold, 167
the Great Acceleration, xi, 39–40, 54,
    135
Green Modernism (McCarthy, J. M.),
    xiv
The Green Studies Reader (Coupe), xiv
Gregory, Elizabeth, 186

Haeckel, Ernst, 118
Haldane, J. B. S., 83, 139–40
Hamilton, Clive, 123, 129n11
Haraway, Donna, xiv, 153, 169–70,
    171nn8–9, 192
Hardy, Thomas, ix
Harrison, Andrew, 8, 10, 17
Hayles, Katherine, 148
Hayot, Eric, 212
Heart of Darkness (Conrad), ix
Hegel, G. W. F., 103–4
Hegglund, Jon, 224
Heidegger, Martin, 212, 219–20, 224
Heise, Ursula, 28, 98, 158, 176
Helmreich, Stefan, 112n3
Henry, Holly, 139
Heraclitus, 41
Heringman, Noah, 146–47
Herman, David, 154–56, 159
Herriman, George, 153, 160, *165*, 165–
    66, 168–69, 171n7
hibakusha stories, 209, 221–22, *222*,
    227n10
Hillis, Danny, 142, 144–46
"Him with His Tail in His Mouth"
    (Lawrence), 12
Hiroshima bombing, xvii–xviii, 209,
    212, 217–19, 221–23, 226

historical time, xii–xiii
Hoberek, Andrew, 141
Holley, Margaret, 187n1
Holocene, xi, 40–42, 135
Homer, 41, 49, 217
Hornborg, Alf, 59
The Horse's Mouth (Cary), xvii, 209,
    214–18, 220
Howell, Ted, xvi
Hubble, Edwin, 83, 88
Huizenga, Kevin, 166–67
human and cosmic scales, 82–83,
    86–90, 93
human and non-human agency, in *The
    Unnamable*, 61–73
human ecology, 121–24, 126–28,
    129n9
human history, natural history and, 123,
    127
humanism: anthropocentrism of, 16;
    Enlightenment, 59–60, 65–66;
    posthumanism and, 11, 17–18,
    153, 169, 174; twentieth-century
    philosophical, 211
humanity: climate and, 220; Earth and,
    11, 17, 121, 125; environment and,
    127; geology and, 127; nature and,
    ix, 5, 9–12, 15–18, 59–60, 115, 119–
    20, 212, 219–20, 223–24
human nature, 211, 223
humans: animals and, 13; dethroning,
    Lawrence on, 9–12; Earth and,
    110, 126–27; ecology and, 116; as
    geological force, 59; human species
    as hyperobject to, 41; nonhumans
    and, x–xi, 4–5, 9–10, 12–18, 23–24,
    59–73, 153, 168–69; oil and, 45;
    technology and, ix–xi
human species, 62; Anthropocene and,
    79, 81, 91–92, 103, 120–21, 213–14;
    cosmic scale and, 86–89; extinction
    and, 213–14; as hyperobject, 41; in
    Last and First Men, 124, 126; plastic
    and, 191; *Star Maker* and, 85–93,
    125–26

human timescales: downscaling, 133–34; geologic timescales and, 42–43, 79–80, 83–84, 93, 115, 125
Huntington, John, 129n12
Husserl, Edmund, 216–17
Huxley, Julian, 92, 116–23, 128n5, 129n9
Hyatt, John Wesley, 194
hyperobjects, xvii, 41, 173–77, 179–81, 183–87, 187n2, 192

Ibuse, Masuji: *Black Rain* by, xvii–xviii, 209, 217–25, 227nn9–10; Cary and, xvii, 209, 212, 218–19, 223–24; on Hiroshima bombing, xvii–xviii, 209, 212, 217–19, 221–23; Watsuji and, 209, 212, 219, 221
Iliad (Homer), 41, 49
The Illustrated London News, 183
Impressionist painters, 34
indigenous ecology, 22
industrialism, 3, 6, 29, 32–33, 80, 91
industrialization, 39, 92, 100, 129n8, 134
industrial modernity, xv, 29, 33, 80–81, 84–86, 91, 93, 120, 137
Industrial Revolution, 32, 125
infrastructural unconscious, 41
Inniss, Kenneth, 8
International Geological Congress, 2016, 135
interplanetary scales and relationships, 104–6
Isle of Pines hurricane, 46–47
Italian Futurism, xvii, 26, 29, 33

Jaffe, Aaron, 137
James, Henry, 187
Jameson, Fredric, 31, 102, 126, 138, 142
Janik, Del Ivan, 6–7
Jazvac, Kelly, 191
Jeans, James, 83, 94n5
Johnson, Clifton, 179, 188n6
Jolas, Eugene, 46
Joyce, James, 147, 214

Kaun, Axel, 73
Keese, Andrew, 4
Kern, Robert, 24
Kerridge, Richard, 31, 59–60
"Kew Gardens" (Woolf), ix
King, Frank, 167
Krazy Kat (Herriman), 160, *165*, 165–66, 168, 171n7
Kuhn, Elizabeth, 12

land ethic, 24
Lang, Fritz, x
Last and First Men (Stapledon), 115–16, 124–27, 128n2, 129n12
"The Last Judgement" (Haldane), 139–40
Latour, Bruno, 23–24
Lawrence, D. H., xv; on American Indians, 6–8, 11; on animals, 4–8, 10, 13–16; on animosity of nature, 14–16; Anthropocene and, 3–5, 11–13, 16–18; *Apocalypse* by, 18; ecology of, 17–18; "Him with His Tail in His Mouth" by, 12; on humans, dethroning, 9–12; on humans and nature, 5, 9–12, 15–18; on humans and nonhumans, 4–5, 9–10, 12–18; on interruption, of modernity, 6–9; "The Man Who Loved Islands" by, 16–17; "Multiplied Man and the Reign of Machine" by, 6; on nature and civilization, 3–5, 7, 13; on nonhuman revolt and nonhuman agency, 13–18; "Pan in America" by, 5; primitivism of, 4, 8, 13; *The Rainbow* by, 6; "Reflections on the Death of a Porcupine" by, 5; *St. Mawr* by, 4, 6–8, 10–11, 13–17; "To Let Go or to Hold On" by, 3–4; "The Triumph of the Machine" by, 6; "Wild Things in Captivity" by, 9; *The Woman Who Ran Away* by, 6–8; *Women in Love* by, 6, 11
Leavis, F. R., 5

LeCain, Timothy James, 60, 62, 67
Lem, Stanislaw: *Fiasco* by, 112;
    Solaris by, xvi, 101, 106–12, 112n3;
    Stapledon and, xvi, 99, 101, 106–7,
    109, 112, 126
Lenton, Tim, 135
Leopold, Aldo, 24
Lewis, Simon L., 59
Lewis, Wyndham, xv; *Blast* and, 21–23,
    26–34; on Futurism, 26–27, 29, 33,
    35n9, 36n14; Vorticism and, 21,
    30–33
"Life and the Planets" (Teilhard),
    94nn4–5
Life Force, 118
Little Nemo in Slumberland (McCay),
    160–65, *162*
Little Orphan Annie (Gray), 167
long now, 135–36, 142–43, *143*
Long Now Foundation, 142–44
longue durée, 80–81, 148
Lorrimer, Jamie, 5
Lovecraft, H. P., x, 169
"Love Songs" (Loy), 198
Loy, Mina, xvii, 194, 197–200, 204
Luciano, Dana, 146
Lumière Brothers, x
Luyten, W. J., 83
Lynas, Mark, 121
Lyytikäinen, Pirjo, 155

machines and technology, 6; Crane on,
    39–40, 44–45; Futurism on, 21–22;
    Vorticists on, 32–33
Mackay, Robin, 148
Mackenzie, Adrian, 136
Malm, Andreas, 59
Man, Paul de, 54
Manhatta, x–xi
"Manifesto of Futurist Dance"
    (Marinetti), 196
"A Man of the Week: Marinetti"
    (Lewis, W.), 26–27, 29
"The Man Who Loved Islands"
    (Lawrence), 16–17

Man with a Movie Camera, x–xi
Marinetteism, 21–22, 29, 33
Marinetti, F. T., 6, 21–22, 26–27, 29,
    34, 195–96, 198
Markley, Robert, xii
Marshall, Kate, 141
Martell, Jessica, xv
Marxism and Literature (Williams, R.),
    xiii
Maslin, Mark A., 59
"The Material Construction of a Plastic
    Complex" (Balla and Depero), 196
materialism, capitalism and, 9
materialist ecocriticism, xiv
materiality: of form, xvii; of modernists,
    plastics and, 193–94, 197–98
material sublime, 15, 54–55
Matthes, F. E., 188n7
McCarthy, Jeffrey Mathes, xiv
McCarthy, Patrick A., 94n3
McCay, Winsor, 153, 160–65, *162*, 169
McClanahan, Annie, 140–41
McCloud, Scott, 156–57, 159, 170n4
McGurl, Mark, 149n1
Meikle, Jeffrey L., 194, 200–201
Méliès, Georges, x
Meredith, Jack, 187n4
Merleau-Ponty, Maurice, 128n1, 221–22
metageographies, 224
Metropolis, x
Mills, Tarpé, 153, 160, 167–69, *168*,
    171n7
Mimesis (Auerbach), 217
Mirrlees, Hope, 195
misanthropocene, 12
misanthropy, biocentrism and, 9–12
Miss Fury (Mills), 160, 167–69, *168*,
    171n7
Mitchison, Naomi, 81
Modern Animalism (Willmott), 164
modernism: aesthetic, xv;
    Anthropocentric, xvii, 134, 174;
    clocks and, 134, 136–39, 142, 147;
    comics and, 169–70; ecocriticism
    and, 115; ecological perspectives

on, xiii–xiv; ecomodernism and ecomodernists, 116–21, 124, 129n8; green, xiv; as interruption of modernity, 6; nature and, xiv, 25, 35n5; noosphere and, 81–88; planetary, 98–99; planetary thinking of, 98; plastics in modernity and, xvii, 193–98; poetics of plastic and plasticity in, 192–93, 195–96, 204; primitivism and, 8; resource-based capitalism and, xiii; scalar thinking and, 80, 93; second modernism, xvi, 134, 136–38, 140, 142–43; technology and, 35n5; time and timescales in, 134–40, 142–43, 147–48

modernism and the Anthropocene. *See specific topics*

Modernism/Modernity journal, xiii–xiv

modernist Anthropocene, xvii, 137–38, 153, 209–12

modernist planets, 99

modernist poetry, xv

modernist studies, planetary turn in, 97–99

Modernist Studies Association, xiii–xiv

modernity: Anthropocene and, 97, 135; Earth and, 97; industrial, xv, 29, 33, 80–81, 84–86, 91, 93, 120, 137; industrialism of, 3, 29, 32–33, 80; interruption of, 6–9; Lawrence on, 5–9; plastic in, xvii

modernization, 5, 86, 97–98, 111, 122, 137

"Modern Poetry" (Crane), 39–40

Modern Times, xi

monoculture *versus* symbiocultures, 169–70

Moore, Alan, 159

Moore, Charles J., 191

Moore, Marianne: Anthropocene and, 174, 176, 187; composition process of, 187n1; "An Octopus" by, xvii, 173–87, 187nn3–4, 188nn5–6; on plastic, 195

Moraru, Christian, 98

Morton, Timothy, xiv, 35n3, 55; on hyperobjects, xvii, 41, 174–76, 179, 183, 186, 187n2, 192

Mount Tacoma, 175–76, 178, 182, 187nn3–4

movie camera, x–xi

Mrs. Dalloway (Woolf), 138

Mt. Rainier National Park, 173, 177, 179, 181, 183, 187n3, 188n5

"Multiplied Man and the Reign of Machine" (Lawrence), 6

Nagasaki bombing, 221–22, *225*

Narratology (Bal), 154

Nash, Paul, ix

Nash, Roderick Frazier, 178

nationalism, British, 30, 36n14

National Park Service (NPS), 173, 175–79, 181, 184, 187n3, 188n5

Native Americans, *The Bridge* on, 42

natural history, human history and, 123, 127

naturalism, 211–12, 220

natural sciences, Anthropocene and, 59

nature: animal and, 14–15; animosity of, 14–16; in Anthropocene, 9, 40, 223–24; art and, 25, 31–33; artificial ecology, plastic and, 198–200; in *The Bridge*, 40–42, 44, 55; civilization and, Lawrence on, 3–5, 7, 13; culture and, 22, 31–32, 34; ecology and, xiv, 55; green modernism and, xiv; Heidegger on, 219–20; humanity and, ix, 5, 9–12, 15–18, 59–60, 115, 119–20, 212, 219–20, 223–24; industry and, *Blast* on, 22–23, 26, 32–33; in literature, ecocritics on, 23–24; modernism and, xiv, 25, 35n5; sky and, 210; technology and, 33

Needham, Joseph, 80

Nelson, Cary, 203

Nevinson, C. R. W., 35n9

new modernist studies, xiii–xiv

A New Theory for American Poetry
　(Fletcher), 40
New Weekly, 26
New York Evening Journal, 165
New York Herald, 161
Nietzsche, Friedrich, 12, 16
Night and Day (Woolf), 139
Nishida, Kitarô Zenshû, 227n8
Nixon, Rob, 133
nonhuman animals, 6–7, 10, 13–14, 16
nonhumans, xiv; agency of, 15–17;
　humans and, x–xi, 4–5, 9–10, 12–18,
　23–24, 59–73, 153, 168–69; revolt
　of, 13–18; subjectivity and agency,
　61–73
noosphere, 89; biosphere and, 84,
　100–101; modernism and, 81–88;
　Star Maker on, 90–91, 106; Teilhard
　on, xvi, 80, 84, 86, 92, 94n6, 100;
　Vernadsky on, 100–101
NPS. *See* National Park Service

"O, Carib Isle!" (Crane), xv, 40–41;
　anagrams in, 48, 50, 52–55; Genesis
　and, 48–49, 51; geological sublime
　in, 55; on human absences and
　ghosts, 51–52; Isle of Pines hurricane
　and, 46–47; on names and speaking
　a name, 50–51, 54; on Satan, 52–54;
　Wordsworth and, 53–54
"An Octopus" (Moore, M.), xvii;
　avalanche in, 176, 185–86; Carey,
　M. C., and, 182; glacier in, 173–87;
　hyperobjects and, 173–77, 179–81,
　183–87; Johnson and, 179, 188n6;
　Mount Tacoma and, 175–76, 178,
　182, 187nn3–4; Mt. Rainier National
　Park and, 173, 177, 179, 181, 183,
　187n3, 188n5; Pycraft and, 183, 185
"The Octopus in the Chanel Island"
　(Carey, M. C.), 182
oil: blood and, 44, 46; boom, US, 39;
　coal and, 124–25; fossil fuels and,
　40–46, 55, 116, 119–20, 124–25;
　humans and, 45

Orta or One Dancing (Stein), 196
Others: A Magazine for the New Verse,
　198
The Outline of History (Wells, H. G.),
　115, 117–18
Oventile, Robert Savino, xv

The Pageant of the Stars (Luyten), 83
"Pan in America" (Lawrence), 5
Papini, Giovanni, 198
Parrinder, Patrick, 125
Patel, Raj, 12
"Paterson" (Williams, W. C.), 200
Pendrell, Luke, 148
Peppis, Paul, 28, 30, 36n1
Phaedrus (Plato), 45
Phelan & Collender, 194
The Phenomenon of Man (Teilhard), 80,
　84–87, 92, 94n6
Pindar, 39, 54
place-based aesthetics, of *Blast*, 27
planetarity, xiv, xvi, 98, 102, 213, 223,
　226, 226n2
planetary consciousness, xvi, 213
planetary frame, 97, 212
planetary modernism, 98–99
planetary politics, 80–81, 85
planetary scale, 97, 112, 126, 146, 223;
　interplanetary scale and relationships,
　104–6; in *The Shape of Things to
　Come*, 122; of *Star Maker*, 101–6;
　Teilhard on, 88, 94n4
planetary thinking, 98–99
planetary time, xiii, xvi–xvii, 85
planetary turn, in modernist studies,
　97–99
planetary worldmaking, in comics, 158
planetology, comparative, 98–101, 106–7
planets: Earth, 98–99, 101–2, 110–12;
　ecology and, 122–23; *Last and First
　Men* on, 124–26; modernist, 99;
　psychology and psyche of, 104–12;
　Solaris on, 106–12; *Star Maker* on,
　101–6, 111–12, 125–26; wandering,
　98–99

plastic: annual consumption by Americans, 204n1; Anthropocene and, 191–92, 194; artificial ecology and, xvii, 193, 195, 198–201, 204; Bakelite and, 195, 198–99, 204nn3–4; the Baroness on, 202–3; celluloid and, 192–96, 198–203, 204n5; Futurism and, 195–96, 204; Gillespie on, 203; hyperobjects and, 192; Loy and, 198–200; in modernism and modernity, xvii, 193–98; Moore, M., on, 195; plasticity and, 193–94, 203–4; poetics of, 192–93, 195, 204; semiotics of, 193, 198, 204; water bottles, 196–97

Plastic Age, 193–94, 196, 198, 201

"The Plastic Foundations of Futurist Sculpture and Painting" (Boccioni), 195–96

plasticity: of form, xvii; of Gillespie, 203; plastics and, 193–94, 203–4; poetics of, 193, 196; of Stein, 196; Williams, W. C., on, 201

plastiglomerate, 191

Plato, 45, 49–50

Pocahontas, 42, 44–46

poetics, of plastic and plasticity, in modernism, 192–93, 195–96, 204

Poetry (magazine), 46–47

Poirier, Richard, 25

"'Poison Gas' in Nature" (Ward), 183

Pope, Alexander, 210

population boom, US, 39

posthumanism, 11, 17–18, 153, 169, 174

postmodernism, 203

Pound, Ezra, 21, 134, 149n1

Powell, Nate, 166–67

The Prelude (Wordsworth), 53–54

primitivism, 4, 8, 13, 36n14, 166, 169, 171n7

psychoanalysis, 105, 109, 112n2

psychology and psyche, of planets, 104–12

Pueblo people, 6–8

Purdy, Jedediah, 35n4

Pycraft, W. P., 183, 185, 188nn9–10

Pynchon, Thomas, 45

Quran, 53

radioactive nuclear fallout, xvii–xviii

radioactive skies, 219, 224

The Rainbow (Lawrence), 6

Raine, Anne, xiv, 60

Rakosi, Carl, 193

realist comics, 157, 160, 166–67, 171n7

"Recent Developments in Cosmical Physics" (Jeans), 94n5

"The Red Wheelbarrow" (Williams, W. C.), 200

"Reflections on the Death of a Porcupine" (Lawrence), 5

Reiss, Robert, 205n10

Rilke, Rainer Maria, 5

Robinson, Jennifer, 226n1

Robinson, Kim Stanley, 128n2, 141

Rohman, Carrie, 13

Rose, Alexander, 143–44

Rose, Gillian, 226n1

Russell, Bertrand, 81

Ruttmann, Walter, x–xi

Sagan, Carl, 98–99

Satan, 52–54

Sawyer, Stephen, 148

scalar thinking, xvi, 80–81, 84–85, 88–93, 146–48

scalar zoom, 134, 147

Schulze, Robin, 184

Schuster, Joshua, xiv, xvi

science fiction (SF), 80, 104–6, 115–17, 128n2, 138–39, 142–44, 154

The Science of Life (Wells, H. G., Wells, G. P., and Huxley), 116–23

second modernism and second modernity, xvi, 134, 136–38, 140, 142–43

semiotic modes, of comics, 156, 170n3

semiotics, of plastics, 193, 198, 204

The Shape of Things to Come (Wells, H. G.), 116, 121–24, 129n10
Shaw, G. B., 118
Sheeler, Charles, x–xi
Shelley, Percy Bysshe, 49
Simpson, Sally, 47
skies, xvii–xviii, *211*, 212; of Anthropocene, 210, 221, 223, 226; in *Black Rain*, 218–19, 221–25; Cary on, 214–18, 220, 224; deep ecology and, 226n2; in *The Horse's Mouth*, 214–17; radioactive, 219, 224
Skim (Tamaki, J., and Tamaki, M.), 166–67, 171n7
"A Slave to Modern Improvements" (Fitzgerald), 204
Sloane, Michael D., xvii
smoke: in *Black Rain*, 217–23; Lawrence on, 10–11
Snyder, Gary, 195
Solaris (Lem), xvi, 101, 106–12, 112n3
"Songs to Joannes" (Loy), 198–99
space and time, xvi–xvii, 83–86, 93
space-time, 88–89, 173–74
Spivak, Gayatri Chakravorty, 212–13
Spring and All (Williams, W. C.), 200
Stalking the Subject (Rohman), 13
Stapledon, Olaf: Anthropocene and, 116–17, 124, 126; on ecology, 116, 126–28; geopsychoanalysis of, 112n2; *Last and First Men* by, 115–16, 124–27, 128n2, 129n12; Lem and, xvi, 99, 101, 106–7, 109, 112, 126; modernism of, 80–81, 93; Teilhard and, xvi, 80–81, 84–90, 92–93; vitalism and, 126, 129n13; Wells, H. G., and, 115–18, 124, 126–28, 128n3; Woolf and, 81–82, 115–16, 128n2
Star Maker (Stapledon), xvi; on cosmic and atomic structures, 90–91; cosmic scale of, 81–83, 86–91, 93; on human species, 85–93, 125–26; on industrial modernity, 85–86; on interplanetary scales and

relationships, 104–6; Lem on, 107; on noosphere, 90–91, 106; on planets and planetary scale, 101–6, 111–12, 125–26; scalar thinking and, 80, 88, 93; utopia and, 89, 92, 101–6, 125; Woolf on, 81–82, 115
steam engine, xi, 134–35, 191–92
Stein, Gertrude, xvii, 193–94, 196–97, 204
Stettheimer, Florine, 193
Stevens, Wallace, 210
St. Mawr (Lawrence), 4, 6–8, 10–11, 13–17
Stoermer, Eugene, xi, 121, 134–35, 176, 191
"storm from the North" symbol, in *Blast*, 27, *27*, 29
storytelling, Earth and, 24
storyworlds, in comics, 154–60, 165–67, 169–70
Strand, Paul, x–xi
stratigraphy, 59, 135
stream of consciousness, xii–xiii
subjective agency, 61–62
subjective identity, 60–61
subjectivity, in *The Unnamable*, 59–63, 66–70, 73
subjectivity, stratigraphy and, 59
Sultzbach, Kelly, xiv, 128n1
Suvin, Darko, 117
Swallow Me Whole (Powell), 167
Swamp Thing (Moore, A.), 159
Symposium (Plato), 49
synchronization, 136, 138

Tamaki, Jillian and Mariko, 166–67, 171n7
Taos, 6
technological sublime, 39–40, 146
technology: CLN and, 145–46; film, x; humans and, ix–xi; modernism and, 35n5; nature and, 33. *See also* machines and technology
Teilhard de Chardin, Pierre: on cosmic scale, 86–88; "Life and the Planets"

by, 94nn4–5; on noosphere, xvi,
80, 84, 86, 92, 94n6, 100; *The
Phenomenon of Man* by, 80, 84–87,
92, 94n6; on planetary scale, 88,
94n4; Stapledon and, xvi, 80–81,
84–90, 92–93; vitalist philosophy,
83–84

Thacker, Eugene, 141

Thompson, Virgil, 193

Thoreau, Henry David, 25, 35nn3–4

time: CLN and, xvi, 134, *142*, 142–
46, *143*; cosmic, 82, 88–90; in
modernism and modernity, 134–40,
142–43, 147–48; planetary, xiii, xvi–
xvii, 85; space and, xvi–xvii, 83–86,
93; space-time, 88–89, 173–74; in
The Time Machine, 147–48; Woolf
on, 138–39

time-lapse photography, 147–48

The Time Machine (Wells, H. G.), x,
127, 139–40, 147–48

Titanic, HMS, ix

Toadvine, Ted, 223

"To Let Go or to Hold On" (Lawrence),
3–4

Tōmatsu Shōmei, 210, *211*, 222, *222*

topographical poems, 40

To the Lighthouse (Woolf), ix, 139

Trafford, James, 148

Trexler, Adam, 12, 117

tri-partite model of temporality, in post-
climate change world, xii–xiii

"The Triumph of the Machine"
(Lawrence), 6

Tsing, Anna, 169

Tung, Charles, xvi

Turner, Fred, 145

the unconscious, 100–101, 109–11;
ecological, 153, 158, 161, 165–66;
infrastructural, 41

The Unnamable (Beckett), xv–xvi;
on human and non-human agency,
61–73; on knowledge, 64–66, 70;
obsessive-compulsive preoccupations

in, 61–62, 66–68, 70–71; on reason
and reasoning, 65–67, 70; on self-
expression and language, 67–73;
silence in, 71–72; subjective identity
in, 60–61; on subjectivity, 59–63,
66–70, 73

Urugami Tenshudo Church, Nagasaki,
225

utopia: digital, 145; *Miss Fury* and, 169;
The Shape of Things to Come and,
122; *Star Maker* and, 89, 92, 101–6,
125

Vancouver, George, 187n3

Van Hulle, Dirk, 61

Vernadsky, Vladimir, xvi, 99–101

Vertov, Dziga, x–xi

vitalism, 83–84, 118, 126, 129n13

vortex, 21, 26–29, 136

Vorticism and Vorticists: Anthropocene
and, 23, 32; in *Blast*, 21–23, 26–31;
on climate and ecology, 22; on
climate and industry, 32; Lewis, W.,
and, 21, 30–33; on machines and
technology, 32–33; on Marinetteism,
21

Voyage à la Lune, x

Wallace, Jeff, 9

Ward, Francis, 183

Ware, Chris, 159

Wark, McKenzie, 41

The War of the Worlds (Wells, H. G.), x

The Waste Land (Eliot), ix, xiii

Watsuji Tetsuro, 209, 212, 219–21,
223–24, 226n3

Watt, James, xi, 191–92

The Waves (Woolf), ix

The Way Things Go (Jaffe), 137

We Are Making a New World, ix

Weller, Shane, 61

Wells, G. P., 116–23

Wells, H. G., xvi, 81; Anthropocene
and, 116–17, 120, 123, 127; on
ecology and human ecology, 116–24,

126–28, 129n9; ecomodernism and, 117–21; *The Fate of Homo Sapiens* by, 127; on humanity and nature, 119–20; *The Outline of History* by, 115, 117–18; *The Science of Life* by, 116–23; *The Shape of Things to Come* by, 116, 121–24, 129n10; Stapledon and, 115–18, 124, 126–28, 128n3; *The Time Machine* by, x, 127, 139–40, 147–48; *The Work, Wealth, and Happiness of Mankind* by, 117, 122

weltbildend, 220–21, 223–24

Wenzel, Jennifer, 212–13, 226n2

"What is the Anthropo-Political?" (Colebrook), 54–55

"'What to Make of a Diminished Thing'" (Costello), 25

What to See in America (Johnson), 179

White Buildings (Crane), 49

Whitehead, Alfred North, 129n13

Whitman, Walt, 42–46, 54–55, 215

Whole Earth Catalog, 142, 145

Wiegand, Charmion von, 41

Wientzen, Timothy, xvi

Wilder, Thornton, x

Wild Kingdom (Huizenga), 166–67

Wildlife in the Anthropocene (Lorrimer), 5

"Wild Things in Captivity" (Lawrence), 9

Williams, Raymond, xiii

Williams, William Carlos, xvii, 194, 200–202, 204

Willis, Patricia, 181

Willmott, Glenn, xvii, 164

Wilson, Edward O., 124

Wolf, Mark, 155

The Woman Who Ran Away (Lawrence), 6–8

Women in Love (Lawrence), 6, 11

Woodring, Jim, 159

Woolf, Virginia, 128n1; *Between the Acts* by, 115; on clocks and time, 138–39, 147; *Mrs. Dalloway* by, 138; *Night and Day* by, 139; Stapledon and, 81–82, 115–16, 128n2; *To the Lighthouse* by, ix, 139; *The Years* by, 81–82

Wordsworth, William, 53–54

The Work, Wealth, and Happiness of Mankind (Wells, H. G.), 117, 122

world, sky and, 212

worldedness, 212–13, 223–24

worlding, 212–13

worldmaking, in comics, xvii, 153–58, 160–61, 165–67, *168*, 169–70; worldbuilding, 154–60, 166, 170; worldreading, 154–57

World War I, 21, 44–45

World War II, 91, 94n4, 101

Wyndham, John, 15

The Years (Woolf), 81–82

Zalasiewicz, Jan, 23

Zelazo, Suzanne, 198

Zukofsky, Louis, 195

About the Editors and Contributors

ABOUT THE EDITORS

Jon Hegglund is Associate Professor of English at Washington State University, where he teaches courses in modernism, ecocriticism and environmental writing, and narrative theory. He has published on geography, spatiality, ecocriticism, and narrative in publications including *ISLE*, *Twentieth-Century Literature*, and the edited collection, *Environment and Narrative*. His book, *World Views: Metageographies of Modernist Fiction* (2012) was nominated for an MLA First Book Prize. Currently, he is completing a book on anthropomorphism as an embodied mode of narrative cognition and serving as a faculty mentor for the *City Scripts* project, an interdisciplinary graduate research group based at Ruhr University in Bochum, Germany.

John McIntyre is Associate Professor of English at the University of Prince Edward Island where he teaches courses in twentieth- and twenty-first- century American and British literature. He is the co-editor of *Rereading the New Criticism* with Miranda Hickman. He has published articles in the *University of Toronto Quarterly* and the *Canadian Journal of Native Studies*.

ABOUT THE CONTRIBUTORS

Joseph Anderton is Senior Lecturer in English Literature at Birmingham City University, UK. He is the author of *Beckett's Creatures: Art of Failure after the Holocaust* (2016), which examines Beckett's post-war prose and plays through the concepts of the "creature" and "creaturely life." Joseph has published various articles on animals, dehumanization, and modernism in relation to Beckett, Franz Kafka, J. M. Coetzee, and Paul Auster, including work in *Modernism/modernity, Twentieth-Century Literature, Samuel Beckett Today/Aujourd'hui, Beckett and Animals, Beyond the Human-Animal Divide*, and *Performance Research.* He is currently working on a new project on homelessness in contemporary British literature.

Emily Chester completed her PhD in 2019 at the University of Bristol, UK. Her doctoral thesis was on the topic of the phenomenology of obsessions and compulsions in Samuel Beckett's writing, and, as well as Beckett's work, her research interests include modernism and illness, the psychological and psychiatric representation of literature, writing and therapy, and refugee narratives. In 2017 she published an article for the journal *Samuel Beckett Today/ Aujourd'hui* entitled "Obsessive Compulsive Ir/rationality in *Watt*," and she continues to write in the field of Samuel Beckett and illness.

Stuart Christie is Professor and Head of the Department of English Language and Literature at Hong Kong Baptist University. He is the author of *Worlding Forster: The Passage from Pastoral* (2005; paperback ed., 2013), *Plural Sovereignties and Contemporary Indigenous Literature* (2009), and the co-editor, along with Zhang Yuejun, of *Modern American Poetry and the Chinese Encounter* (2012). He has published articles in venues such as *Modern Fiction Studies, College Literature, PMLA, Foreign Literature Studies* (外國文學研究), *The American Indian Quarterly*, and *Modernism/modernity Print+.*

Julia E. Daniel, Associate Professor of English at Baylor University, is the author of *Building Natures: Modern American Poetry, Landscape Architecture, and City Planning* (2017), and the co-editor of *Modernism in the Green: Public Greens in Modern Literature and Culture* (2020). She also serves as the co-editor of the *T. S. Eliot Studies Annual* (Clemson UP). Her research interests include modern American poetry, urban ecocriticism, and modern material culture. Her work has also appeared or is forthcoming in *Eliot Now, The New Wallace Stevens Studies, Ecomodernism, The Cambridge Companion to* The Waste Land, and *Critical Quarterly.*

Ted Howell is Lecturer in Writing Arts at Rowan University, where his teaching and research focus on environmental and sustainability issues, specifically climate change.

Jessica Martell is Assistant Professor of Interdisciplinary Studies at Appalachian State University in the Blue Ridge Mountains of North Carolina. She is the author of *Farm to Form: Modernist Literature and Ecologies of Food in the British Empire* (2020) and co-editor of *Modernism and Food Studies: Politics, Aesthetics, and the Avant-Garde* (2019). Her work has also appeared in *Modernist Cultures, Journal of Modern Literature, Nineteenth-Century Literature*, and *Gastronomica: The Journal for Food Studies.*

Robert Savino Oventile is Professor of English at Pasadena City College. He has published essays and book reviews in *Postmodern Culture, Jacket, symplokē*, and *The Chicago Quarterly Review*, among other journals. His poetry has appeared in *The New Delta Review, Upstairs at Duroc*, and *The Denver Quarterly*. He is the author of *Impossible Reading: Idolatry and Diversity in Literature* (2008) and of *Satan's Secret Daughters: The Muse as Daemon* (2014). He is co-author with Sandy Florian of *Sophia Lethe Talks Doxodox Down* (Atmosphere, 2021).

Joshua Schuster is an Associate Professor of English and core faculty member at the Centre for the Study of Theory and Criticism at Western University. He is the author of *The Ecology of Modernism: American Environments and Avant-Garde Poetics* (2015) and co-author with Derek Woods of *Three Critiques of Existential Risk* (2020).

Michael D. Sloane teaches in the School of Language and Liberal Studies at Fanshawe College in London, Ontario, Canada. With research specializing in ecological objects in American modernist poetry, his writing appears in publications like *Literature, Rhetoric and Values*; *Critical Perspectives on Veganism*; *The Goose*; *William Carlos Williams Review*; and *Modernism in the Green: Public Greens in Modern Literature and Culture.*

Charles M. Tung is Professor and Chair of English at Seattle University, where he teaches courses on twentieth- and twenty-first-century literature, temporal scale, and representations of racial anachronism. He is the author of *Modernism and Time Machines* (2019). His recent work on time and modernity has appeared in *Timescales: Ecological Temporalities across Disciplines, Time and Literature, ASAP/Journal, Modernism/Modernity*, and *Configurations*. His current book project is on big clocks and ethnofuturist timescales.

Timothy Wientzen is Associate Professor of English at Skidmore College, where his teaching and scholarship focus on twentieth-century British literatures, contemporary fiction, and science fiction. He is the author of *Automatic: Literary Modernism and the Politics of Reflex* (2021). *Automatic* explores how the science of reflex challenged prevailing theories of political behavior in the twentieth century, and informed a host of modern institutions, including modernist literature. Work on this and other topics has appeared in journals like *Novel*, *Genre*, and *Journal of Modern Literature*.

Glenn Willmott is Professor of English and Cultural Studies at Queen's University in Canada. He studies modernism and popular culture from social-political and ecological perspectives, and is a past president of the Canadian Society for the Study of Comics and of the Association for Literature, Environment, and Culture in Canada. Recent books include *Reading for Wonder: Ecology, Ethics, Enchantment*, and *Modern Animalism: Habitats of Scarcity and Wealth in Comics and Literature*.